AF740564

Psychoanalysis and Literature

Psychoanalysis and Literature

The Stories We Live

Marilyn Charles

ROWMAN & LITTLEFIELD
Lanham • Boulder • New York • London

Published by Rowman & Littlefield
A wholly owned subsidiary of The Rowman & Littlefield Publishing Group, Inc.
4501 Forbes Boulevard, Suite 200, Lanham, Maryland 20706
www.rowman.com

Unit A, Whitacre Mews, 26-34 Stannary Street, London SE11 4AB

Copyright © 2015 by Rowman & Littlefield

All rights reserved. No part of this book may be reproduced in any form or by any electronic or mechanical means, including information storage and retrieval systems, without written permission from the publisher, except by a reviewer who may quote passages in a review.

British Library Cataloguing in Publication Information Available

Library of Congress Cataloging-in-Publication Data

Charles, Marilyn.
Psychoanalysis and literature : the stories we live / Marilyn Charles.
pages cm.
Includes bibliographical references and index.
ISBN 978-1-4422-3183-2 (cloth) -- ISBN 978-1-4422-3184-9 (electronic)
1. Psychoanalysis and literature. 2. Psychoanalysis in literature. I. Title.
PN56.P92C46 2015
809'.93353--dc23
2015000225

™ The paper used in this publication meets the minimum requirements of American National Standard for Information Sciences Permanence of Paper for Printed Library Materials, ANSI/NISO Z39.48-1992.

Printed in the United States of America

This book is dedicated to Grant Justin King and to Carson Laura King, and to all the other shining stars who guide us toward a better future.

Contents

Acknowledgments

I feel profound gratitude to my patients and supervisees, who challenge me to grow beyond my limits, and who generously allow me to share their efforts in the hope that these might prove useful to others who are trying to find their way.

I offer this book to all of the young people who are courageously determined to find their way into this difficult but rewarding work, having in mind also those who will benefit from their efforts.

I would like to acknowledge Julia Brown, whose enthusiasm for my writing on literature and psychoanalysis afforded the spark that gave rise to this volume.

I am also grateful to Joseph Mauch, William Orme, Trisha Ready, Sandra Ullmann, and Stuart Weir, whose comments and encouragement have helped to shape the volume.

Last but not least, I would like to acknowledge Bruce Charles, the person who gave me a home in this world, and my children, Devon King, Justin Charles, and Jonathan Charles, and my son-in-law, Bryan King, who have taught me how to live, and love, in it.

Foreword

Suzanne Langer writes that "artistic form is congruent with the dynamic forms of our direct sensuous life: works of art are projections of 'felt life,' as Henry James called it, into spatial, temporal, and poetic structures. They are images of feeling that formulate it for our conception" (1942, p. 26).

Dr. Marilyn Charles has written a book worthy of Langer's comment on form and formulation via an engagement with the art of the novel. I imagine Dr. Charles with her patients; the presences in the room on her side are voices of other psychoanalysts to be sure, but quite likely also the voices of the novelists she has read, each providing a form for her listening. In this book we, the readers, get to listen in second-hand on her thinking about these two rich veins that inform clinical work, that most private of spaces and experiences.

The book creates the warp and weft of a vast weaving like one of those medieval tapestries, or perhaps a rug from Turkey, an old one, with the trademark of the maker's flaw embedded, to mark it as human. One can read lines in the book as warp, the lengthwise threads held in tension on a frame, the frame psychoanalysis. We call the yarn woven over and under the warp the weft, or woof. Suddenly, a dog barks in the midst of my thinking, so like that flaw, that interruption or gap so necessary to weaving, writing and psychoanalysis. Lines of warp: voices of other analysts from a span of traditions, speaking about the unconscious, creativity, dreams, memory, ambiguity, desire. Lines of weft: encounters with epiphany, catastrophic change, relationships gone awry, intergeneration al trauma, collisions of culture, identity, community, aging and death. Warp means "that which is thrown across." Dr. Charles throws across to us, her readers, her reading of passages from novels alongside her experience as an analyst with patients. What can we learn, by taking up these threads and making them our own? To speak of this, I will go to just a few places in the book and say a little about what I gleaned from reading this book of layered renderings.

* * *

Julian Barnes writes "I know this much: that there is objective time, but also subjective time, the kind you wear on the inside of your wrist, next to where the pulse lies. And this personal time, which is the true time, is measured in your relationship to memory" (2011, p. 122). I found four passages through the subjective time of this book; there are many more, but I chose these four. As a reader you can begin anywhere, choose your own passages.

I

In the midst of reading Dr. Charles' first chapter I realize that a reading can be, itself, a series of epiphanies, parallel to analytic clinical encounters. Dr. Charles considers epiphany in a moment between Mr. and Mrs. Ramsey in the garden in Virginia Woolf's *To the Lighthouse*.

> Woolf perhaps speaks most explicitly to the issue of epiphany when she writes: *suddenly the meaning, which, for no reason at all . . . descends on people, making them symbolic, making them representative, came upon them, and made them in the dusk standing, looking, the symbols of marriage, husband and wife. Then, after an instant, the symbolic outline which transcended the real figures sank down again.* Woolf highlights this type of epiphanic moment and she also invokes it, bringing the reader into a transcendental reality in which distinctions blur.

In this spirit of making space for epiphany Dr. Charles meets with her patient, Jane, with Woolf as a companion. Dr. Charles encounters a void in her patient, and the necessity to sustain such an encounter, rather than cover it. As an analyst she realizes that hearing what the unconscious might have to say, an epiphany or a sudden startling recognition, depends on such moments when nothing is certain because nothing is there.

II

Since I, too, have been immersed in reading Woolf, and particularly her most daring final work, *The Waves,* I was intrigued by Dr. Charles rendering of that novel and her construction of Woolf's artistry in writing it.

In her second chapter, Dr. Charles writes: "Part of what is so exquisitely inviting about this novel is the formal interplay of content and structure. Woolf's concern with form is immanent throughout. In her attempts to bring to bear the power of the formal elements of design and order without losing touch with the vitality of the lived moment, she created a work that is lyrical and evocative. One becomes caught in the rhythms of the text."

Dr. Charles traces the ways that Woolf's language, especially in this novel, is musical—intentionally so. Listening to human speech is also fundamentally musical, consisting of phrases, rhythms, and repetitions. The result is that we, the readers, become attuned to hearing within language its musical sense and nonsense. Before trying to pin down what it means, there is language as an experience of "being." Here is Dr. Charles again:

> In *The Waves* Woolf dives deeply into her own being, thereby articulating a language of the unconscious and exploring the processes by which inspiration informs creation. In this way, she challenges us to believe in our own voices sufficiently that we can imagine surviving the encounter with the incredible and terrible richness of our own inner beings.

Dr. Charles moves back and forth between reading Woolf's diaries about the creation of *The Waves* and the book itself, returning to the world of her own thought and practice as an analyst. In doing so, she shows us how to take our bearings and believe ourselves in clinical work.

III

I turned to chapter 12, "Standing Outside the Gates," randomly, and could not stop reading. Dr. Charles turns to *Pola X*, a French film inspired by Herman Melville's novel, *Pierre*, to explore her work with Peter, a young man in the midst of an identity crisis who had lost his bearing with respect to his family and his place in the world.

Dr. Charles finds striking parallels between the Melville's Pierre, "... a young man of privilege, who becomes disillusioned in the transition to adulthood, when the semblance of the father breaks open and familiar guideposts can no longer be relied on," and her patient. Melville's Pierre has met a woman who claims to be his sister, the unacknowledged daughter of his father, a sister who identifies as an exile. Dr. Charles describes this meeting: "Pierre's enchantment with Isabel and his disillusionment with his father and his life are profound, and he gives up everything to take care of her. This break with family and community leave him at the fringes of society, destitute."

Her patient, Peter, "was similarly preoccupied with issues of meaning and morality" at a point when he feared he was "losing his mind." Dr. Charles, understanding implicitly that psychosis can be a place of both exile and identity, offers her patient a new way through his crisis: "Rather than naming his experience as a psychotic process, I chose to call it an identity crisis. In so doing, I took a stand with both Peter and his family, endorsing the importance for Peter of having time and resources to find his way through this crisis, while having a psychoanalytic interpreter to guide him on that journey."

I read this chapter and thought "what a strangely perfect intervention." A young man in an identity crisis could, potentially identify to psychosis and to a life path as a mental patient, but here is another offer: take a journey through an identity crisis, a turning point into a life of your choosing through psychoanalysis.

IV

I chose chapter 17 because there is so little we know about aging and coming to the threshold of dying with respect to listening. In this chapter Dr. Charles uses several sources to inform her thinking about her patient, but the parallels are strongest with respect to "Tony," the protagonist of Julian Barnes' *The Sense of an Ending*. Dr. Charles explains that Tony, "looks back on a life characterized by relationships that largely elude his understanding. We see the story evolve and alter from the narrow scope of adolescence, through the greater wisdom of age, and then finally coalesce through the recognition of alternative viewpoints that highlight ways in which memory can seal over the past."

Dr. Charles explores the ways that his place in time, late in his life, gives Tony a sense of history. But history, as Tony's friend Adrian Finn has said, "is that certainty produced at the point where the imperfections of memory meet the inadequacies of documentation." Aware of this undertow in the novel, Dr. Charles points out, "At the end of the novel, Tony is left with his shame at the enormity of what he has been unable to see, what he had been unable to face. The reader, however, is left with the bigger picture of what remains invisible, largely because of Tony's inability to move beyond the frame of his own imaginings."

In her work with "Guy, an aging artist who struggles to locate himself in a story in which his humor and creative capacities have effectively masked the shame at his core," Dr. Charles seeks a third perspective on his life, a perspective that will come through his dreams. A sequence of dreams disrupts his life story and offers something true to this man in what he has passed on to the next generation.

Identified to the position of Dr. Charles' "reader"—we are given in this chapter, and throughout the book, a way to approach the world of clinical practice from a wider vantage point, outside the ways we might imagine either our patients or ourselves.

As Dr. Charles shows us, the function of the analyst is to receive the the startling knowledge that comes from the unconscious. To do so means entering something mysterious in its very heart—without a knowledge of what's coming, without a ready interpretation to give your patient. What you have, sitting there listening, is a radical ignorance of what is to come, coupled with an attuned and skilled way of listening. Read the book and hear it!

* * *

Through my Lacanian formation as an analyst, and listening as a writer and poet, I appreciate the distinctive ways that Dr. Charles reads both literature and the speech of her patients. But I would be remiss not to put a final spin on my own reading, and what I gleaned from the opportunity to peruse Dr. Charles' book—from the point of view of erasures and deletions—returning silence to listening, and the white page to writing.

Jacques Lacan called literature "the cloud of language" which "constitutes writing." He describes writing as "a bunch of strokes and what erases them." Literature, he argued, consists of holes and erasures. This writing of "letters" from and of the body involves the white space of silences, letters written in vanishing ink. The Real returns, after we have had some say about experience, some representation around the holes in language that make language work. The Real is ready to swallow any and all possible renderings, any readings. Yet language is all we have. In fact, novelists, poets, playwrights, are each compelled to try to bring something of what is written on the body into an original, audible art.

In this sense, writing and analytic listening work on parallel courses, making a space for what is not possible to know or say otherwise, even as the snow of not-saying falls, erasing us, reforming us for the next version.

Annie G. Rogers, PhD
Professor of Psychoanalysis and Clinical Psychology
Hampshire College
Author of *A Shining Affliction* (1995) and *The Unsayable* (2006)

Prologue

> "Why do you stay in prison
> When the door is so wide open?"
>
> —Rumi

Joseph Campbell describes the search for identity as a labyrinthian challenge, in which we are invited take on the hero's quest as an investigation into the depths of our being. Although this may seem like a solitary endeavor,

> we have not even to risk the adventure alone, for the heroes of all time have gone before us. The labyrinth is thoroughly known. We have only to follow the thread of the hero path, and where we had thought to find an abomination, we shall find a god. And where we had thought to slay another, we shall slay ourselves. Where we had thought to travel outward, we will come to the center of our existence. And where we had thought to be alone, we will be with the world. (1988, p. 151)

That quest is also the challenge of psychoanalysis, to find a quiet space through which to enter into that realm of mystery that is the human experience. Psychoanalysis attempts to provide one point of entry into that realm and yet, long before psychoanalysis began, literature was a way of exploring the deeper questions and dilemmas that face us as human beings. In turn, Freud used myth and literature to point to some of the crucial questions at the core of human development. In this way, he intuitively recognized the utility of what Bion (1977) later termed *binocular perspective*, the capacity to look at complex issues from more than one vantage point. In this volume, I use material from literature alongside clinical work as a way of highlighting salient issues and developmental passages that can be understood, explored, and worked through from a psychoanalytic perspective. I hope that this method will prove useful both to clinicians in helping to locate some of the dilemmas confronted in the consulting room within the greater societal context, and also to academics in their applications of psychoanalytic theory as a lens on culture.

Because literature often explores the same territory encountered by the clinician, being able to look at a case alongside a piece of fiction can expand and enrich our understanding. The novel offers the reader something that can be experienced directly, as opposed to the case, which is of essence always second hand. Using, then, a piece of fiction as a counterpoint to the clinical case invites the reader to enter into the exploration more fully and directly, in a more experience-near fashion. Contextualizing the clinical case in this way helps to pull the focus toward the existential human dilemmas we share with our patients and away from the medicalized terms that may accurately describe particular behaviors but may also be distancing and dehumanizing.

Using literature in this way also encourages the reader to be thinking in metaphor, which is especially useful from a psychoanalytic perspective. The metaphor helps us to move from the particular to the universal, highlighting important patterns, essential elements, and functional relationships underlying the topic at hand. We will be exploring themes endemic to the human condition, such as ways in which tensions between creativity and trauma, and between culture and meaning, affect identity development. Literature affords a means for getting outside the case, from which vantage point the particulars are less likely to obscure the underlying patterns and structures in place. Paradoxically, that *view from the outside* can point to the heart of a matter that has become obscured because we are too much inside it. Feeling directly implicated in a dilemma can heighten the intensity too much to allow for reflection. At such times, being able to recognize the dilemma in the displacement can afford sufficient breathing room for reflection. Clinically, the ability to look obliquely rather than directly allows meanings to come together and emerge over time, as they manifest in personal narratives or in dreams, or in the projective tests that crystalize and highlight salient patterns of relating and other aspects of character. Inevitably, the life dilemmas being explored are implicated in the form and structure of the work itself, which lends an affective tone that affects our reading of the narrative, in whatever form it presents itself, further enhancing our engagement and, with it, the passion Bion (1977) points to as a unique and valued instrument in the analyst's arsenal.

Winnicott (1971) suggests that the core dilemma at the heart of the psychoanalytic journey is to discover one's own potential for creativity, a view that parallels Lacan's (1992) developmental stance that the work should enhance the analysand's ability to recognize his or her own desires, to become the Subject of the inquiry. The psychoanalyst relies on the creativity inherent in each individual's unconscious to organize, explicate, and bring to life the salient issues requiring attention. From that perspective, it is important to allow material to emerge rather than try to force our data into an order that may obscure more than it illuminates. Following Freud, Bion (1990) observes that at times we need to be able to deepen the darkness sufficiently to allow hidden truths to reveal themselves. In this volume, I hope that the theory will help to organize the material without overshadowing it.

I

Literature, Psychoanalysis, and Sensory Experience

Introduction

> "Art is the nearest thing to life; it is a mode of amplifying experience and extending contact with our fellow-men beyond the bounds of our personal lot."
>
> —George Eliot, *Essays*

Literature affords the possibility of a vicarious experience. It is arguably crafted to provide just such an experience, to transport us into an imagined world. Much as the psychoanalyst tries to invite the dreams and free associations that will provide a commentary on the more linear narrative of daily life, the novelist often counterposes two or more narrative threads to open up the possibilities within a story. This type of structure allows us to encounter the possibility of a misreading or alternative reading, thereby affording the type of *binocular vision* that can be so important in breaking through ostensible truths so that we might consider alternatives (Bion, 1977).

In *The Blind Assassin,* for example, Atwood (2000) offers us a story within a story, providing through newspaper clippings the illusion of a "real life," an ostensibly objective relating of facts that offers a counterpoint to the narrative threads. Woven into the story is the fantasy novel written by one of the characters that provides a more primary process rendering of the relationships being considered. As the novel proceeds, we are carried along a narrative thread only to realize that our reading of the facts may be a mis-reading, that the blind assassin is not so easily or clearly located but rather likely lies waiting in each of us to the extent that we are willing to turn a blind eye to another's pain or desire. We will find this type of structure in several of the novels we will consider, a structure that allows the novelist easy entry into the realm of primary process that provides a commentary on our waking lives in ways that are potentially illuminating. This literary device models the consulting room, in which we are always seeking the story behind the story that will help to more fully reveal ourselves to ourselves.

The narrative form is a particularly useful structure for inviting us to reflect more deeply on the challenges entailed in becoming more fully ourselves. Research has shown that narrative text is more likely to prompt vivid autobiographical memories than other forms of text (Mar and Oatley, 2008). We seem to be hard-wired, through identification processes, to simulate and vicariously experience the experience of others (Gallese, 2009). Studies on the functions of fiction show that literary narratives offer models of the social world through which readers derive information from literature that they can then apply to their own life experiences (Gerrig and Rapp, 2004).

Through the processes of abstraction, simplification, and compression, fiction offers a deep immersion into a simulated experience of social interaction. It allows us to try an experience or way of being or thinking on for size. Kuiken, Miall, and Sikora (2004) note that readers not only consciously identify with aspects of the text, perhaps more fundamentally they also identify with the characters themselves. This latter mode of identification is involved in what these authors term *self-modifying feelings,* through which readers, at times, "find themselves participating in an unconventional flow of feelings through which they *realize* something that they have not previously experienced—or at least not in the form provided by the text" (p. 175). These types of reading experiences have been termed *expressive enactments,* thereby marking the prevalence of kinaesthetic imagery and the evocation of metaphor that occurs as the identificatory voice of the reader mingles with that of the author to elicit "feeling, prompt reflection on felt meanings, and loosen the boundaries that normally delimit conceptual understandings" (Sikora, Kuiken, and Miall, 2011, p. 266). This heightened affectivity and loosening of conceptual edges brings us into the realm of primary process, augmented by the aesthetic dimension through engagement with the narrative form itself.

These lines of inquiry into the functions of literature have helped to illustrate ways in which self-understanding is deepened through reading. In part, literature performs this process through metaphors of self-identification with characters in the text (Cohen, 1999). This process does not seem to be one of conscious simulation or imagining but rather of direct engagement with the feelings presented in the text (Hanfling, 1996; Turvey, 2006). Turvey contends that "we can respond with feeling to something regardless of whether it is real or not, fictional or not, if it is presented in a vivid enough way" (p. 119). From this perspective, our emotional responses to fiction can be located, at least in part, in the "concrete presentational qualities, a properly aesthetic domain, not just in the thoughts or imaginings they arouse in our minds" (Turvey, p. 119). In other words, we respond directly to the structure, rhythms, and other formal aspects of the work, along with the vivacity that invites greater absorption into the text.

Findings regarding the mirror neuron system show that there is a simulation aspect to our experiences in reading fiction, through the process of social identification or what Gallese (2009) calls *embodied simulation*. Research on mirror neurons shows that the same areas of the brain are activated when expressive acts are perceived as when they are executed. According to Gallese, "a common underlying functional mechanism—embodied simulation—mediates our capacity to share the meaning of actions, intentions, feelings, and emotions with others, thus grounding our identification with and connectedness to others" (p. 520). Notably, this system is not solely dependent on visual information. Mirror neurons also code meanings based on related sounds, leading Gallese to propose that "mirror neurons by mapping observed, implied, or heard goal-directed motor acts on their motor neural substrate in the observer's motor system allows a direct form of action understanding" (p. 520). These mechanisms provide a means for implicit knowledge about others' feelings and intentions at the bodily, rather than the cognitive, level.

The concept of embodied simulation provides a useful way of understanding the empathic engagement that can be both traumatizing and healing in the therapeutic dyad. Notable for our purposes here, the mirror neuron system affords the clinician the capacity to vicariously experience the pain and the pleasure of others. As we listen to the stories of trauma, or watch them unfold through the child's play or through artistic creations, we enter into that world at a deep and fundamental level. It is only from that place that we can, perhaps, find our way through, together, to a better place. Through our joint struggles to attenuate the distress and heal from the trauma, we are both afforded the potential for *posttraumatic growth* (Tedeschi and Calhoun, 2004).

According to Joseph Campbell (1949), our myths are the stories that hold the essential mysteries of the human spirit. From this perspective, the basic underlying patterns are the same, the details colored by the culture from which they are derived. Campbell recognizes that psychoanalysis exposes these myths in these modern times in which "in the absence of an effective general mythology, each of us has his private, unrecognized, rudimentary, yet secretly potent pantheon of dreams" (p. 4). At the core of our myths about the hero's quest to penetrate the mysteries of life, to reach the center of the labyrinth and slay the minotaur within, we can recognize tensions between early maternal dependency and the need to eventually separate and move out into the world, that crucial juncture of separation individuation in which so many become mired.

For Campbell, psychoanalysis affords a means "to conduct people across those difficult thresholds of transformation that demand a change in the patterns not only of conscious but also of unconscious life" (p. 10). Myth marks meanings and provides "the symbols that carry the human spirit forward" (p. 11). The Cretan story of the labyrinth is one such story of rites of passage. For Campbell, the hero's journey is to

> retreat from the world scene of secondary effects to those causal zones of the psyche where the difficulties really reside, and there to clarify the difficulties, eradicate them in his own case (i.e. give battle to the nursery demons of his local culture) and break through to the undistorted, direct experience and assimilation of the underlying patterns of experience. (p. 17)

For Campbell, the Ariadne thread that enables us to find our way through the labyrinth is the capacity to see the underlying pattern of the journey and recognize what is at stake. Notably, literature can provide the key: "Modern literature is devoted, in great measure, to a courageous, open-eyed observation of the sickeningly broken figurations that abound before us, around us, and within us" (p. 27). In an age in which we have lost touch with the religious structures and rituals that sustained us in times past, the essential patterns of human experience are revealed to us in our dreams and, collectively, in the stories of our age. The hero's quest is a journey inward through which the universal tragedies are transcended *through their recognition*. A fundamental aspect of this journey is the return and reintegration with society to face the troubles of the world rather than merely retreating from them.

Campbell (1949) contends that in contemporary society meaning is largely unconscious, and resides in the individual rather than in the collective coordinating mythologies. From that framework, coming to full maturity in contemporary culture requires "rendering the modern world spiritually significant" (p. 388). In today's largely secular society, we need to be able to recognize the new symbols that will emerge to help hold meaning, faith, and hope, colored by cultural context. "Therefore, it is necessary for men to understand, and be able to see, that through various symbols the same redemption is revealed" (p. 389), a dilemma that will be highlighted in our consideration of Fowles' (1977) *The Magus* in chapter 12. In times past, the challenge was to identify with the external beings that represented both danger and sustenance, whereas for Campbell it is now man himself who is the crucial mystery.

> Man is that alien presence with whom the forces of egoism must come to terms, through whom the ego is to be crucified and resurrected, and in whose image society is to be reformed. Man, understood however not as "I" but as "Thou": for the ideals and temporal institutions of no tribe, race, continent, social class, or century, can be the measure of the inexhaustible and multifariously wonderful divine existence that is the life in all of us. (p. 391)

The paradox of penetrability and impenetrability is fundamental to the psychoanalytic discourse, which can be seen as a search for knowledge that defies containment, the labyrinth that both entices and repels, obscures and reveals. The labyrinth has been linked to Lacan's (1977a) ideas of anamorphosis (something that may be visible only when viewed in an unconventional way, from a different perspective), which refers to the possibility of coherence emerging in relation to something that is not actually present (Scott, 2008). We are always in the paradoxical position of trying to become more (and less) than we are, in the face of what is known, not yet known, or likely unknowable.

Beginning with the arena Bollas (1987) refers to as the *unthought known*, in Part I, we will explore ways in which perceptual (and apperceptive) experience organizes very primary meanings that inform all of our understandings. We will introduce the idea of primary sensory experience and ways in which the writer and psychoanalyst share the challenge of bringing that primary sensory experience into words. Work from Virginia Woolf, who explicitly struggled with that challenge, will be used to illustrate ways in which the formal structures of experience can carry meaning above and beyond—and sometimes in opposition to—the words being used.

In Part II, we will consider trauma and the ways in which traumatic experience can disrupt the ability to bring experience into words. We will discuss the importance of narrative as a way to order and organize events, and ways in which the form of the traumatic novel disrupts and disregulates, thereby invoking the type of chaotic fragmentation that typifies traumatic experience.

In Part III, we will turn to the dreams that often reveal aspects of experience that cannot yet be integrated into working consciousness. Dreams pull us into the realm of primary process, thereby elucidating links and meaning structures that may not be visible to the conscious, rational mind.

In Part IV, we will discuss ways in which myth and other narratives structure universal understandings that mark aspects of meaning and of meaning-making. In particular, we will explore the added difficulties of cultural dislocations and ways in which people can be driven mad by tensions between different cultural expectations. In spite of increasing knowledge regarding the ways in which culture shapes experience, there is often the expectation that we will be *of one mind*, making subtleties of differentiated experience linked to cultural variation at times invisible.

In Part V, we will take a developmental perspective and consider the search for an autonomous identity that is nested in and related to the cultural contexts in which it arises. Tensions between the individual and the collective will be considered. In particular, we will focus on the labyrinth as a trope that marks the complexities of the quest for knowledge in the service of autonomous identity development. In that context, we will also explore art and madness, and the ways in which the creative individual can find him or herself *standing outside the gates*. Although the outside perspective can usefully inform the inside view and thereby provide a useful vantage point, marginalization can be destabilizing, thereby inhibiting the consolidation of a secure identity.

In Part VI, we will close the conversation with a consideration of later life tensions between identity, relatedness, aging, and death. Age affords its challenges and its rewards, as the external demands by others diminish and we can more fully face issues related to generativity, personal meanings, and fulfillment.

ONE

Epiphany: The Poet's Art, The Analyst's Instrument

Formal Structure as a Vehicle for the Expression of Primary Experience[1]

> "What was the meaning of life? That was all—a simple question; one that tended to close in on one with years. The great revelation had never come. The great revelation perhaps never did come. Instead there were little daily miracles, illuminations, matches struck unexpectedly in the dark. . . . In the midst of chaos there was shape; this eternal passing and flowing."
>
> —Virginia Woolf, *To the Lighthouse*\

Human beings straddle two worlds, beginning life as sensual beings, unformed by the language that will eventually come to categorize, organize, and thereby supersede our more primary ways of knowing. Analysts must sit with one foot in each of these worlds, attempting to empathically consider the experience of the other and then to try to bring that experience into language that can be more overtly reflected on and considered within the dyad. Artists are compelling to us in part because they find a way to speak to us of the timeless truths that we encounter but have difficulty making rational sense of without losing the essence. Much like the task of the analyst, writers such as Virginia Woolf have attempted to bring into language essential truths first intuited in moments of inspiration or *epiphany*. I will use Woolf's writing as a way of looking more closely into the process of bringing such moments into language.

In this chapter, we will explore ways in which essential meanings are lodged in nonverbal aspects of communication. Psychoanalysts are in the paradoxical position of using words to earn our living and yet, at a deeper level, being utterly dependent on the nonverbal exchanges that shape and moderate those verbalizations. We have long relied on primary sensory experience as a means for encountering, metabolizing, and integrating nonverbal communication. Slower to develop has been a language for discussing these more primary ways of knowing. We tend to valorize rational understanding and yet the very difficult work of psychoanalytic psychotherapy demands our ability to co-exist in both primary and secondary process realms, and to also tolerate the inevitable moments of disequilibrium. What may feel like an empathic or interpretive failure is often an opportunity to obtain, at the level of personal experience, a sense of where the patient may be stuck. The feel of these ungrounded, seemingly unbounded moments is inevitably regressive, resonating with the primitive moments of disequilibrium and dedifferentiation linked to traumatic memory (Charles, 2007; Krystal, 1988).

We begin life as sensory beings, in a world not yet informed by the language that will eventually categorize, organize, and thereby supersede our more primary ways of knowing. Before language is acquired, parent and child communicate, often effortlessly and seamlessly, through patterned exchanges of touch, gesture, and tone (Trevarthen, 1989, 1995). Many primary experiences have never been encoded into verbal memory but rather become part of the nonverbal, implicit system in which interchanges are highly patterned and occur more rapidly than we can consciously think *about* them (Fogel, 1992). Memories of this sort tend to be experienced as truth without inviting reflection.

The crucial organizing factor structuring these nonverbal meanings is affect, which has been described as "the supra-modal currency into which stimulation in any modality can be translated" (Stern, 1985, p. 53). Affect has its own prosody, which we recognize implicitly when we hear or see its various manifestations through voice or facial gesture. These affective prosodies are highly patterned, inviting artists such as Gauguin and Van Gogh to use musical metaphors as a way of referring to the subtleties of their own responsiveness to hue, tone, and variation (Rose, 1996; Charles and Telis, 2009).

As we grow, the primary rhythms of human being and interchange are attached to experiences in ways that are both communal and idiosyncratic. A good-enough early environment helps us to be present in our experiences and to begin to organize them in relation to the amodal aspects of nonverbal communication, in which:

> the dimensions of experience such as shape, texture, and location in space, all come to carry meanings beyond any specific representation. We learn to "read" nuances of line in works of art as in faces. The slope, the turn, the sweep, the rhythm: each in some important way seems to mirror the type of affective prosody described by such disparate theorists as Stern (1985) and Tomkins (1962, 1987). Although we may not be

> able to decode them in verbal terms, these types of meanings become reference points, (Charles, 2002a, p. 111)

anchors that facilitate further meaning-making and other creative endeavors. The aesthetic element adds another dimension to these experiences, through the formal properties of art that lend their own particular emotional resonance to the encounter (Langer, 1953).

In fact, our aesthetic encounters can sometimes function analogously as an aid in the process of finding our way through the confusing realms of the unconscious, realms that can be so treacherous that we may be reluctant to inhabit them, even in dreams or fantasy. Although we use symbols and categories as ways of naming and organizing these experiences, and then communicating our understandings to others, there is also the beauty and freedom of primary process—what Ehrenzweig (1967) refers to as the *hidden order* of the unconscious—that enables us to explore in fantasy what may be out of reach through more pragmatic means. This domain of primary sensory experience is also the realm of the transcendent moment, providing that point of juxtaposition between being both grounded and unbounded that has been referred to as *epiphany*. These moments of inspiration call to and elude us, often taking the form of essential realities—what Bion (1977) terms *O*, Lacan (1977b) the *Real*—that we can intuit in the moment but never entirely capture in retrospect. These realities can be truly awesome, tantalizing us as they invite our interest and also, at times, our terror.

For the artist, this type of primary sensory experience often carries a sense of truth or imperative order that captures the attention and demands to be given form, thereby transforming exactly what is most uniquely idiosyncratic into something that might be shared. Artists are compelling to us in part because they find ways of speaking to us of these timeless truths that we have difficulty making rational sense of without losing the essence, and do so in a way that is sufficiently personal to engage us affectively.

With the advent of technology, the artist's internal world has increasingly come to the fore as a legitimate object of inquiry, in which it is often the articulation of feeling rather than the documentation of external reality that is at issue (Charles and Telis, 2009). One of the prevalent characteristics of modern art is the search for ways to more overtly explore and express primary experience, to derive new forms through which to articulate feelings (Rhode, 1998). That challenge heightens the tension between the internal experience and the medium of articulation that is fundamental to the aesthetic moment, so that contemplative immersion provides the opportunity for profound transformation for artist and audience alike (Rose, 1980).

From this framework, art is at essence a personal experience in which the "work of art, whatever its content, or subject . . . must be an externalization, through its shapes and lines and colours, of the unique psychophysical rhythm of the person making it. Otherwise it will have no life in it whatever, for there is no other source for its life" (Milner, 1957, p. 230). These patterns, because they are deeply personal, seem particularly compelling, evoking a direct resonance that reminds us that affect, at base, is a patterned phenomenon that joins us all, regardless of the particularities ascribed by cultural context. Art also speaks a language that is potentially comprehensible by all people, communicating directly and "powerfully because it makes systematic expression of deep and spontaneous 'images' or 'impulses,' that are subjective, emotional, and therefore, immediately transferable" (Trevarthen, 1995, p. 160). This universality invites us into the realm of myth, in which we encounter timeless truths through a narrative form that enables us to hold the complexity beyond our ability to grasp the particulars in any given moment (Charles, 2010). Even with abstract art, the audience experiences the aesthetic moment while also in some sense telling him- or herself a story that organizes that experience. Art personalizes the universal and universalizes the particular, thereby providing an opportunity to encounter complex experiential truths at a far enough remove that they might be easier to grasp, and perhaps also easier to bear.

Expressing in language these essentially preverbal moments of inspiration or intuition is particularly challenging. Bion (1977) has defined intuition as information not yet sufficiently metabolized to be capable of articulation. Paradoxically, language provides a structure through which to organize complex meanings but in so doing can limit the affective power and range of the message. Virginia Woolf (1953) was one writer who spoke explicitly of this dilemma as, for example, in her descriptions of the *play-poem* idea that was eventually published under the title *The Waves* (1931, see chapter 2). Adrienne Rich also describes this type of transformative experience, using poetry as her vehicle, articulating a language of the body through which epiphany becomes art (Charles, 2002a).

Poetry is one medium that provides a bridge between words and experience, in part because the structure itself carries meaning. Through the use of metaphor and the affective power of the prosody of the line, poets can convey to the reader a sense of wonder at the ineffability of the world around. In poems such as "Planetarium," for example, Adrienne Rich (1984) describes her felt experience of absorbing and attempting to translate sensory experience into usable symbols, depicting at once an awareness of meaningfulness and also the utter elusiveness of the keys by which those meanings might reveal themselves. At times, as in "Sibling Mysteries" (1978) and "Shooting Stars" (1984), Rich brings the reader directly into contact with a language of the body, depicting how the self becomes profoundly patterned through interactions with the world around. These depictions put us in touch with the nonverbal realm in which the self becomes an instrument through which experience registers and becomes translated into symbolic forms (Charles, 2002a).

The psychoanalyst knows something of being such an instrument. In our work with more deeply disturbed individuals (whose experience may be largely inaccessible through words), we rely on our intuitions—or what Bion (1977) refers to as the *common* senses, the *confluence* of the senses—to apperceive through the unconscious whatever is imperceptible through conscious, rational thought. In our work with less troubled individuals, our intuitions serve as guides through the narratives that have formed like hardened brittle crusts over the more vulnerable facts still to be integrated.

Not unlike the fiction writer, the psychoanalyst builds narratives through attention to Ehrenzweig's (1967) *unconscious order* of nonverbal experience. Narrative provides a structure that helps us to track transformations of relationships between elements across time (Ricoeur, 1984), such that we can perhaps come to distinguish the functional relationships from the various masks or characters they inhabit. Attuning herself to the prosodies of the patient in much the same way as observed in cross-modal communications between mother and child, the analyst learns to anticipate, translate, and transform the types of patterned data—such as affective prosodies—that inform the nonverbal sphere (Charles, 2002a; Fogel, 1992; Stern, 1985). There is always a tension between form and substance such that any interpretation is open to transformations over time as our understanding is augmented and amended by the lived moment.

Exquisitely attuned to the nether regions of dream, phantasy, and primary sensory experience, Virginia Woolf tried to move beyond the constrictions of narrative form in order to bring primary sensory experience—the language of the body—into conscious awareness (Charles, 2002a). She invites the reader into resonance with the feeling by capturing its essence in words. This work parallels the analytic endeavor, as the analysand labors to vivify inchoate experience so that the analyst's elaboration might be more fully grounded in the analysand's inner world. Contemporary Kleinians (Shafer, 1997) elaborate how fundamentally the analyst relies on nonverbal communications, particularly in our work with traumatic experience that has remained outside the rational order. The term *projective identification* marks a communication in which the analyst experiences some aspect of the analysand's internal world that is split off and therefore inaccessible to reflection aside from through the countertransference experience. In tandem, to better understand the multiple levels through which such meaning is constructed, we can consider Woolf's descriptions of *her* struggles and take note of the transformations through which she resolves sensory experience into narrative form.

Woolf had a finely tuned ear for prosody. In her diaries, she writes of the importance of using her imagination to play more freely with ideas gathered by the rational mind. She describes this endeavor almost as though she were composing a symphony of images in which she might keep "the sound of the sea and the birds, dawn and garden subconsciously present, doing their work under ground" (1953, p. 169). Through such endeavors, Woolf shows her poet's ear and poet's heart, balancing the demands of conscious and unconscious mind in her attempts to give voice to sensory experience. This attention to prosody, or pattern, is in line with Miall and Kuiken's (1994) description of how the reader derives meaning from a text: We "begin to anticipate the recurrence and development of certain affective meanings, perhaps only in imprecise intuitions at first, but increasingly explicitly as these recurrences accumulate" (p. 349). Such is the task of the analyst—coming to anticipate both idiosyncratic and universal symbols and to configure threads of meaning as they begin to manifest in the material. In avoiding saturating the present moment with presumed knowledge, the analyst hopes to be open to a new experience that transforms what had been known into something fresh and new. These moments often have the feel of an epiphany: an encounter with "truth" such that our vision feels profoundly altered. This type of heightened awareness is what Oately (1999) refers to in his depiction of the experienced truth value of emotional simulation that occurs in reading fiction.

In searching for a new, more highly refined way of articulating primary experience, Woolf attempts to provide the reader with an experience of an epiphanic moment. Like the poet, she uses her resonance to inchoate meanings to provide condensed, tightly packed images in her art. Like the analyst, she configures these metaphors into narrative form. In speaking to her attempt to combine these two modes of expression, she writes:

> What I want is to saturate every atom. I mean to eliminate all waste, deadness, superfluity: to give the moment whole; whatever it includes. Say that the moment is a combination of thought; sensation; the voice of the sea. Waste, deadness, come from the inclusion of things that don't belong to the moment. . . . The poets succeed by simplifying: practically everything is left out. I want to put practically everything in: yet to saturate. That is what I want to do in *The Moths*. It must include nonsense, fact, sordidity: but made transparent. (1953, p. 139)

In this description, Woolf points to the multi-determined nature of psychic experience, paralleling Freud's insights about the dreamwork. Perhaps, in part, Woolf feeds the mind of the psychoanalyst because her creative journey seems to have been such a personal one. Through her writing, she plumbs the depths of human experience—the human psyche—attending to both conscious and unconscious dimensions of meaning in her search for answers to elusive truths. In *To the Lighthouse,* for example, from the very first page she sets up the dilemma to be explored through James, who:

> belonged, even at the age of six, to that great clan which cannot keep this feeling separate from that, but must let future prospects, with their joys and sorrows, cloud what is actually at hand, since to such people even in earliest childhood any turn in the wheel of sensation has the power to crystallize and transfix the moment upon which its gloom or radiance rests (1927, p. 9).

How, Woolf wonders, might such a person find his way in the world? In tandem, we analysts might wonder how to help our patients (and also ourselves) navigate in the world while also keeping faith with the prosodies of affective life. Using the character of the artist Lily Briscoe, Woolf poses another question: how one might capture an epiphanic moment in such a way as to communicate some essence of that moment to an other. Like a composer, always weaving the strands of her thematic melodies together, Woolf allows her themes and characters to play upon one another, in this way building up experiences and attendant sensitivities in the reader, and allowing these experiences to speak directly, in this way *doing their work underground.*

From the first scene in which James and his mother sit nestled, endowed with "heavenly bliss" (p. 9), only to have their union cut by the knife of the father's gaze, this novel has the flavor of an oedipal voyage. Seen through James' eye, the father comes "grinning . . . with the pleasure of disillusioning his son and casting ridicule upon his wife" (p. 10). In the background stands the Lighthouse, that metaphor of maternity and allure that the mother promises and the father spoils, casting a harsh light upon "the passage to that fabled land where our brightest hopes are extinguished, our frail barks founder in the darkness" and survival is based on "courage, truth, and the power to endure" (p. 11). Here we have a vivid depiction of the oedipal dilemma as cast through the lenses of Bion (1977) and Steiner (1985), as a struggle between light and darkness that too easily leaves us yearning for the soothing obscurity of willful blindness. In this struggle, our desire for the grand light stands in counterpoint to as great a darkness. Like Icarus, we are warned away from that beckoning brilliance so that the allure of heavenly bliss might give way to a terrible but potentially life-saving fall from grace. In this way, using Woolf's own metaphors, our bark might find solid ground rather than becoming caught—like Woolf herself—too soon, too desperately, in the dark, endless waters of the unconscious.

In reference to this struggle, Woolf writes of her sense of a preordained order that whispers around the edges of her consciousness and can be neither grasped nor ignored. These *moments of being,* as she calls them, emerge in her novels in *a fin that turns* in the distance or something that "moved, flashed, turned a silver wing in the air" (1927, p. 33). Woolf uses her characters to represent aspects of self, interposing them such that they become threads playing in relation to the metaphors she has fixed. In this way, she creates exactly the type of symphony of which she writes in her diaries in which the elements play and interplay, doing their work underground. For example, Woolf depicts Lily as a representation of the creative self who stands before her empty canvas and the scene before her, caught by an "avalanche" of feeling such that she feels "herself transfixed by the intensity of her perception" (p. 39) and *knows* "without having learnt" (p. 46).

In *To the Lighthouse*, Woolf plays with this opposition between two truths in many forms, counterposing the "Genius"—that can grasp the elusive products of intuition—with the "plodding and persevering" of the rational mind (p. 55). Another theme threading through this novel is the power of love to connect two individuals but also to obstruct and obscure essential aspects of self, configured for example by James in relation to his father. Woolf, as is her habit, uses the *scene* to note relationships and mark patterns (Charles, 2004b). "Most of all," she writes of James, "he hated the twang and twitter of his father's emotion which, vibrating round them, disturbed the perfect simplicity and good sense of his relations with his mother" (p. 58).

This opposition is configured along the lines of a larger tension between women and men and the price for each of engagement with the other. Through Lily's musings on the creative process, Woolf explores the woman's conflict between creating her own products versus becoming the muse for another. She paints a striking contrast between her portrayal of the creative acts of men versus women. For the man, the creative act is portrayed in relation to the other as a "homage to beauty," but also one can be "redeemed by having won the beauty" (p. 57). For the woman, there is a tension between the desire to *be* Beauty, which in some sense means becoming annihilated as a Subject, versus pursuing one's creative endeavors in spite of the fact that one likely will merely plod rather than purveying Genius or Beauty itself. From this framework, one cannot be redeemed without betraying either the other or oneself. The choice for either the man or the woman, then, is between embracing the illusion of greatness or embracing the truth that unfolds in the living of one's life.

For Woolf, these tensions afford an impossible choice, particularly for the woman who is pulled toward the "rapture of creation" (1927, p. 61). Poignantly, Woolf notes the exhaustion left in the wake of these encounters. Through Mrs. Ramsey, we see the dilemma of the wife who, in locating her value in relation to her husband, becomes a slave to his wellbeing. "Ominously," Woolf tells us, Mrs. Ramsey hears "a wave fall" (p. 61) "at the very moment when it was painful to be reminded of the inadequacy of human relationships" (p. 62) and of her own vanity that keeps her tied, somewhat blindly, in this way. In this image, the trope of the waves that is to organize Woolf's later prose-poem is introduced, presaging her later preoccupations. In this novel, however, we see how Woolf struggles with this issue of how being in love seductively invites us to blissfully obscure painful truths. As Lily contemplates through loving eyes the "magic" that is Mrs. Ramsey, she brings to mind the essence of the woman by starting "the tune of Mrs. Ramsey in her head" (p. 76). Lily searches for insights through Mrs. Ramsey, wondering: "What art was there, known to love or cunning, by which one pressed through into those secret chambers? . . . for it was not knowledge but unity she desired . . . intimacy itself" (p. 79).

Woolf perhaps speaks most explicitly to the issue of epiphany when she writes:

> suddenly the meaning which, for no reason at all . . . descends on people, making them symbolical, making them representative, came upon them, and made them in the dusk standing, looking, the symbols of marriage, husband and wife. Then, after an instant, the symbolical outline which transcended the real figures sank down again. (pp. 110–11)

In the novel, Woolf highlights this type of epiphanic moment and she also invokes it, bringing the reader into a transcendent reality in which distinctions blur. Much as the analyst attempts to ground herself in the multidimensional experience of being both mother and child, persecutor and victim, Woolf uses the characters of Mrs. Ramsey and Lily Briscoe to consider timeless dilemmas, such as those anchored in the Oedipal myth. From this point of paradox, we are challenged to find the sense *and* the nonsense, and to tolerate both, as the other finds his or her own way through. So, for example, through the transparency of her observations of mother and child, we find Mrs. Ramsey encountering transference as she divines:

> through her own past, some deep, some buried, some quite speechless feeling that one had for one's mother at Rose's age. Like all feelings felt for oneself, Mrs. Ramsey thought, it made one sad. It was inadequate; what one could give in return; and what Rose felt was quite out of proportion to anything she actually was. And Rose would grow up; and Rose would suffer, she supposed, with these deep feelings. (1927, p. 123)

Continuing her exploration of the multiplicity inherent in human experience, Woolf also considers from two sides the woman's desire for the ephemeral, for Beauty. Juxtaposing her characters, we see that whereas Lily takes her own path, Mrs. Ramsey is elevated in relation to the man who places her on a pedestal. Woolf locates Mrs. Ramsey in a similar position to that of the analyst, who narrates the story of the other, aware of the importance of the part she plays and at times able to enjoy being equal to this task. At other times, however, Mrs. Ramsey feels lost, without purpose or meaning, as though life has passed her by. By creating an outer perspective through Lily, Woolf is able to observe the Woman from inside and out, first noting Mrs. Ramsey's internal awareness of being lost: "But what have I done with my life?" she wonders. "She had a sense of being past everything," as though it had "all come to an end" (p. 126). Then we see Mrs. Ramsey from the outside as Lily Briscoe watches her "drifting into that strange no-man's land where to follow is impossible and yet their going inflicts such a chill on those who watch them" (p. 127). From this perspective, for Mrs. Ramsey, the place of Beauty becomes the place of Death.

This novel, cast in three parts, has a ternary structure in which we have the prelude, the intermezzo and the conclusion. Seen as parts of the human life, we can see a preliminary text, rife with pre-oedipal themes, such that young James still holds the hope of attaining the lighthouse even though his father bars the way. In her turn, his mother attempts to hold togethe—for each member of the household—the vitality embraced by this type of fantasy. In part one, no one seems able to move beyond this essential dilemma. Jouissance seems achievable, beckoning just out of reach. In the second portion, however, time intervenes and sweeps away the illusion of endless life and fantasies fulfilled. Then, in the final section, we see how life fares in a world in which fantasies cannot be sustained. Mothers do die too soon and, in the wake of such a momentous event, some fantasies must yield and even life itself cannot necessarily be sustained.

Perhaps Woolf's greatest gift is her ability to use her unconscious resonance to bring forward complexities that continue to elude her. Like a composer, she weaves together strands that are sufficiently in tune with her own epiphanic experience that they evoke an affective resonance in the reader, pulling us toward a deeper engagement with our own struggles. And so we find that she has placed the threads of her internal struggles—children who die in far-off wars; mothers who predecease them; tensions between survival as a woman and as an artis—and woven them in tight melody such that we still hear the "sound of sea and . . . birds, dawn and garden subconsciously present, doing their work underground" (1953, p. 169). Such is her genius that these elements of experience come alive in the reader and ripple into the unconscious, doing their work underground.

In Woolf's novels, exquisitely counterposed are the conscious and unconscious realms as she fights to bring into words sensory experiences that to some extent must always elude language. Female and male, fantasy and reality confront one another, as do tensions between the death of fantasy versus death itself, inextricably intertwined. Woolf puzzles through these enigmas in ways that speak of and beyond her own being, yet sufficiently anchored in her experience, in her voice, to bring us into that realm of timeless truths and timeless terrors; the realm of artistic creation.

This is also the realm of the psychoanalyst, in which we encounter ourselves in relation to an unknown other who has come to us for assistance. The process, then, is inevitably one of coming up against this otherness, taking it in, metabolizing it, and offering something back such that whatever is being offered can be struggled with, worked, and reworked. Although we may not consciously know where we are going, clinicians have incorporated other such experiences of not knowing where we are going and yet finding our way. That paradox helps us to tolerate the current experience of being lost in the darkness without shining the light of our own brilliance such that the path becomes further obscured (Bion, 1990). The psychoanalyst works best in the twilight of the preconscious, with one foot in the lived reality of the moment and the other in the unconscious resonances always at play.

As we attempt to meet the other in this place of potential, we use whatever we can from our experience and our theory to approach the place where the other has become caught while also trying to offer something that will be useful. In this process, we come up against the inevitable otherness that separates us, but we also come up against the inevitable sameness that marks us as co-travelers in the all too human journey of living a life. I experience this both—and as a Jacob's ladder in my mind's eye that turns endlessly and can never quite be captured or contained. The inevitable otherness of being marks the rupture between self and other beyond which we cannot know. Noted by Freud (1900–1901) in his idea of the navel of the dream, and by Lacan (1977b) in his demarcation of the inevitability of giving up the hope of omniscient omnipotence, there is always a gap between our desire to know and the limits of our ability to do so. This is the point of yes and no that Bion and Lacan notably mark for us. It is both the frustration of the work and the remarkable hope of it that one can continually move toward the light, or the darkness, without becoming impossibly frustrated, engulfed, or destroyed.

When we enter the realm of primary experience, we are in the magical, mysterious territory of dream, myth, and legend, where the rules of daily experience are suspended and the unconscious order holds dominion. In this twilight domain, we come closer to the more primary aspects of experience, the levels underneath the stories we have learned to tell ourselves repetitively, like rosary beads, to keep the demons at bay.

For the artist caught between her creativity and the pragmatics of daily living, being oneself can feel like an impossible conundrum. Moving now to the consulting room, we can consider "Jane," a young writer of great promise, who had come to an impasse as her creative products became increasingly studied and empty. This emptiness stands as a stark concretization of the emptiness she encounters inside, seemingly cut off from her own internal vitality and considerable resources. Pale, wan, and seemingly frail, Jane is a study in contrasts, with a downward turn to eyes that flare brilliantly in flashes of smile when her intellect is engaged by a comment that connects.

Jane presents a story that is not easily told or received, in which nothing is quite as it seems and the very beauty of her productions is a trap she recedes from. She seems to be faced with an ethical demand in which the beauty of one's productions is insufficient if not infused with that psycho-physical energy Milner (1957) alludes to. Caught by a family history in which need and desire cannot be acknowledged, however, she is cut off from that very vitality, without even marking this detachment as a dilemma. Underneath her concerns over her ability to think and write cogently, her deeper underlying questions have to do with her personhood. Coming into being as a character-who-creates will necessarily entail reclaiming her body and the primary sensory experience that might enliven her being and suffuse her works with the personal encoding that is inevitably our best route to the universal.

At this juncture, in which the epiphanic experience that moves towards expression meets questions of value, we come up hard against the void that Jane encounters as she worries around the edges of her own hopes and fears. Fundamental to the psychoanalytic process is our willingness to sit with uncertainty. Meeting in such moments carries the desire and dread of profound intimacy, as we allow ourselves to touch and be touched in the areas of greatest vulnerability, encountering the *sensory signatures* (Fabiani, Stadler, and Wessels, 2000) of our patients' memories. These encounters reactivate what psychoanalysts have referred to as "memories in feeling" (Klein, 1957, p. 254), a *language of the body* (Charles, 2002a) through which nonverbal understandings are stored and speak their truths in patterned form. It is through this type of articulation that trauma longs to heal itself, an urge toward transformation that we see in Woolf's writing and in Jane's symptoms. This urge seems to be one facet of what Bion calls the *truth instinct* and Gadamer (1988) refers to as the deadly serious domain of *play*, which affords the possibility of transforming despair into something true that speaks *of* the universal *through* the individual.

Although we cannot know where an individual journey will take us beforehand, over time our sensory instruments become more finely attuned, resonating to the realities of the lived moment, such as they are. In those moments, our only guiding star may be the integrity—culled from all we know of being human—that leads us toward truth as best we can find it (Grotstein, 1981). It is important for the psychoanalyst to be respectful of how much is learned directly through our bodies about what it means to be human and how to make our way in the world (Olds, 2008). The recent work in neurobiology on mirror neurons affirms what we know from experience regarding how fundamentally bein—-with another imprints itself upon us and is integrated at the sensory, bodily level (Gallese, 2009; Rizzolatti and Craighero, 2004). The Unconscious is at essence a domain of patterns, in which understanding takes the form of pattern recognition. Being with the patterns of another person over time imprints those patterns upon us, which we then *know* from our own experience and also *understand* via whatever reason we can bring to bear.

Psychoanalysts have intuited the essential relation between being-with and becoming, and have spoken of it in many ways. Perhaps Winnicott (1971) points most clearly to the fundamental relationship between being—with a receptive other and being able to discover one's self and one's creative potential, such that it is in one's ability to play that one is most real. And so, for Jane, for Rich, for Woolf, and for all of us who endeavor to transform moments of epiphany into forms that can be shared with others, it is paradoxically our ability to create from a space in which we can be most fully ourselves that we are most likely to touch something true and profound in the other. That truth may be terrible to contemplate, inviting our resistance, but it is also compelling, a siren's call that holds the eternal in relation to the sweet and painful knowledge of our finitude. That knowledge puts a limit to our narcissism, reminding us of the need to pass along whatever is precious to those who will come after.

Returning to Lily, we can envision her standing before the empty canvas, contemplating the Beauty that is Mrs. Ramsey. We can weave into this picture the words of Gadamer (1988): "the absolute moment in which a spectator stands is at once self-forgetfulness and reconciliation with the self. That which detaches from everything also gives him back the whole of his being" (p. 113); "the transformation is a transformation into the true" (p. 101). That ability, to be present with, recognize, and further integrate truth as one has experienced it, forms the foundation on which self-development and creative capacities can be built, cherished, and passed along. That place is one in which the psychoanalyst hopes to stand sufficiently to be able to invite her patients into this space of potential as well.

NOTE

1. This chapter is an amended version of a paper originally published as: Marilyn Charles, "Epiphany: The Poet's Art, The Analyst's Instrument: Formal Structure as a Vehicle for the Expression of Primary Experience," *The Psychoanalytic Review* vol. 97, no. 3 (2010): pp. 451-467. Copyright Guilford Press. Reprinted with the permission of The Guilford Press. Excerpts from *To the Lighthouse* by Virginia Woolf. Copyright 1927 by Houghton Mifflin Harcourt Publishing Company. Copyright © renewed 1954 by Leonard Woolf. Reprinted by permission of Houghton Mifflin Harcourt Publishing Company. All rights reserved.

TWO

The Waves

Tensions Between Creativity and Containment in the Life and Writings of Virginia Woolf[1]

> "I am made and remade continually. Different people draw different words from me."
>
> —Virginia Woolf, *The Waves*

In this chapter, we will consider the fine line between genius and that *edge too far* alluded to in chapter 1. Many creative individuals have struggled to bring their individuality to bear without completely losing touch with their grounding in reality (Charles, 2003a). Some, like Icarus, have flown too close to the flame, whereas others have greatly enriched our lives with treasures mined in travels through their own less conscious regions. Virginia Woolf is one artist who straddled that line, leaving behind a rich legacy through which we can watch an artist struggling both implicitly and explicitly to bring forth her genius without losing hold of her sanity.

For Woolf, the roots of her creativity seem to be inextricably entwined with the roots of her madness. In her diaries (1953), we see her struggling to contain the threats posed by the unconscious without losing touch with the bounty offered there, explicitly depicting the unconscious as the container of important patterns she is trying to understand. In her fiction, these same themes often play as a background melody. They emerge more explicitly as we see her playing out, through her characters, tensions between insanity and creativity and between freedom, containment, and constraint. These tensions between creativity and madness are perhaps most apparent as we look through the successive revisionings of Woolf's (1931) novel *The Waves*.

The Waves may be viewed as an attempt to descend into and explore the unconscious and to bring forth its riches into the light through the use of metaphor. In this endeavor, Woolf (1953) explicitly attempts to move beyond the constrictions of the narrative form in order to produce a work that is both dense and transparent, thereby vivifying her original inspiration, which was profound but ephemeral. Metaphor provides a means for playing with complex realities so that we can consider and reconsider them (Charles, 2004a). Works of art that stand the test of time do so in part because they provide a means for the observer to encounter and more deeply consider these complexities. The interplay between reader and text can be extremely enriching, inviting us to share vicariously in the moment of illumination.

In Woolf's fiction, we see her creating characters and scenes as a way of considering aspects of self, other, and world from the relatively safe vantage of distance. As we join with her in this process, we are offered an opportunity to reflect on these relationships from the inside out and from the outside in. This type of exploration is perhaps best exemplified in *The Waves*, a novel that provides us with a complexity of voices and perspectives from which to consider what it means to be human. Explored, in particular, are the interrelationships of whole to part, conscious to unconscious, and passive to active. The novel is composed of multiple voices speaking collectively for the individual domain, segmented reciprocally with passages reflecting the impersonal realm. Woolf (1953) refers to the former as *soliloquies* or *monologues* and to the latter as *interludes*. The interplay between these two elements sets up a basic rhythm within the text that frames and enriches the themes being explored.

Woolf (1976a) left behind two drafts of the finished novel, replete with notes and extensive revisions. The holograph drafts preserve Woolf's ongoing editing, including strikethroughs and errors of grammar and punctuation. As we compare the earlier drafts of *The Waves* with the completed version, we can see quite vividly how her inner turmoil was projected out onto the printed page and then contained, condensed, and refined. Being able to view the evolution of this work affords a unique vantage point from which to consider relationships between the inspiration and the creative product.

Creativity involves the sometimes-competing urges between the desire to divest the self of self (and the turmoil of not understanding) and the desire to project the self upon whatever stage has become the medium of choice. Each of these paths provides a means for containing our ambivalence and mastering the trauma of not understanding. Our lack of comprehension is often a function of our inability to integrate information experienced as assaults upon the self. These assaults may be due to a lack of recognition of positive aspects of self (lack of valuing) or from active devaluing of aspects of self. Not understanding can be a way of avoiding encountering the "bad" self. The avoidance, however, affirms the badness and thereby further entrenches it. We find ourselves at odds with our own ambivalence, the type of dual motive that can obscure but can also bring to light whatever has been deemed unseeable.

Duality is inherent in *The Waves*. This novel may be viewed as an attempt to descend into the unconscious, mine it, and bring forth its riches into the light. It is also, however, an unconscious attempt to *dump the refuse onto the shore* (using the language of Woolf's own metaphors): to bring our creations—in the forms of our children or our words—to life and to tolerate that, though uniquely ours, they are also merely one more creation in the larger scheme.

For Woolf, who had hoped to bear children but was barred from doing so, her words were in many ways the children she had longed to bear. Her barrenness, linked as it was to a history of mental instability, became linked also to a sense of inherent deficit (Bell, 1972a, 1972b). In light of this vulnerability, it is with great poignancy that we are struck by how carefully she considered her words and how fearful she was of bringing those words into the light. There is an urgency to give flight to her ideas and a corresponding fear of being annihilated in the process. We see her caught between the urgent pressure to bring forth her words and the fear of letting them go, playing with these competing urges so that she might allow her progeny to stand on the shore and find their own place among the others. Always in the background are the lingering doubts and questions that plagued her. Would her works be recognized? Would they be valued? Or would they become mere refuse upon the shore?

I have been fascinated by the abundance and richness of the material left by this woman who struggled so valiantly to be known and valued. Tensions between the need to create and the need to maintain one's bearings in the pragmatic world can pose a dilemma for any artist but were particularly problematic for women in an era in which the roles prescribed for them were so constricted. Woolf did not have access to some of the means available today that might have enabled her to work through these dilemmas within the containing bounds of a therapeutic environment. She did receive sustenance from her family, however. The value they ascribed to the written word helped to provide Woolf with a vehicle for expression and recognition.

Woolf seems to have used her writing as a way of bringing forward her own primary process material (the seemingly relatively free associations to be found in earlier drafts of her manuscript) and then elaborating it, using the formal structuring of secondary process to refine and contain it. In this way, she was able to provide the reader with a clear, recognizable story line in most of her novels, augmented by the condensed depth and layering traditionally found in poetry.

Because her earlier novels had worked on both of these levels, Woolf had been able to be read, appreciated, and accepted. The overlay of the narrative provided sufficient structure to invite the reader in, whereas the underlying depth engaged the reader at a deeper, more profound level. As Woolf's writings progressed, however, her work became more daring. Much like the waves that had so captured her imagination, her daring ebbed and flowed, producing alternations between the more innovative pieces that taxed and strained her resources versus the more conventional, less taxing pieces that enabled her to continue to ply her art and trade during the periods of recovery between the more arduous endeavors.

Woolf originally conceptualized this particular novel through the metaphor of moths flying ostensibly freely but drawn inexorably to the flame that is both light and death, another nexus in the oedipal prohibition against knowledge (see Bion, 1977). In keeping with this sense of disquiet and foreboding, the metaphor of the moths seems to represent, for Woolf, a sense of the imminent coming together of random elements in a way that eventually intrudes into and impacts upon the human drama. Over time, this inevitability came to have a different rhythm that was embodied in the metaphor of the waves. Although the image of the waves evokes the arbitrary randomness and nonrational order of the original metaphor, it is less chaotic and carries more of a sense of a relentless, patterned order than is evoked by the image of individual moths propelled into flight by some mysterious, unknown force.

The common element here would seem to be that the moths are ultimately drawn to (and destroyed by) the light, much as the waves break upon the shore, discharging some of their vitality. In the ongoing interludes with which Woolf intersperses the final text, we encounter the inexorable, inevitable sounding of the waves, the ceaseless eternal bringing to birth. In this metaphor, there is no intent. The urgency is primal and without desire. The inevitable receding of the waves is less salient in the text. Ultimately, however, the ebbing that must precede and follow the flow is brought to the fore as the characters face their own ebbing, their own mortality.

I have discussed previously how patterns come to be reference points for marking metaphors and for making sense of self and universe (Charles, 2002a). Formal elements constrain and circumscribe our realities at a very primary level. For Woolf, the primary formal element in her fiction is the scene. The scene marks the configural space and offers a way of pondering the intricacies of existence. In her autobiographical writings, Woolf notes that scenes provide

> a means of summing up and making innumerable details visible in one concrete picture . . . [but also] I find that scene making is my natural way of marking the past. Always a scene has arranged itself: representative; enduring. This confirms in me my instinctive notion: . . . the sensation that we are sealed vessels afloat on what it is convenient to call reality; and at some moments the sealing matter cracks; in floods reality; that is, these scenes—for why do they survive undamaged year

> after year unless they are made of something comparatively permanent? (1976b, p. 122)

These musings find their way into the final novel, as well, as Woolf ponders and marvels at the incredible richness that can impregnate and vivify a visual image. It is Bernard, the character who speaks for the writing self in the novel, who marks the pivotal images as they recur:

> Leaning over this parapet I see far out a waste of water. A fin turns. This bare visual impression is unattached to any line of reason, it springs up as one might see the fin of a porpoise on the horizon. Visual impressions often communicate thus briefly statements that we shall in time to come uncover and coax into words. (1931, p. 134)

This image—of a waste of water—is incredibly poignant in light of Woolf's longing and inability to bear children. From this waste of water emerges a fin: something deadly and yet alive. Woolf wrestles repeatedly with this fin, it emerges recurrently in her work.

As Woolf talks about the experience of creating this novel, there is always the urgency of the inspiration lurking just below the surface. At times, this urgency can seem quite treacherous, as in the image of the fin, whereas at other times it can feel benign, prescient, or pregnant with possibilities. In finally coming to the end of the work, Woolf describes the experience as one of "moments of such intensity and intoxication that I seemed only to stumble after my own voice, or almost, after some sort of speaker (as when I was mad) I was almost afraid, remembering the voices that used to fly ahead" (1953, p. 169). At this pivotal juncture, she remarks on the transformation that had occurred over time regarding the metaphors and images through which she had conceptualized the work.

> What interests me in the last stage was the freedom and boldness with which my imagination picked up, used and tossed aside all the images, symbols which I had prepared. I am sure that this is the right way of using them—not in set pieces, as I had tried at first, coherently, but simply as images, never making them work out; only suggest. Thus I hope to have kept the sound of the sea and the birds, dawn and garden subconsciously present, doing their work underground. (1953, p. 169)

In this way, Woolf manages to achieve a balance between conscious and unconscious. She finds a way to elaborate the unconscious sufficiently to bring it to life in words, without overriding its power by overly refining the elements.

In allowing the images to speak to the reader, Woolf demonstrates an implicit faith in her ability to convey some essence of the affective experience that inspired the text. That faith is affirmed by the responses of readers over the generations and also by evidence gleaned by literary theorists. Miall and Kuiken (1994), for example, have found that the reader responds not only to the semantic meanings of the words but also, more fundamentally, to patterns in the text, to the ways in which affective meanings recur and are developed so that they begin to accumulate meanings for the reader. This ability to anticipate and to come to know the work in this primary fashion helps to promote a sense of familiarity that can be extremely engaging and thereby potentially transformative (Oately, 1999).

The Waves has its underpinnings in a patterned, elusive form that took hold of Woolf's consciousness and would not let go. We find early intimations of the inspiration that gave rise to this novel in passages from her diaries. On September 30, 1926, for example, she writes:

> I wished to add some remarks to this, on the mystical side of this solitude; how it is not oneself but something in the universe that one's left with. It is this that is frightening and exciting in the midst of my profound gloom, depression, boredom, whatever it is. One sees a fin passing far out. What image can I reach to convey what I mean? Really there is none, I think. The interesting thing is that in all my feeling and thinking I have never come up against this before. Life is, soberly and accurately, the oddest affair; has in it the essence of reality. I used to feel this as a child— couldn't step across a puddle once, I remember, for thinking how strange—what am I? etc. But by writing I don't reach anything. All I mean to make is a note of a curious state of mind. I hazard the guess that it may be the impulse behind another book. . . . I want to watch and see how the idea at first occurs. I want to trace my own process. (1953, pp. 101–102)

In this passage, we see the juxtaposition of inspiration and creative process as alternate means for exploring one another. There is also a growing fascination with form and structure as vital elements of a greater whole that is, as of yet, a formless intuition. We see Woolf attempting to create a style that will be evocative of the transformational process through which the novel is being born. She refers to this evolving wellspring recurrently in her diaries, attempting to vivify it, to give it form. In 1927, for example, she comes back to "the play-poem idea; the idea of some continuous stream, not solely of human thought. . . . I do a little work on it in the evening when the gramophone is playing late Beethoven sonatas" (1953, p. 108).

In November of 1928, she writes: "The Moths still haunts me, coming, as they always do, unbidden, between tea and dinner while L. plays the gramophone" (1953, p. 138). Woolf writes of her desire to integrate the inner and the outer, and to keep the spontaneity of her earlier writing while incorporating an imposed order. Preoccupied by the idea of meanings that emerge from a lived moment, she can envision a text in which she might be able to capture such a moment so as to "give the moment whole whatever it includes" (1953, p. 139). She notes that what she is searching for is almost the opposite of a poem, in which meanings are stripped down to their very essence. Rather, she imagines what she terms a *play-poem* that communicates the essence through the inclusion of all the various bits of experience of which a moment is made.

In early 1929, Woolf's ideas begin to coalesce as she explicitly juxtaposes the mystical and ephemeral with the solid and enduring, contrasting the uncertain flight of the moths with the recurrence of the waves. She writes:

> Now is life very solid or very shifting? I am haunted by the two contradictions. This has gone on forever; will last forever; goes down to the bottom of the world—this moment I stand on. Also it is transitory, flying, diaphanous. I shall pass like a cloud on the waves. Perhaps it may be that though we change, flying after one another, so quick, so quick, yet we are somehow successive and continuous we human beings, and show the light through. But what is the light? I am impressed by the transitoriness of human life. (1953, p. 141)

The weight of the transitory seems to press upon her in her urgency to give words to her intuitions without betraying their essence.

The process of writing *The Waves* seems to parallel the intent to give the moment whole, to provide the reader with an experience of absorption into aspects of life's mysteries. It is in this work, more than any other, that Woolf pushes herself and her art to their limits. "I sacrifice nothing to seemliness. I press to my centre" (1953, p. 151). Woolf was explicitly attempting to break through the external bounds of convention, even as she broke through the internal constrictions that inhibited the relatively free elaboration of her ideas. In this endeavor, she seems to be grappling with the same type of dilemma that Bion (1977) faced in his attempts to extricate pivotal conceptualizations from the mass of preconceptions that can cloud and obscure them. This is an important facet of art and theory, each of which can potentially vivify or highlight reality in a way that shakes us free from habitual modes of seeing and feeling (Shklovsky, 1917).

Decontextualizing reality in this type of way enables us to see anew what we may have ceased to notice due to inattention or habituation. In May 1930, Woolf writes:

> Unlike all my other books in every way, it is unlike them in this, that I begin to re-write it, or conceive it again with ardour, directly I have done. I begin to see what I had in my mind; and want to begin cutting out masses of irrelevance and clearing, sharpening and making the good phrases shine. One wave after another. (1953, p. 159)

Then, in August of that year, she notes that the book is "resolving itself . . . into a series of dramatic soliloquies. The thing is to keep them running homogenously in and out, in the rhythm of the waves" (p. 159).

In the form and structure of the book, we see the same configural and affective elements that are evoked more explicitly by the content. We are pounded by the waves created by the segmenting enforced by the intervals within the book, as we encounter the various personages and then the waves and then the voices once again. This repeated encounter confronts us with the added layer of the passage of time in a much more direct, experience-near form than was the case in *The Years* and *To the Lighthouse*. In those novels, Woolf (1927, 1937) *told* us about the passage of time. She illustrated it for us. We were able to encounter the passage of time but only from a distance. In *The Waves*, by contrast, we are not afforded the safety of distance. We *experience* the passing of time in this novel. We are drawn into it. It takes us in and then disgorges us, much like the waves themselves.

My sense is that it was this very phenomenon that Woolf was exploring and trying to capture in this work, so that the form and structure mirror the ideas being portrayed. It was also, according to Woolf, the process that was taking place within her in the act of creation, as she wrote and rewrote the material in successive waves of inspiration and refinement. Like the waves, Woolf put herself forward and then drew back to see what she had left upon the shore. Because she is able to convey her meanings on multiple levels, we are invited into an experience of the phenomenon she is attempting to convey while also taking in these ideas through the more highly elaborated channels of language: the word. It was, perhaps, precisely Woolf's genius to be able to become aware of complexities in unique ways and then to communicate these complexities so effectively that many generations have been able to resonate to and be touched by her images, meanings, and words.

Woolf's greatest asset, which was also her greatest vulnerability, was her ability to access these less conscious configural meanings. Her psychic survival was built on her ability to give words to these meanings in rich and vital ways that were sufficiently idiosyncratic to capture the stamp of her personality but also sufficiently accessible that we are able to share in them and to find our own meanings. This, truly, is the beauty and the richness of art—that a person can "read" the universe through her own sensibilities and pass along to us through that peculiar vertex an invitation to discover whatever we might discover for ourselves.

This novel is dense, with musical, mystical underpinnings. In many ways, it has the feel and intensity of poetry, which essentially "attempts to convey something beyond what can be conveyed in prose rhythms" (Eliot, 1943, p. 23). Poetry moves beyond the surface text to include rhythm and structure as fundamental derivatives of meaning (Miall and Kuiken, 1994). Throughout the writing of *The Waves*, Woolf was preoccupied with the form of it, how to integrate the disparate voices into a whole in which the disparate voices could still sound their own notes.

One formal aspect of this work that is very powerful is the rhythmic nature of the text, which invites a descent into the most basic, primordial underpinnings of self. In this way, we are drawn into the type of primary rhythms within which the book seems to have been conceived and shaped. In her diaries, Woolf describes music as the medium within which the work was birthed. Its rhythmic power is ever present in the background and then emerges into the foreground in the final text, in the form of the interludes.

The power of the rhythmic structure in this text is such that we are not surprised to hear that it was Beethoven that Woolf was listening to in the evenings during the period when this novel was gestating. In December 1930, she writes:

> It occurred to me last night while listening to a Beethoven quartet that I would merge all the interjected passages into Bernard's final speech and end with the words O solitude: thus making him absorb all those scenes and having no further break. This is also to show that the theme effort, effort, dominates: not the waves: and personality: and defiance: but I am not sure of the effect artistically; because the proportions may need the intervention of the waves finally so as to make a conclusion. (1953, p. 162)

Part of what is so exquisitely inviting about this novel is the formal interplay of content and structure. Woolf's concern with form is immanent throughout. In her attempts to bring to bear the power of the formal elements of design and order without losing touch with the vitality of the lived moment, she created a work that is lyrical and evocative. One becomes caught in the rhythms of the text. McConnell (1986) describes the novel as "serial music" (p. 57), in which each movement is initiated by a speech by Bernard, aside from the fifth section, which breaks this pattern to introduce the ultimate break in life's rhythms through the death of Percival. As she writes about the process of writing this novel, Woolf uses musical metaphors to describe her desire to pull the pieces together and to create a unity of the fragments:

> What it wants is presumably unity; but it is I think rather good. . . . Suppose I could run all the scenes together more?—by rhythms chiefly. So as to avoid those cuts; so as to make the blood run like a torrent from end to end—I don't want the waste that the breaks give; I want to avoid chapters; that indeed is my achievement, if any, here: a saturated, unchopped completeness; changes of scene, of mind, of person, done without spilling a drop. (1953, pp. 163–64)

The metaphor of musical form is also explicit in the text itself, as Woolf plays her characters like strings of an instrument she is sounding as she composes. Through the character of Bernard, Woolf fingers the faces lovingly, the faces that have merged to the foreground from all the lives, all the moments. "Faces recur, faces and faces—they press their beauty to the walls of my bubble. . . . How impossible to order them rightly; to detach one separately, or to give the effect of the whole—again like music. What a symphony with its concord and discord, and its tunes on top and its complicated bass beneath" (1931, p. 182).

Although the musical form underlying *The Waves* might be viewed as fugal in nature, Levin (1986) describes it as contrapuntal, suggesting that it moves beyond the fugal toward a newer form:

> The novel moves overall through continuous variation, not through a repetition of experiences and perceptions, towards a final "resolution of forces"—without finally achieving it in actual experience. Even in the long concluding monologue that, in Bernard's words, seeks to "sum up," subjective and objective reality are indistinguishable. The purpose of musical style in *The Waves* is to maintain this sense of ongoing experience through a structure that never seems to end. (p. 222)

This novel emerged through evolving metaphors, from moth to wave. From one perspective, this work may be seen as an attempt to create through words some of the affective responsiveness evoked by great music, while interposing the imagery attendant to Woolf's moments of illumination. The idea of *The Moths* was particularly fascinating to me because it seemed to take the form, in Woolf's experience, of the kind of patterned, configural element that can be so important in marking essential meanings in human discourse (Charles, 2002a, 2004a). Richter (1985) suggests that "the moth embodies the continuous struggle of the mind to bring form out of chaos: the universal and often desperate condition of the artist" (p. 209). The moth, as a metaphor, seems to have very rich and deep meanings for Woolf, for whom the hunting of moths and butterflies was a particularly evocative memory from childhood (Bell, 1972a, 1972b). Woolf refers to moths repeatedly in her diaries and fiction, and the metaphor seems to take particular force as it begins to become embodied in the conceptualizations that ultimately give rise to the novel *The Waves*.

Richter (1985) notes the multifaceted nature of the figure of the moth in Woolf's writings. Woolf uses this image as a metaphor for the writing self and also for the act of imagination: "not only the mind which creates, but also the very process of creating" (Richter, 1985, pp. 199–200). Notably, Woolf explicitly likens herself to a moth, describing her mind as a chrysalis and her recurring descents into illness in terms of a chrysalis stage that infuses her creativity. In this way, she also speaks to her ambivalent relationship with her illnesses, which she dreads but longs for as a source of fertilization, an entry point into the deep wellsprings of her inspiration.

In her diaries, we watch the inspiration begin to take form from its vague but powerful beginnings. There is an urgency and a reverence as Woolf describes her persistent sense of something profound in the making, gestating within her. Initially, there are merely "premonitions of a book—states of soul in creating—[that] are very queer and little apprehended" (1953, p. 145). In a later diary entry, Woolf describes this process more fully.

> I had a tremendous sense of life beginning; mixed with that emotion which is the essence of my feeling, but escapes description. . . . I felt the spring beginning . . . and all the doors opening; and this is I believe the moth shaking its wings in me. I then begin to make up my story whatever it is. (1953, p. 154)

The image of the moth emerges as one of fertility, gestation, and birth. These themes become transformed into the image of the waves, recurrently bringing forth their gifts from the unconscious.

In the symbol of the moth, there is not only the idea of birth but also the idea of inevitability and ultimately of death itself. The moth is drawn to the very flame that will eventually extinguish it. As Woolf tries to capture the ideas and images that mass in her unconscious, ever present are the fragility of the receptacle through which the ideas must pass and the insufficiency of the vessel that contains them. Although Woolf has transformed the major metaphor of the novel from the moth into the waves, remnants of the original imagery remain, particularly in regard to the character of Rhoda, who is the most ephemeral of the six voices speaking within the text.

We encounter the image of the moth in the earliest pages of the novel, as Jinny likens Rhoda's eyes to "those pale flowers to which moths come in the evening" (Woolf, 1931, p. 11). Rhoda's resemblance to the moth becomes a means of affirming her fragility, her ephemeral nature. "Her shoulder-blades meet across her back like the wings of a small butterfly. . . . She has no body as the others have" (1931, pp. 15–16). In an earlier version, this passage reads: "she is the least embodied of us all. She is the most distant" (1976a, p. 420). Woolf is more overtly metaphysical in this earlier version: "There are moments of illumination when everything becomes plain" (1976a, p. 217).

This allusion, however, is also a way of marking an inner vulnerability that is deadly and destructive. We are confronted, once again, with the exigencies of prohibition that warn against that edge too far. Rhoda is not only the moth that will be consumed by the flame; she is also the flame that consumes all life and beauty. "What fear wavered and hid itself and blew to a flame in the depths of her grey, her startled, her dreaming eyes? . . . The willow as she saw it grew on the verge of a grey desert where no bird sang. The leaves shriveled as she looked at them, tossed in agony as she passed them" (1931, pp. 178–179). It is Rhoda who ultimately enacts Woolf's urge toward self-destruction. It is Rhoda who takes the leap into the abyss/flame/void that presages Woolf's final immersion into the watery womb in which she ultimately acts out her own destiny.

The book itself was composed in waves—in successive drafts through which the metaphors merged, emerged, or diffused, allowing us to watch the evolution of the text. Woolf (1953) describes repeated difficulties in breaking off from the novel entirely. She would barely come to an end point when the urgency would rise once more and she would find herself absorbed, once again, into the text. More than any of her previous works, Woolf found herself haunted and enveloped by *The Waves*. She seems to have become immersed in an ongoing process of reaching into the depths and then containing the images and refining them, in striking parallel to the themes elaborated in the text. In the early drafts, we see tantalizing hints of what is to come or, alternatively, we encounter chaotic and tortuous outpourings, written and rewritten in repeated attempts to speak to what seems both essential and true.

In her second draft, Woolf speaks, through the character of Bernard, of "that 'I' . . . who has been most mysteriously composed; ~~from the~~ waves breaking & leaving some sediment" (1976a, p. 718). In the final typescript, this passage reads: "the man who has been so mysteriously and with sudden accretions of being built up, in a beech wood, sitting by a willow tree on a bank, leaning over a parapet at Hampton Court" (1931, p. 201). The waves are gone in the final version: they have receded, once again, into the background and are known largely through their rhythms and the reminders interspersed throughout the text.

Through the characters in the novel, Woolf struggles to give voice to her sense of awe and appreciation at the complexity and beauty of existence. Much as he has come to appreciate himself as a constellation and sum of experiences, Bernard also comes to cherish all the fragments of experience that surround him. They are richly perceived and apperceived:

> all these peelings, fragments of bread, & plush & gilt as the loved relics of some windblown garden; ~~the~~ lovely shapes; the astonishing gift that lies; something, like that pear, at once desirable, but so beautiful, mottled like a thrushs breast, cool, firm, & if you peel it the skin lies in thin spirals, all mottled, veined, like the shells sea shells; so that I hear again the murmur the incessant murmur, which met my ear in the nursery, of breaking waves. (1976a, p. 729)

Woolf seems dissatisfied by her attempts to capture the essence of what she is trying to convey and continues her efforts through several passages, ending with:

> Far, far away I hear the perpetual wave fall; but its shock scarcely ~~d~~ no longer troubles ~~my~~ me: ~~I seem~~ out of the surge of the sea.
> ~~And then,~~ So, for a moment, we seem ~~to have~~ capable of anything; of understanding. Taking upon ourselves the mystery of things—appareled in darkness; ~~I could now~~ I could go now like a spy I seem to hear all that has been sung. (1976a, p. 730)

These passages become condensed in the final version into the following:

> The shock of the falling wave which has sounded all my life, which woke me so that I saw the gold loop on the cupboard, no longer makes quiver what I hold.

> So now, taking upon me the mystery of things, I could go like a spy without leaving this place, without stirring from my chair. (1931, p. 207)

In the first draft, Woolf denies her ambivalence. She sets the final scene in somber tones that maintain a balance, an equilibrium, as though Bernard might make his peace with life before he leaves it. In the second draft, however, we see the chaos that has been denied in the earlier version. Exhaustive and exhausting, this passage is marked by many strike-throughs and repeated attempts to bring the essence of the images to life.

Having allowed the chaos relatively free rein, in the final draft Woolf contains the chaos without denying it. Early on, she writes of Bernard being torn by longing and regret, by memories that haunt and tease him. "Yet this shadow, this vanity, this mask that watches me, has the power to drive me back again, among all those other faces; to make me suffer again, & long laugh; & beat about like a moth, caught in a room, dashing from light to light" (1976a, p. 736). This chaotic passage, worked and reworked, becomes: "Yet this shadow which has sat by me for an hour or two, this mask from which peep two eyes, has power to drive me back, to pinion me down among all those other faces, to shut me in a hot room; to send me dashing like a moth from candle to candle" (1931, p. 208). In this last passage, it is only the repeated blows as the moth moves from candle to candle that sustains the intense assaultiveness of Woolf's original passage.

This theme is picked up one final time in the last two paragraphs of the finished novel, as Bernard accepts his essential aloneness. He separates himself from the "eye" that he kept as the external observer, the self-object who alternately embraced and annihilated him. As he embraces his solitude, "there is a sense of the break of day," which he does not call dawn but rather a "general awakening. The stars draw back and are extinguished. The bars deepen themselves between the waves. . . . Yes, this is the eternal renewal, the incessant rise and fall and fall and rise again. And in me too the wave rises. It swells; it arches its back" (1931, pp. 210–11). This new wave swelling within him is the urge toward death, followed by the waves, breaking once again upon the shore.

Life and death; loss, resignation, and transformation intermingle in *The Waves,* to highlight metamorphosis as an ongoing theme that restlessly and relentlessly forms the backdrop of this text, from images of moths and chrysalis to water and birth. Ever lurking in the background is Woolf's despair at the losses she has endured. Her urgency to transform her agitation into illumination—her despair into glory—gives the text some of its rhythmic, driving pulse. There is also, in this, the urgency to leave something of value behind and to make sense of that which is left behind by others, their residue that resides within us. Woolf expresses some of her own urgency through Bernard as he faces death. At this juncture, Bernard attempts to put forward his life but finds it difficult to separate self from other: the "parts of me that belong to others, that have been dipped in them" (1976a, p. 727). That line note in draft two becomes incorporated into the following passage in the final draft, as Woolf attempts to communicate her sense of the intermingling, and yet ultimate separation, of individual lives:

> And now I ask, "Who am I?" I have been talking of Bernard, Neville, Jinny, Susan, Rhoda and Louis. Am I all of them? Am I one and distinct? I do not know. We sat here together. But now Percival is dead, and Rhoda is dead; we are divided; we are not here. Yet I cannot find any obstacle separating us. There is no division between me and them. As I talked I felt "I am you." This difference we make so much of, this identity we so feverishly cherish, was overcome. (1931, p. 205)

This sense of immersion and intermingling is a recurrent element of *The Waves*, evoked not only by the fluidity of the voices as they entwine with one another but also through references to water. That element is ever present in the text, from images of gestation, pregnancy, and birth, through those of baptism and, ultimately, death. Water comes to stand for many things, from the original source of life, to that which washes one clean, to the final immersion enacted by Woolf in her ultimate return to the source.

The sea as source is closely intertwined with the maternal presence in Woolf's life and in her writings (Charles, 2004b; Wolf and Wolf, 1979). Images of sea and water seem to bind together childhood and memory for her in many ways (Bell, 1972a, 1972b). In Woolf's fiction, the sea is always present at whatever distance, just as her mother forms a distant presence as well. Images of waves breaking and receding are a recurrent theme, reminding us of the terrible losses Woolf encountered through the early deaths of her mother and her beloved brother Thoby. The intertwining themes of life, death, water, creativity, and the maternal presence are nowhere stronger than in *The Waves*. "What is illustrated via this elastic, aquaceous volume is precisely the double, synechdocal link between the maternal body, reservoir of all beings and all objects, and the whole universe—their imaginary interchangeability and the conjunction of their destructive powers" (Ferrer, 1990, p. 70).

Ferrer (1990) notes that water enlarges and tends to become infinite in Woolf's writings. The most striking example is her recurrent allusion to an experience from childhood in which "I was suspended; I could not step across the puddle; I tried to touch something . . . the whole world became unreal" (Woolf, 1976b, p. 78). That experience seems to have provided a benchmark for Woolf. It was one of those moments in which she had a heightened sense of being, the type of epiphany described in chapter 1. Inspiration, for Woolf, often came in the form of an "involuntary rush," in which "one thing burst into another" (1976b, p. 81). In this process, "I suppose that I did for myself what psycho-analysts do for their patients. I expressed some very long felt and deeply felt emotion. And in expressing it I explained it and then laid it to rest. But what is the meaning of 'explained' it?" (1976b, p. 81) she wonders.

Much as Woolf alludes repeatedly to the puddle as a pivotal moment in her own development, Bernard returns repeatedly to the moment he refers to as his own psychological birth, which he describes almost as a psychic baptism:

> Yes, ever since old Mrs. Constable lifted her sponge and pouring warm water over me covered me with flesh I have been sensitive, percipient. Here on my brow is the blow I got when Percival fell. Here on the nape of my neck is the kiss Jinny gave Louis. My eyes fill with Susan's tears. I see, far away, quivering like a golden thread, the pillar Rhoda saw, and feel the rush of the wind of her flight when she leapt. (1931, p. 205)

In this passage, Bernard pulls together the fragments—the disparate aspects of being that Woolf has fleshed out in the text—and enfolds them into self. To do this requires an inner immersion—another type of baptismal fire.

> Thus when I come to shape here at this table between my hands the story of my life and set it before you as a complete thing, I have to recall things gone far, gone deep, sunk into this life or that and become part of it; dreams, too, things surrounding me, and the inmates, those old half-articulate ghosts who keep up their hauntings by day and night; who turn over in their sleep, who utter their confused cries, who put out their phantom fingers and clutch at me as I try to escape—shadows of people one might have been; unborn selves. (1931, p. 205)

The preceding passage takes us far from the immersion in and emersion from liquid that characterizes this first psychic birth, into another realm, less substantial and more elusive. We are carried toward the mystical realm—the ephemeral realm of inspiration Woolf refers to in her diaries. Omitted, however, in the final typescript, is the repetitive sound of the sea that is still in the foreground in the previous draft: "Surely I have had the sound of the sea in my ears always" (1976a, p. 727). In that earlier draft, the sound of the sea is repeated within the text itself, rather than having been removed largely to the refrain that separates the chorus of voices in between.

These voices are always juxtaposed so that we are never free from our ambivalence, the tensions of our essential multiplicity. If Bernard can be seen as the part of Woolf that soothes and loses herself in her phrases, Rhoda would seem to represent the part of Woolf that cannot or will not be appeased and stands always at the edge of this world and the next. Rhoda's ephemeral presence confronts us with another subtext in this multilayered work, drawn from the intermingling themes of death, loss, and resignation.

Death enters the novel most pointedly with the untimely demise of Percival. As we encounter the magnitude of the reverberations of this loss upon each character, we wonder to what extent Woolf is speaking to the terrible sorrow she endured in the wake of her brother Thoby's death. As she reels with the news of Percival's death, Rhoda reflects on her solitude, her utter permeability in the face of despair:

> But I will not make phrases, blinding myself like a bull with silk streamers. ~~I will accept this gift,~~ The heavens have cracked asunder; & here~~, at last,~~ is my flash of light. here is the rent in the world. through which I see ordinary things like trees gashed with lightning. . . . I will do usual things, but ~~with~~ understanding; under this illumination; as an offering to Percival, a bunch of violets, something given him by me. (1976a, pp. 572–73)

Woolf seems to feels the need to dignify the occasion with her despair and, through Rhoda, projects her anguish and hostility onto the world about.

> I am out alone in a hostile world. I do not want things I know, & touch & handle, about me. I want indifference & violence & to be ~~tossed up~~ & dashed down like a stone on the rocks. I want to taste the ferocity & power of this universe. (1976a, p. 573)

In the same draft, Woolf rewrites these passages, making another attempt to speak to the chaos experienced in the wake of the first intensity of sorrow. In this passage, the dark anguish is transformed into a yearning for release:

> I will loose the tumult in my heart—which is like the waves. I will let fly my arrow; & the chained hounds shall race, & I shall give myself to the waters—I shall ~~come~~ no longer restrain this leaping, this bounty this insensate desire, rough & [undulant?], great & powerful like the waves of the sea, to be out of this quit of this free of this, away & away. (1976a, p. 581)

In the final typescript, these tumultuous passages have been tamed. Rhoda imagines a woman going out to the sea, blown by the wind, vanishing:

> Now I will relinquish; now I will let loose. Now I will at last free the checked, the jerked-back desire to be spent, to be consumed. We will gallop together over desert hills where the swallow dips her wings in dark pools and the pillars stand entire. Into the wave that dashes upon the shore, into the wave that flings its white foam to the uttermost corners of the earth, I throw my violets, my offering to Percival (1931, p. 117)

This galloping mirrors the movements of the waves, as we are invited to lose ourselves in their relentless pounding toward shore. In this novel, it is the movement from the source that is always salient, rather than the ebbing that marks the course of the waves' eventual return. The waves pound upon the shore and leave their refuse there. It is the shore that is affected, it is there that our attention is drawn. This directionality would seem to be in keeping with that of the moths, as well, in their movement from some unknown source toward the light that calls to them but also presages their doom. The waves evoke this latter aspect more compellingly. They would seem to be a deeper and more enigmatic metaphor, bringing to mind all the dark complexities of the womb and of primary unconsciousness.

I wonder if the moth imagery represents, in some sense, an attempt to escape from the maternal legacy—from the frightening, albeit generative and creative, darkness of her own unconscious—and to believe that she might *fly free*. This idea of flying free is linked conceptually to the moths who, like Icarus, fly too close to the sun (too far from the parent) and are destroyed in this very flight. In some sense, we carry the longing for flight—for escape—but also the knowledge that the act is ultimately doomed, that it is an act of suicide.

Inherent in these metaphors—the refuse on the shore, the moths to the flame—is the sense that we are all captives, ultimately, of the inexorability of fate. This inevitability would seem to form the core of the resignation with which Woolf must have walked finally into that dark river. As we trace her evolving thoughts about and through this work, we encounter Woolf, transfixed between, on the one hand, this sense of doom and her desires to evade it and, on the other, the seduction of it: her desires to give way to it and submit herself to fate. Recurrently, she returns to the notion of the random yet patterned order that was the source and inspiration for the novel. Although this order was too diffuse and distant to be accessible to the conscious mind, she sensed it, hovering, not merely waiting in the wings, but rather imminent and impinging.

This sense of the parts coming together from more diffuse beginnings—of parts coming together to form a whole—this is our experience in reading *The Waves*, as we are given fragments, pieces of a larger whole that is disparate and diffuse and difficult to organize into a coherent unity. Woolf carries us along with her, allowing us glimpses of some of the enigmas with which she was struggling at the time. The experience is somewhat chaotic and unsettling, resulting in part from the fragmented nature of the text and characters. My sense is that the individual voices speak for aspects of self, projected outward as fragments of character (this was to have been a book without characters), so that we are left with a sense of pieces of the whole—fragments from disparate vertices—and we try to understand these differences and their potential meanings as parts of some greater whole. This is the task taken up more explicitly by the various characters as they attempt to piece together fragments of self and other within the text and grapple, ultimately, with Time.

In line with the musical metaphors, another theme that emerges is that of repetition as rhythm, a prosody that marks for us the passage of time.

Woolf was looking for a new form through which she could depict not only the passage of time, but also the sense of transformation embodied therein. In her first draft of the novel, she writes of

> trying to find, in the folds of the past . . . such fragments as time having broken the complete perfect vessel, . . . still keeps safe. . . . The perfect vessel? But it was not by any means made of durable stuff. For it was only ~~in [ ] looking~~ when the thing had happened . . . & the violence of the shock was over that one could [-] ~~gathe receive~~ understand, or . . . really; live; . . . only when one had left the room & was walking home at dead of night. Then ~~indeed~~ in that ~~vas deep jar,~~ darkness, which had no limit ~~for I am thinking of a~~ very dark ~~midnight, which, & no light, the fact that. what the~~ whose shores were invisible; whose ~~memory, lat~~ whatever had just happened, expanded; & ~~while som~~ something dropped away. (1976a, p. 9)

This is a passage in which the repeated attempts, strikethroughs and new beginnings give some sense of the urgency with which Woolf was attempting to capture something quite elusive yet essential.

This urgency helps to shape the final text, in which themes are recurrent and repeated. The structure of the book is one of voices and interludes within which the same characters are revisited. The six characters speak in turn, each from his or her own perspective. It is often not clear, however, whose voice we are hearing, whose lens is coloring the universe. In this way, we are forced to become involved in the process of discovering the characters and coming to know them more fully for ourselves.

Through the interludes, we are reminded of the passage of time. In the beginning, it is morning: Life is beginning and the children are young. Time passes and the afternoon light

> had brushed a cabinet, & then gilt it. Here made the window on the side of the jar waver. ~~And~~ in an uncertainty ~~an~~ ambiguity, as if some shadow were released, a moths wing flight through the immense solidity of cup & chair & table; which flapping its wings left hanging high spaces; such as those in a cathedral, where the voice fails, & descends, fluttering lost; & dies before it reaches the ground. (1976a, p. 607)

In the final typescript, this text becomes: "All for a moment wavered and bent in uncertainty and ambiguity, as if a great moth sailing through the room had shadowed the immense solidity of chairs and tables with floating wings" (1931, p. 130). In that final version, Woolf has highlighted for us the repeated theme of the interplay between that which is substantial, corporeal and ostensibly real, and the ephemeral.

In the next section, Bernard picks up this theme of time passing and in its very passage illuminating the real. Through Bernard, Woolf gathers her thoughts, as she tries to make sense of the interplay between the form and the scene, the story and the design.

> Why stress these little individual events, & make them into shapes which can be sold like toys on trays? I sometimes think there is no story whatever. And that is part of my curious predicament. And that is also the extraordinary interest; for if it suddenly seems possible that there is after all—something. I talk of "time falling." I talk of "drops forming." I have glimpses of a rhythm; & of an order which is imposed by that rhythm; & of myself being one of those who are able to perceive that rhythm (now & then)—~~que~~ in moments of haste & surrender (1976a, p. 611)

The final version of this passage is crisp, condensed down from the previous iterations through which Woolf had attempted to capture this insight.

> "And time," said Bernard, "lets fall its drop. The drop that has formed on the roof of the soul falls. On the roof of my mind time, forming, lets fall its drop. . . . All through the day's work, at intervals, my mind went to an empty place, saying, 'what is lost? What is over?' . . . This drop falling has nothing to do with losing my youth. This drop falling is time tapering to a point. . . . Time tapers to a point. As a drop falls from a glass heavy with some sediment, time falls. These are the true cycles, these are the true events. Then as if all the luminosity of the atmosphere were withdrawn I see to the bare bottom. I see what habit covers." (1931, p. 131)

Bernard is attempting to deal with the passage of time, with meaning, illusion and, ultimately, with death. He ponders on the "fin in the waste of waters" as he hangs over the parapet, interposed, as it were, between earth and water. Then Susan asks: "Where can the shadow enter? What shock can loosen my laboriously gathered, relentlessly pressed down life?" (1931, p. 136). Each of the characters in middle age affirms the passing of time and acknowledges the that-which-is-not, alongside the that-which-is. Perhaps in Bernard's drop, these dualities have met, acknowledged one another, and parted, but now with greater awareness of their coexistence on some plane of existence.

Neville, in his turn, describes the diminished urgency of age. "The old corrosion has lost its bite—envy, intrigue and bitterness have been washed out. We have lost our glory too" (1931, p. 139). "But now in this room, which I enter without knocking, things are said as if they had been written. . . . I listen. I am marvelously on the alert" (1931, p. 141). The poem he has sought, he is finally encountering. He has come upon the essence of it, this poem that seems to be being written through the living of it. He refers to this poem as the residue that one might glean from casting one's own illuminations upon the fragments, moments, and images that make up a life. To read it,

> one must have myriad eyes. . . . One must put aside antipathies and jealousies and not interrupt. One must have patience and infinite care

> and let the light sound, . . . unfold too. Nothing is to be rejected in fear or horror. . . . One must be sceptical, but throw caution to the winds and when the door opens accept absolutely. Also sometimes weep; also cut away ruthlessly with the slice of the blade soot, bark, hard accretions of all sorts. And so (while they talk) let down one's net deeper and deeper and gently draw in and bring to the surface what he said and she said and make some poetry. (1931, pp. 141–42)

Ultimately, however, it is Louis to whom falls the task of creating the poem that will make sense of it all. "My destiny has been that I remember and must weave together, must plait into one cable the many threads, the thin, the thick, the broken, the enduring of our long history, of our tumultuous and varied day" (1931, p. 144). This destiny, played out across the life span, finds its roots, its sustenance, and its rejuvenation in the fluid waters of the unconscious and its maelstroms of memory and desire. We are brought back, once again, to the source. "I revive myself," he says, "in the waters of childhood" (1976a, p. 470).

In many of Woolf's other novels, we are reminded of the tensions that she experienced between living and dying and between sanity and creativity. Through characters such as Septimus, the poet in *Mrs. Dalloway* (1925), or Lily, the artist in *To the Lighthouse* (1927), we see her attempting to reconcile the two sides of the split between being able to use her art and being overwhelmed by it. In this way, Woolf raises questions regarding the extent to which we use or are used by our art. In addition, how do we balance the need to become immersed versus the fear of becoming overwhelmed by the richness of our unconscious process? In *The Waves,* Woolf dives deeply into her own being, thereby articulating a language of the unconscious and exploring the processes by which inspiration informs creation. In this way, she challenges us to believe in our own voices sufficiently that we can imagine surviving the encounter with the incredible and terrible richness of our own inner beings.

NOTE

1. This chapter is an amended version of a paper originally published as: Marilyn Charles, "*The Waves*: Tensions between Creativity and Containment in the Life and Writings of Virginia Woolf," *The Psychoanalytic Review* vol. 91, no. 1 (2004): pp. 71–97. Copyright Guilford Press. Reprinted with the permission of The Guilford Press. Excerpts from *The Waves* by Virginia Woolf. Copyright 1931 by Houghton Mifflin Harcourt Publishing Company. Copyright © renewed 1959 by Leonard Woolf. Reprinted by permission of Houghton Mifflin Harcourt Publishing Company. All rights reserved.

II

Trauma

THREE

Falling Man

Encounters with Catastrophic Change[1]

"What you see is distracted by memory, by being who you are, all this time, for all these years."

—Don DeLillo, *Falling Man*

Trauma makes a cut into our experience, forcing us to reconsider—or perhaps to consider for the first time—aspects of experience that had previously been hidden by virtue of their very familiarity. In this way, trauma can serve a similar function to art in providing a moment of disjunction that invites us to look at the world in a new way. Whereas art provides a relatively protected space for such an encounter, trauma, by definition, pushes us beyond the bounds of what we can take in tolerably without disturbance. Bion (1965) describes *catastrophic change* in terms of a new idea that forces a fundamental shift in the person. He links this idea to Keats' (1935) conceptualization of *negative capability*. The assault on the twin towers thrust Americans into an encounter with catastrophic change. Previously protected by the illusion of security fed by our relative imperviousness to others' points of view, we are harshly awakened to our defensive blindness. This rupture helps us to see the particular beyond the seeming universality, locating culture as a variable frame defining meanings through the narratives that hold complexities of human experience in conceptual space. Don DeLillo's *Falling Man* (2007) offers a reading of catastrophe as a forced encounter with fallibility, breaking apart illusions of sameness and difference, toward integration of that which trauma excludes from awareness.

In the wake of the havoc wreaked by the 2001 assault on the Twin Towers, we are thrust into an encounter with catastrophic change. Their insistent absence marks an element that had perhaps been missing from

American consciousness, a recognition of our profound vulnerability. Fortunate not to have known war within our borders for many generations, this intrusion shook us to our very core. The illusion of inviolability broken, we are precipitously reminded that we can never be entirely safe from attack, intrusion, or hatred and we find ourselves dragged reluctantly to consider the ravaging effects of such hatred.

Visible now is the extent of the hostility we evoke in others, inviting us to consider what we *might have been missing* that could have provoked such an assault. Although our government has been quick to locate *the problem* in terrorists who seek to destroy us from the outside—and thus to wage war *over there*—this cataclysm also points to other collisions that are occurring in this age of diminishing physical distance between disparate groups whose values can be fundamentally at odds with one another. We increase our peril by accepting the invitation to wage war over there rather than reflecting on the ways in which we are implicated in wars over here. In a nation founded to safeguard the rights of free speech and freedom of belief, it is not clear to what extent we are able to live according to those principles when we encounter major differences in world views or when fear impedes reflective function (Charles, 2006a, June 27–28, 2007, 2008a).

Psychoanalysts know something of the danger of projecting badness into the other such that we are inevitably persecuted from without by whatever we fail to attend to within (Klein, 1935). When fear is triggered, however, it is easy to lose perspective and to accept dichotomous notions of good and bad, right and wrong, as though these simplified versions reflect a larger Truth. Descriptions of the inevitable *return of the repressed* have real implications for the need to grapple as a society with those who have been oppressed or excluded, written over and spoken through. At some level, we know that whatever we ignore still exists and yet the tendency to turn a blind eye persists, leaving our symptoms to serve as reminders of whatever has been excluded from conscious awareness (Bion, 1963; Steiner, 1985). At the societal level, those individuals most fundamentally excluded often speak most eloquently through their actions, potentially offering useful information about breakdowns in the social links, as mounting social, economic, and environmental problems press more insistently for recognition.

Trauma interferes with our ability to form and sustain links with one another, through the overwhelming affect that ruptures our sense of going-on-being in the present moment, thereby divorcing self from self and self from other (Krystal, 1988). The psychoanalytic endeavor provides the possibility of healing such ruptures, as patient and analyst work toward meeting one another and enduring the distress together rather than avoiding it or splitting it off. "What is at stake, then," write Davoine and Gaudillière, "is precisely the coming into being of the subject, the subject of a history not so much censored as erased, reduced to nothing, and yet inevitably existing" (2004, p. 47). In pointing to the perils of becoming complicit in such erasure, Davoine and Gaudillière highlight the potential in psychoanalysis for rediscovering the person-as-subject through the narrative as it evolves.

The complexities of human experience are captured in the parables, myths, and stories through which we mark and pass along our fears, our questions, and our understanding. These narratives provide structures that help us to consider specific aspects of a dilemma in relation to the whole (Bion, 1977; Charles, 2010), thereby also helping us to recognize our common humanity even when this humanity is being tested seemingly beyond human endurance. The testimony of traumatic stories offers an opportunity for repair for both the individual who has been traumatized—and thus thrust outside of the social fabric—and for the witness who otherwise is also barred from a commonly held humanity.

In the research on psychosis and social exclusion we have been conducting through the Erikson Institute at the Austen Riggs Center, we have seen how profoundly coherence can be disrupted by misunderstanding and, alternatively, how cogency can be called into being by an empathic and respectful interviewer (Charles and O'Loughlin, in progress). Felman (1995) marks this same dilemma in relation to the individual whose ability to contextualize his or her own narration in space and time depends on an other who can empathically enter the experience but also remain separate. "The narrator herself does not know any longer who she was except *through her testimony* . . . In itself, the knowledge *does not exist,* it can only *happen* through the testimony: it cannot be separated from it" (p. 53). Evidence from the developmental literature shows how we develop self-coherence in relation to the ability to construct a cogent self-narrative through our engagements with others (Fivush, 2007). From this perspective, it is through the process of narrativization that the subject emerges. Felman depicts a two person negotiation in which one person's ability to be fundamentally touched by another is reparative in and of itself. Bringing the traumatic experience back into the continuum of space, time, and corporeal reality provides a foundation from which a coherent story may ultimately be told and received, and thereby more fully experienced as if for the first time.

In this way, the relation between a teller of trauma and a witness who can be both separate and engaged with a real other invites back into the conversation elements that have been left out. Our intention to respectfully embrace what had been unspeakable is both an ethical and a definitional stance. For the clinician, the close links between trauma and psychosis, and the very different meanings and ideas about care marked by these two designations, invite us to consider our own reflexive responses and to eschew the desire to split off primal terrors and project them into the other. Davoine and Gaudillière (2004), for example, make an ethical stand when they contextualize madness in the annals of a history that has become unspeakable, stating that "people said to be crazy, in the ordinary sense of the term, show us what it was necessary to do in order to survive. . . . In our experience, the successive shocks that constitute the rhythm of an analysis of madness always lead back to the same region, the field of historical and social traumas" (pp. xxii–xxiii).

The willingness to tolerate, resonate with, and begin to assimilate these rhythms can be crucial when working with individuals whose experience has been disrupted by trauma and who therefore in fundamental ways cannot know, much less consistently value, themselves. Because trauma disrupts encoding in verbal memory, communications often occur at the level of the body, through affect that is displaced or through other somatic experiences. In work with such individuals, the disparate worlds of verbal and nonverbal discourse meet and interpenetrate one another, inviting us to either sit with our discomfort as best we might or else further deny and distort the messages we are receiving. Truths at this level tend to be experienced as intuitive or uncanny, often seeming to intrude unbidden into our awareness, a type of truth perhaps more accessible to poetry than to prose. In the words of Lévinas, "The poem situates itself precisely at that level which is pre-syntactic and pre-logical . . . but which is also prior to 'unconcealment': at the moment of pure touch, of pure contact, of that grasping, that pressing" (1978, p. 17).

Although such experience resists being brought into language, novelists at times attempt to give voice to this realm of the uncanny, to speak to something that feels vitally true but as yet has no words. In DeLillo's *Falling Man* (2007), the reader is offered such an experience, invited in as witness to a story uniquely characterized by the fragmentation, repetition, and lack of coherence of the traumatic narrative. In this novel, the reader's expectation of linearity is continually disrupted in a world that has been turned on end. In creating a narrative in which no single perspective claims sovereignty, DeLillo keeps us off balance. At times, we do not even know from whose perspective the story is being told, resulting in feelings of conceptual vertigo as we struggle to regain and retain our bearings in a world in which the reliable markers of certainty have been taken away. As we shift from one perspective to another, moving inevitably toward the catastrophe that has already happened, DeLillo moves beyond the constraints of the personal life narrative to point toward the underlying meanings embedded in the stories as they unfold. By offering multiple vertices that speak together rather than supersede one another, DeLillo creates a modern-day myth while also pointing to ways in which the characters are co-constructing their own myths as they desperately search for meaning.

By offering disparate perspectives, each through the eyes of one for whom trauma has become impossibly personalized, DeLillo exhibits how "facts" are inevitably artifacts of the particular cultural and personal lenses though which they are viewed. Culture marks meanings, much as personal experience colors perceptions of self and other. To the extent that views are shared, the view itself can become invisible, and we can lose sight of even the idea that there might be other possibilities. Collective trauma is particularly vulnerable to this type of distortion, further dichotomizing self versus other and denying the negative effects of trauma by subverting it into a designation of superiority as opposed to inferiority under the auspices of a worldview organized around the *chosen trauma* (Volkan, 2001).

DeLillo's novel juxtaposes one chosen trauma with another, thus breaking into our presumptions through encounters with the Other. In this way, he invites us to consider ways in which individual experiences can be complicated by what LaCapra (1999) calls *structural trauma*. In LaCapra's formulation, the abstract and ahistorical nature of structural trauma lends itself to the type of ecstatically redemptive solutions noted by Volkan (2001) that tend to deny or devalue harm that might befall the other. As one example, LaCapra points to Derrida's (1995a) exposition of the story of Abraham and Isaac, in which the killing of one's child is transformed from a human act of betrayal into proof of an ethic anchored in an abstract higher order. This dangerous turn, in which we are all implicated, is marked explicitly in *Falling Man* through the character of Hammad, the terrorist.

In offering us various and disparate subjectivities through which to view a traumatic event and its sequellae, DeLillo points to the individual, the group, and tensions between the two in ways that afford us an angle into the more complicated truths that can be glimpsed in the spaces that stand between one view and another. In this way, the lenses of culture, themselves, are highlighted and we can recognize ways in which those colored lenses skew meanings. This skewing of meaning can lead to collisions because of disparities that are insufficiently respected or they can lead to collusions that make meanings more opaque because there is no possibility of respectfully encountering another view. In refusing to fully endorse any particular perspective, DeLillo invites us to consider the price of failing to reflect broadly on a particular human dilemma in real time.

In depicting a move into the realm of an abstract Other who must be annihilated in order to ensure our survival, DeLillo illustrates a collapse in the distinction between what LaCapra (1999) terms *absence*, which is general, abstract, and ahistorical; and *loss*, which he describes as inevitably personal and historicized. Seen through LaCapra's lens, the absent towers mark for Americans a structural trauma, in that they invite awareness of our essential and irreversible vulnerability above and beyond any particular event in real time and therefore also beyond any particular resolution. As DeLillo reminds us, they also mark what has been less visible to Americans regarding the plight of Hammad, the character in the novel who represents the denigrated other. Denigration erases whatever legitimacy underlies the dilemma of Hammad, thereby creating fertile soil for the eruption of violence (Žižek, 2008). The erasure of the Other inevitably creates vulnerability in the social fabric, a vulnerability DeLillo depicts by suggesting that Hammad's trauma had remained relatively invisible in American culture until it exploded onto the world stage.

If we think of modernity in terms of the disruption of the subject through the encounter with events that defy integration (Newmark, 1995), then the novel that attempts to engage with both the subjective and transpersonal aspects of trauma becomes an ethical act that is potentially transformative, in pushing us toward facing this demand (Felman, 1995). In distinguishing between the structural trauma that marks a deficit within the social fabric, versus the personal trauma that has been experienced in and marked by real time, LaCapra points to some essential dilemmas inherent in any conversation between the individual whose trauma has remained unspoken and the witness who enables the testimony to unfold.

This engagement in a traumatic moment can be arduous. Felman suggests that the reader of traumatic literature—much like the clinician who is called upon to register the patient's traumatic experience—must be willing to accompany the writer "into the very places—the very night, the very silence" (p. 44) that gave rise to the work. To work through trauma, we must be willing to be pulled into it, to experience it, to be played on by it. In this way, the form of traumatic literature itself must startle us, fragmenting and breaking apart our comfortable resting place and inviting us into a shocking reality in which we might become lost. Only then, suggests Felman, from within the darkness, within the void, "within the woundedness . . . the event, incomprehensible though it might be, becomes accessible" (p. 34). In line with clinical experience, Felman contends that it is in this realm beyond words—in the counterpoint between imposed elements and silence—that meaning emerges.

Much as testimony is made possible in the context of a relationship in which one can witness oneself being witnessed (Laub, 1995), culture and its effects are made visible when there is more than one vantage point to help us catch sight of what we might otherwise be missing. In line with Bion's (1967a) admonition to leave aside memory and desire in order to better encounter whatever we might discover if we can avoid foreclosing on alternative possibilities, Lévi-Strauss (1984) suggests that in order to understand universal problems, we must pull back from our presumptions so as to look from both inside and out, in order to see "what is peculiar to each culture in the form of myth, ritual and language—that is, in domains where the oppositions are both identifiable and unconscious" (p. 22).

As the underlying patterns emerge, we can better see the work of culture, which Ricoeur (1970) describes as similar in form to the dreamwork. In both cases, desire can be located through the ways in which it is disguised within a given frame. In the realm of myth, universal truths are located in relation to an ethos framed by culture and then further colored by personal experience (Charles, 2010). Much as the dream provides an encapsulated picture of complex webs of desire and fear cloaked in symbolic forms, myths and other narratives passed along within cultures help us to hold in mind complexities of human experience so that we can consider parts without losing the whole. These models enable us to represent, organize, and simplify meanings within a conceptual frame, providing anchors for the primary perceptual elements that speak profoundly and directly, and thus insist on recognition (Cassirer, 1957).

In contrast, DeLillo offers a traumatic narrative in which meaning and meaning-making are disrupted, such that the fragments do not register as coherent elements of a sequence over time but rather as disembodied and dissociated fragments, often experienced as imposed or hallucinated, as uncanny, outside space and time (Caruth, 1991). Much like the dream, the elements coexist without the containing (and also limiting) structure of the normal laws of rational logic. Time, an essential element in meaning-making, is lost, evoking the imminence often experienced by survivors of trauma such that, paradoxically, one feels as though one is in the presence of the danger one has already survived (Krystal, 1988; Winnicott, 1964).

For those whose development has been impeded by traumatic experience, putting together a coherent story can be an important aspect of healing. The narrative provides a frame in which absence can be marked and taken note of, as we stumble over a gap that indicates that something is missing, as we move toward and against unconcealment. When dealing with trauma, which by its nature tends to elude integration into conscious memory, this type of demarcation can be crucial (Charles, 2000a; Krystal, 1988). At times, it is only the gap—a notable absence—that marks the meanings that are latent and can only manifest over time as a narrative unfolds (Lacan, 1977c). "For history to be a history of trauma means that it is referential precisely to the extent that it is not fully perceived as it occurs; or to put it somewhat differently, that a history can be grasped only in the very inaccessibility of its occurrence" (Caruth, p. 187).

Regarding the stumbling that must occur in order to encounter something missing, Felman (1995) points to Celan's description of the importance of obtaining sufficient distance from oneself as subject, to literally dis-locate oneself such that we can set ourselves free and perhaps encounter something new. She quotes from Celan: "Perhaps—I'm just asking—perhaps literature, in the company of the I which has forgotten itself, travels the same path as art toward that which is mysterious and alien" (Celan, 1978, p. 33, in Felman, p. 44). Without this disruption, the traumatic narrative cannot be heard but rather is sealed over in the very act of being articulated. In this way, it betrays itself.

In line with current understanding of the impact of trauma on memory (see Hutterer and Liss, 2006), Lacan (1977d) suggests that these gaps do not merely signify a failure to attend but rather an alienation or denial of meaning, which he terms *aphanisis*. This denial of meaning is similar to what Bion (1967b) describes as an *attack on linking*, through which process an associative link is denied, thereby de-signifying an element of experience. This process of marking the unthinkable helps us to tolerate what feels like an imminent and immanent encounter with catastrophic change (Bion, 1970). Titrating our awareness affords some respite from overwhelming affect by keeping the traumatic element out of sight but not quite out of mind, so that we might negotiate such an encounter in ways that may be catastrophic—in the sense of subverting the prevailing order—without being disastrous.

In *Falling Man*, Don DeLillo (2007) uses the absent towers as this type of marker, bringing to our attention a profound absence that has come to carry multiple levels of meanings. Layering absence upon absence, DeLillo invites an encounter with the traumatic memory that is by its very nature fragmented and cannot be fully represented. Of his main character, DeLillo writes: "He was losing things as they happened. He felt things come and go" (p. 240). In this way, DeLillo points to ways in which trauma fragments experience, such that dream, nightmare, and memory can seem so impossibly interwoven that 'reality' can be difficult to determine or rely on (see chapter 7). So, then, even in a familiar setting, an individual might feel, as DeLillo writes, as though "they were falling out of the world" (p. 212). There can be a sense of déjà vu or prescience, as though one is sleepwalking, finding oneself moving into the present in an uncanny kind of way, as though "he was fitting into something made to his shape" (p. 225). Thus disrupted in space, time, and meaning, the numbness and sense of the uncanny may be ways of attempting to come to grips with whatever seems unendurable.

In creating a story that does not tell itself directly but rather circles around a core marked by trauma, DeLillo brilliantly and evocatively creates a structure that signifies and mirrors the traumatic experience, inviting the reader into a direct and highly personal encounter. The Falling Man haunts the book, invoked indirectly through the memories of those who were at the scene of the tragedy, and directly by the character who repeatedly invokes the image by enacting it. The metaphor of the falling man ripples repetitively, as man, his creation, his body, his dreams, and his life as he had known it topple endlessly throughout the novel.

We begin the novel with a man who might be dead but is not. We end the novel with a greater appreciation of ways in which this man, now so deadened, perhaps always was. Keith's failure to come to grips with tragedy and to embrace living invites us to question what it means to truly live, and to wonder how we might embrace the inevitability of pain, limit, and lack in ways that move, not toward dying, but rather toward living life more fully. We, the readers, are the falling man, inevitably falling toward our own fate, as DeLillo invites us to consider whether we will live our lives casting backwards, trying to make sense of the emptiness yawning behind us, or whether we will find a way to move forward, even though this means coming inexorably closer to our own destiny.

In this way, DeLillo picks up a timeless theme, alluded to, for example, in Kafka's (1946) story, "In The Penal Colony":

> "And how does the sentence run?" asked the explorer.
> "Whatever commandment the prisoner has disobeyed is written on his body."
> "Does he know his sentence?"
> "There would be no point in telling him. He'll learn it on his body."
> "Enlightenment comes to the most dull-witted. . . the man begins to understand the inscription . . . deciphers it with his wounds." (pp. 144–45, 150)

This passage describes how profoundly we can be inscribed by meanings we can never fully comprehend but rather *might encounter* if we can attain sufficient distance to afford some perspective through which to view whatever has become "given" and thus recedes from view. Although trauma impedes cognitive capacities and integration of experience in the moment, it leaves its marks upon us that we may decipher over time, as parts of ourselves are annihilated and reconfigured. Traumatic memory is at once personal and transpersonal, our experience transcribed, not upon a blank slate, but rather upon a slate already etched by the histories of those who have come before.

Metaphors, too, are etched by history. Much like the hanged man of the Tarot deck, the Falling Man comes to represent the rupture of the illusion of control that is experienced as cataclysmic but might also make way for greater understanding. Inevitably, the understanding is hard won. The Falling Man character in the novel repeats the illusion of the fall, over and over, finally dying before he can enact the fall itself. Similarly, Lianne, whose husband survived the falling of the towers, is mesmerized by televised images through which she ritualizes her own inability to make sense of what life has offered. Watching the towers fall over and over becomes a liturgy, like rosary beads passing through fingers, leaving no trace but only perpetuating that terrible moment, outside of time. Her absorption in the traumatic moment is not dissimilar from that of the terrorist in DeLillo's story, who girds himself in his religion in order to move away from the pain of the moment:

> Recite the sacred words
> Pull your clothes tightly about you.
> Fix your gaze.
> Carry your soul in your hand. (DeLillo, p. 238)

Continuing to disorient the reader in space, time, and culture, DeLillo shifts seamlessly between characters who invite very different affective engagements. We encounter Hammad, the terrorist, as he mobilizes his resources so as to endure the pain. We are pulled into what feels like real and terrible time, as he fastens his seatbelt and watches a bottle fall and spin. Then, in a dizzying movement, DeLillo pulls us past our resistance and across frames, watching the bottle fall, spin, "and then skitter across the floor an instant before the aircraft struck the tower, heat, then fuel, then fire, and a blast wave that sent Keith Neudecker out of his chair and into a wall" (p. 239). In this one sentence, we are blasted with the realization that we have entered into known and impossibly traumatic territory. The plane has hit; the terrorist's intention has become the victim's fate, and we are left with whatever had been set in motion through the force of history, "the pious ancestors who had pulled their clothes tightly about them before battle . . . the one who named the way" (p. 239). For Keith,

> Things began to fall, one thing and then another, things singly at first, coming down out of the gap in the ceiling, and he tried lifting Rumsey out of the chair. Then something outside, going past the window. Something went past the window, then he saw it. First it went and was gone and then he saw it and had to stand a moment staring out at nothing, holding Rumsey under the arms.
>
> He could not stop seeing it, twenty feet away, an instant of something sideways, going past the window, white shirt, hand up, falling before he saw it. Debris came in clusters now. (p. 242)

In these passages, DeLillo portrays vividly and evocatively the overwhelming absorption in the present along with the dissociation from meaning that typifies the traumatic moment. In that moment, survival functions take over and there is little room for reflection. "The whole business of being Rumsey was in shambles now," writes DeLillo. "Keith held tight to the belt buckle. He stood and looked at him and the man opened his eyes and died. This is when he wondered what was happening here" (p. 243).

Much like the dream, art affords a means for representing truths directly and powerfully, so that we can feel their impact and allow them to register over time, revealing their truths in layers as we absorb them. "Things came back to him in hazy visions, like half an eye staring. These were moments he'd lost as they were happening and he had to stop walking in order to stop seeing them" (p. 243). Because of the potential for saying and unsaying, art also allows us to represent truths that we are repressing as a culture and thus failing to recognize, truths that may be vitally important but that we are having difficulty integrating into our waking understanding (Lawrence, 2004).

Perhaps most difficult for the Western reader, DeLillo cuts into our shared presumptions and offers a view from the other side. He brings us directly into to the many-layered difficulties of integrating and reflecting upon traumatic experience by confronting us with a personal and personalized rendition of the terrorist-who-has-been-traumatized. The reader is invited to sample the perspective of Hammad's mentor, who is haunted by the high-pitched cries of boys he could hear above the other sounds of battle.

> The boys were sounding the cry of history, the story of ancient Shia defeat and the allegiance of the living to those who were dead and defeated. That cry is still close to me, he said. Not like something happening yesterday but something always happening, over a thousand years happening, always in the air. (p. 78)

The terrorist struggles to keep faith with his own ancestors as he faces imminent death:

> The pious ancestors [who] had pulled their clothes tightly about them before battle. They were the ones who named the way. How could any death be better?
> Every sin of your life is forgiven in the seconds to come.
> There is nothing between you and eternal life in the seconds to come." (p. 239)

In this way, DeLillo points directly to the problematic of the chosen trauma described by Volkan (2001), that resists resolution precisely because it splits off the voice and experience of the Other. Such dichotomous battles invite pseudo-solutions that vanquish and silence the alternative perspective, rather than inviting more stable resolutions in which each might be re-humanized in the eyes of the other. When exploring such affectively charged subjects, metaphor can help to hold in mind the essence of the dilemma while exploring the complexities. Using symbols in this way helps us to organize the complexities of human experience, in spite of the inevitable limits of mind, imagination, and endurance.

In *Falling Man*, it is the not-quite-remembered memory of something falling that becomes the unifying metaphor. By offering repeated views from various angles, DeLillo not only helps us to grapple with the complexity of this symbol but also titrates our distress. He thus helps us to tolerate the traumatic image, itself, through repeated brief encounters with what emerge over time to be painful truths. In insisting on including the terrorist in his exploration, DeLillo rejects the call of *the* chosen trauma, implicitly warning us against foreclosing our understanding by accepting without reflection the types of facile truths that are condoned by culture and thereby too easily become invisible.

Symbols help to mark aspects of lived experience that are difficult to represent in more abstract language. Symbols speak to us directly and evocatively, their meanings anchored in affect (LeDoux, 1996), such that "the expressive meaning attaches to the perception itself, in which it is apprehended and immediately experienced" (Cassirer, 1957, p. 68). As these primary perceptual elements attain both signal and symbol functions, intense affective experience can be transformed from aversive flares into meaningful moments that can be noted, communicated, reflected on, and integrated. We see this type of transformative process in the novel *Falling Man* as terrible images are repeated so that, for example, the various implications condensed into the "man scaled in ash, in pulverized matter" (p. 6) are revealed slowly, over time, as our defenses ebb with the force of repeated engagements.

Aiding in this transformation is the narrative process itself, which provides a containing structure through which universal feelings might be comprehended and communicated by condensing complex experiences into "the unity of an 'image'" (Cassirer, 1957, p. 108). For Cassirer, it is the *representation* of the image that enables it to persist, both as a single instance and also as a symbol for something greater from which the instance emanates. So, then, as DeLillo layers and condenses meanings into an evolving image, unpacked slowly over time, he enables the reader to experience the slow process of coming to grips with trauma through the unfolding of the story. Pulled into the position of witness, we are invited to empathize with an other as other, without entirely splitting off what initially feels alien and alienating.

In the novel, these various representations are linked implicitly through their interrelationships within the narrative, before evolving over time into crisper, more directly accessible imagery. DeLillo uses the narrative structure much like the dream, in which meanings are derived through the juxtaposition or narrational proximity among affectively laden images. The very complexity of these relationships affords an affective power to the story, much as we find in dreams, as we respond directly to the kinesthetic dimensions of the determinants. We experience the kinesthetic dimension through the patterning of the elements, and it is the pattern that carries the affective charge (Schachtel, 1966), communicating a direct and experiential sense of participation or co-creation (Kris, 1952). As we project something of self into our experience, kinesthetic responsiveness links powerfully with empathic understanding.

We register these types of primary, kinesthetic, relational meanings without necessarily being able to articulate them. Because they register so directly, they have a different truth value than information learned through words (Charles and Telis, 2009). Paradoxically, however, it is language that provides a system through which consensual meanings persist and thus can be rediscovered. As a sequentially organized process, language "provides that possibility of 'finding-again' and of recognition by virtue of which totally different, spatially and temporally separate, phenomena can be understood as manifestations of one and the same subject" (Cassirer, p. 108). Our ability to detect patterns or, as Bion (1977) calls them, *constant conjunctions*, helps us to build a narrative that makes sense within the meanings defined and proscribed within the frame of a given culture.

DeLillo uses pattern and the traumatic rupture of pattern as a trope in this novel that is fundamentally a meditation on absent presence and the price of foreclosing on mourning. Even as he repetitively breaks into presuppositions framed by culture, DeLillo also repeatedly offers the experience of finding again, whether through the elaboration over time of the horrifying meanings of the pulverized elements we first encounter in the first chapter, or through the Falling Man himself, who appears at various junctures as an almost glimpsed memory, an elaborately enacted illusion, and a terrible reality. The latter enigma is clarified over time but, in the end, DeLillo leaves us with the utter impossibility of truly integrating traumatic memories: "Then he saw a shirt come down out of the sky. He walked and saw it fall, arms waving like nothing in this life" (p. 246). This "nothing in this life" marks our resistance to knowing things that feel annihilating in the impossible demands that such knowledge might impose.

It is not only trauma that impedes integration. If we think of Cassirer's notion of the realm of myth as one in which meanings are defined and organized in terms of differences within a conceptual order, we can also see how elusive meaning can be as we move from one cultural frame to another. Psychoanalysis points to the universality that underlies human experience and yet each culture has its own version of these universal stories, told through that culture's particular lenses. And so, DeLillo contrasts the ways in which Hammad, the terrorist, soothes himself by organizing his experience within his own cultural frame versus the ways in which Lianne, the New Yorker attempting to come to grips with her own traumatic experiences, organizes hers. Even within a given culture, there may be various ways of making meaning. Thus we see how Lianne's struggles to grapple with horror are tinged with iterative attempts to find meaning, whether from her repetitive immersion in the traumatic scene, from spirituality (the Falling Man as tarot card), or from conventional religion.

Like many other Americans, Lianne finds herself repetitively and relentlessly watching the impossible images as they replay in an endless loop across her television screen. In this effort, she seems to be trying to move past some point of impossibility, trying desperately to find anchors in a universe in which meanings are crumbling. Paradoxically, however, the repetition itself denies the ultimate and terrible ending that has, indeed, occurred. "Headlong, free fall, she thought, and this picture burned a hole in her mind and heart, dear God, he was a falling angel and his beauty was horrific" (p. 222). She tries going to church, searching for solace. "It was a comfort, feeling their presence, the dead she'd loved and all the faceless others who'd filled a thousand churches. . . . isn't it the world that brings you to God? Beauty, grief, terror, the empty desert, the

Bach Cantatas" (pp. 233-34). In the catastrophic moment, beauty and horror mingle into a profound sense of awe.

Lianne longs for an encounter with a God who will make sense of seemingly senseless tragedy, but also dreads the ways in which that encounter might make the tragedy real and unavoidable. "God would consume her. God would de-create her and she was too small and too tame to resist. That's why she was resisting now. Because think about it. Because once you believe such a thing, God is, then how can you escape, how survive the power of it, is and was and ever shall be" (p. 235). Lianne finds herself seeking a truth that she fears is beyond her capacity to tolerate. The fear configures in her mind as a terrible, aching absence.

> She thought that the hovering possible presence of God was the thing that created loneliness and doubt in the soul and she also thought that God was the thing, the entity existing outside space and time that resolved this doubt in the tonal power of a word, a voice. God is the voice that says, "I am not here." (p. 236)

By continually changing perspective and thus pushing past the limits of any one mind, DeLillo both condenses and juxtaposes the various absences marked by the metaphor of the falling man, the absence of mind, memory, and meaning; the absence of God; and the absence of the world as we had known it. There is a rupture that resists our efforts to move forward without first coming to grips with the enormity of what has come to pass and its various ramifications. The form of this novel, as is true of narratives of trauma more generally, enacts metonymically the traumatic rupture and dislocation in space and time being portrayed (Olivier, 2008). As readers, we not only see the type of willful blindness that underlies many of our myths that point to the price of knowledge (Bion, 1977), we can also find ourselves implicated. DeLillo uses the character of Lianne to vivify this dilemma of willful blindness: "She was arguing with herself but it wasn't argument, just the noise the brain makes" (p. 236).

Countering this noise that in part marks our reluctance to make meaning from our experience, DeLillo juxtaposes the efforts of Lianne and Hammad—the wife of the survivor and the terrorist who invokes the cataclysm—to use religion to make sense of impossible experiences. Through this juxtaposition, DeLillo invites us to move beyond the constraining veils of our own cultural perspectives to better see what is universal and what is particular in each vantage point. Pulling back in this way helps us to locate our common humanity while also perhaps being more respectful of the inevitable differences we encounter. This stance invokes what has been termed the *Third* or the *Name of the Father*, locating knowledge or "Truth" beyond either the individual or dyadic perspectives. In his early work, Lacan (1977e) links the Name of the Father with the figure of law that endorses meaning in a way that moves beyond any individual rendering. Such an external reference point can help us to recognize our preconceptions and thus obtain a clearer distinction between the universal and the particular. In this way, the novelist invites us to more reflectively consider the positions we take and thus, perhaps, to catch a glimpse of our own *pathological certainties* (Shapiro, 1982) that may promise redemption at the price of care for the individual or for humanity as an overarching principle.

Preconceptions or acquired knowledge not challenged by or integrated through personal experience can become an obstructive force resisting new learning, thereby impeding our ability to grapple with puzzles as they present themselves to us. "Wisdom" itself can be a hazard, if we impose our understanding on a new situation rather than trying to encounter difference and allow it to make an impression on us. Offering a metaphor that speaks to this issue quite pointedly, Bion suggests that if we are to attempt to understand obscure subjects such as "the most fundamental and primitive parts of the human mind . . . instead of trying to bring a brilliant, intelligent, knowledgeable light to bear on obscure problems," we should instead "bring to bear a diminution of the 'light'—a penetrating beam of darkness; a reciprocal of the searchlight" (1990, p. 20). Likening this discipline to the task of observing a game of tennis being played in the dark, Bion invites us to try to tolerate the darkness enough that we might be able to stop looking for the net and see, instead, the "holes, including the fact that they are knitted, or netted together" (p. 21). If we can accept our ignorance and accustom ourselves to the darkness, the object of our attention might reveal itself as it absorbs some of the light that surrounds it, rather than being overshadowed by our "brilliant" illuminations.

This model encourages ongoing humility in the face of the inevitability of difference. If we can tolerate our ignorance rather than trying to immediately overcome it, we are in a better position to learn. When dealing with unconscious defenses, which by definition resist our efforts to detect them in ourselves, it is useful to have in mind a model that encourages us to hold steady when we would most like to leap away. Having in mind that there is always a larger perspective from which a situation might look different than what we are currently able to see or imagine helps us to inquire into the darkness of what is not yet known rather than accepting presumed knowledge in ways that occlude further understanding. While collisions between opposing viewpoints can be uncomfortable, they also serve as signals of gaps that might be attenuated through further inquiry. These signals alert us to the possibility that we might be so deeply embedded in our own culture that the road signs have become implicit and not easily noted. Often, suggests Lacan (1977j), it is only in our stumbling that some greater truth might be revealed,

> by which we would arrive at the paradox of conceiving that the discourse in an analytic session is valuable only in so far as it stumbles or is interrupted: if the session itself were not constituted as a cut in false discourse, or rather, to the extent that the discourse succeeds in emptying itself as speech, in being no more than Mallarmé's worn coinage that is passed from hand to hand "in silence." (p. 299)

Notably, trauma introduces just such a cut and our stumbling affords an encounter with a truth to which we might respond with interest or with evasion.

DeLillo's novel can be viewed as an insistent intrusion of such cuts that demand the reader's attention. In line with Lévi-Strauss' (1984) recognition of the importance of both internal and external views in order to make sense of cultural meanings, *Falling Man* offers several vantage points, insistently decontextualizing each view so that we cannot easily get our bearings. From the first page, context is denuded and personhood not designated. "It was not a street anymore but a world, a time and space of falling ash and near night. He was walking north through rubble and mud. . . . This was the world now" (p. 3). We are not even sure if the first character we encounter is actually alive.

> He tried to tell himself he was alive but the idea was too obscure to take hold. . . . . an old panel truck appeared . . . and the driver leaned toward the window on the passenger's side and examined what he saw: a man scaled in ash, in pulverized matter. . . . It wasn't until he got in the truck and shut the door that he understood where he'd been going all along. (p. 6)

In this first chapter, we are also introduced to the notion of traumatic memory through the image that is to haunt the reader, much as it does the characters, throughout the recounting. "There was something else then, outside all this, not belonging to this, aloft. He watched it coming down. A shirt came down out of the high smoke, a shirt lifted and drifting in the scant light and then falling again, down toward the river" (p. 4).

By offering a story told in fragments from differing but not clearly differentiated perspectives, DeLillo demonstrates the precarious nature of meaning, a difficulty familiar to clinicians who work with traumatized individuals. Bion (1967b), for example, describes in his early papers the difficult process of making meaning from the disparate fragments offered by those for whom symbols do not *represent* reality but rather are experienced *as* reality, those for whom there is not sufficient distance from the lived experience to be able to reflect on it. In attempting to understand the frame of reference for one caught in such traumatic isolation, Bion learned a deep respect for the experienced immanence of catastrophe that can lead to seemingly bizarre behavior. Such is DeLillo's stance, as he positions his characters in relation to one another, their actions driven by forces they may not currently comprehend but may come to understand over time as the narrative progresses and the story unfolds.

Acutely aware of the precarious nature of meaning, Bion (1977) developed his model of psychoanalytic inquiry using Henri Poincaré's idea of the *selected fact* to mark the powerful effects of perspective on how we organize information. Coherence, therefore, is always in relation to whatever selected facts are organizing the frame, and content can obstruct our ability to take note of whatever underlying factors are at play. Trauma impedes our ability to learn, not only *from* the traumatic moment but also in the wake of it. DeLillo (2007) depicts this dilemma through his characters, who are stunned by tragedy, frozen in time and space. Caught in the moment of catastrophe, the survivors find themselves reliving over and over what cannot be taken in and assimilated. The reader is confronted with the precariousness of such unintegrated meanings. Thus, two characters who had shared a common experience are drawn to one another, sensing that they might be able to speak to one another in ways they cannot speak to others "because it was inside them now and because he needed to hear what he'd lost in the tracings of memory" (p. 91).

In *Falling Man*, DeLillo adds to the complexity by juxtaposing what is lost from mind and memory through trauma, with what is lost through aging. Implicit in this juxtaposition is a question regarding the ephemeral nature of time, meaning, and human experience. Our deep reliance on continuity for security is highlighted as memory is disrupted, whether by aging or by trauma. By contrasting these two types of disruption, each of which tends to isolate us but which we can also share if we can bear it, DeLillo invites us to recapture the common humanity underlying our shared vulnerabilities.

We first encounter the isolating effects of memory dimmed through aging: "The world was receding, the simplest recognitions. She began to lose her sense of clarity, of distinctness. She was not lost so much as falling, growing fainter. Nothing lay around her but silence and distance" (pp. 93–94). We then encounter the possibilities inherent in sharing the difficulties imposed by shared trauma, if we can tolerate the disjunction: "These are the days after. Everything now is measured by after. . . . Do I know how to make one thing out of another, without pretending? Can I stay who I am, or do I have to become all those other people who watch someone walk out the door?" (p. 138). In the wake of this national catastrophe, each individual may feel isolated by the particularities of his or her experience but also shares a common bond. "I don't know this America anymore," says one character. "I don't recognize it. . . . There's an empty space where America used to be" (p. 193).

In this novel, the Falling Man marks an absence that denotes catastrophic change. What remains to be seen is the extent to which any of the characters can use this demarcation as a way of engaging with the trauma and making personal the loss, so that they might create new meanings that accept, acknowledge, and take into account the fact of the catastrophe. As Bion (1977) notes, any action can be used toward growth or evasion. The Falling Man can be experienced as a repetitive shock that lulls us into the numbness of acute trauma, a shock one merely "recovers from," in this way as a denial of the personal link or as in invitation to engage personally with the enormity of the trauma that has befallen. The falling man, as a character, seems unable to engage sufficiently with his own actions to enable him to continue to live.

In developing a complex web in which various positions can be located in relation to one another, DeLillo creates a formal structure in ways that decontextualize meanings and invite reconsideration of presumed truths. This process in some ways mirrors the psychoanalytic inquiry into that which is explicitly not known but becomes revealed *because* it can be sufficiently displaced, disguised, or negated. Such meanings are inevitably personal, a product of both individual and collective histories, and thus can only be known to the extent that we can push past or at least recognize prejudices colored by our own histories and attempt to locate ourselves in the frame of the other.

Psychoanalytic training helps us to recognize various types of cues, verbal and nonverbal, that mark explicit or implicit meanings as they are elaborated over time. One aspect of this training process is to learn to distinguish between empathic resonance and projection. In being willing to learn more about ourselves and how we respond to various cues, we can consider more reflectively what is being aroused in us by the other and to have ideas as to how we might make sense of these experiences. One factor we keep in mind is the tendency to organize experience in dichotomous terms. Such designations are useful simplifications that help us to organize our experience but also confound it, as we lose information in the process of simplification. There is an inherent tension between presumptions of sameness that can cloud our ability to detect difference, and presumptions of difference that can impede our ability to note commonalities (Matte-Blanco, 1975, 1988). Each limit poses its own hazards.

Narrative art can function as a means for marking such hazards and inviting a re-consideration or re-visioning of culture. In creating representations of these difficulties, the writer invites those inside and outside of a given culture to reflectively consider whatever truths might be explicitly known or implicitly revealed in the work, and thus perhaps to move beyond polarized positions toward a more reflective consideration. The provision of multiple vantage points disrupts our remoteness from whatever has been designated as Other, thereby helping to attenuate the tendency to believe in our own distortions.

In *Falling Man,* DeLillo invites an uneasy encounter with the havoc wreaked by the destruction of the towers *in relation to* a havoc that was already in place but insufficiently appreciated, in terms of particular blind spots in western culture that invite disrespectful views of the Other. Even psychoanalysts, who can utilize concepts such as transference and the unconscious with great facility, have our own blind spots such that we forget that transference *is* endemic in human relationships and that the Unconscious *is* unconscious. We, too, try to know enough that we can avoid uncomfortable feelings of uncertainty and so are just as prone as anyone else to moving away from the twinges that invite us to look at precisely whatever we are most fervently avoiding seeing. Fear is a powerful motivating force, threatening to leave us relatively impervious to the very information we might need in order to more constructively counter it (Charles, June 2–28, 2007). Fear can also lead us to engage in fantasies that provide momentary relief.

The empty sky left behind in the wake of the falling of the twin towers marks a fantasy in the United States that was ruptured by 9/11. In that rupture—in that gap—becomes visible whatever we had been repressing having to do with lack and with limit. Staking our claim on a fantasy of American greatness with no limits, we had created a bubble in which we lived as though resources are not limited, pollution and waste take no toll, and money that we do not have might endlessly be spent. The assault on the twin towers also marked a rupture in the illusion that our boundaries are impermeable. Our *reaction* to that—to go to war as though we could control destiny through such an endeavor—can be seen as an omnipotent enactment, a living out of a grandiose fantasy on a staggering scale. From one perspective, moving outward in this way may be seen as a short-sighted and desperate attempt to make the self safe by killing the other, a paranoid-schizoid playing out on the real world stage of our failure to come to grips with the inevitability of limits.

Countering that type of obfuscating tendency. DeLillo uses the novel *Falling Man* as a means for speaking about cultural forces that tear not only the social fabric but also psychic cohesion. The unsaying that characterizes the traumatic narrative allows difficult truths to be revealed in titrated doses such that they might reach us in spite of whatever censors are in place. This unsaying is in some ways the fundamental stance of the psychoanalyst, who must be willing to not *already know* in order to *learn* (Bion, 1967a). We can be so caught by our preconceptions that reality barely intrudes. In contrast, our willingness to not-know helps us to encounter the other as other, speak from our own experience, listen respectfully, and sound the distance between. In so doing, we can gauge our progress and catch glimpses of what eludes us, as we try to bear sitting with painful feelings, noting the ways in which we resist and defend, and inquiring into the dark spaces of whatever remains unknown or unconsidered, and also into the glare of what cannot be glimpsed through our "brilliant" lens.

Much as he was inclined to believe that some things are better seen in the dark, Bion (1977) also had the idea that if you pulled away from the content so that you could see the process, you would have a much clearer vantage point on the patterns of relationships in which meanings reside. At this point in history, we are confronted with evidence of our relative blindness to very real differences in perspective from one culture to another, and to the profound impact of ignoring pieces of reality that have been excluded from American consciousness. As DeLillo puts it: "What we see is the living truth. The mirror softens the effect by submerging the actual face. Your face is your life. But your face is submerged in your life. That's why you don't see it. Only other people see it. And the camera of course" (p. 115). We need others in order to see beyond the limits of our own perceptions and preconceptions. It is through such dialogues with difference that meanings evolve and trauma may, just possibly, be transformed.

Cassirer describes a "revolution" that takes place in the transformation from "action to schema, to the symbol, to representation" (p. 153). In *Falling Man*, DeLillo creates this type of revolution for the reader, marking the point of concealment such that we are invited to push past our inhibitions and re-experience a traumatic moment from our own past. DeLillo insistently decontextualizes our experience so that we cannot easily locate reliable guideposts by which to find our way. He then assaults us repeatedly with traumatic images seen from various angles, thus inviting us to actively reflect and find our way, rather than passively accepting whatever partial meanings have numbed us or lulled us into complacency. That complacency, arising from an incredibly myopic view of the complexities of human consciousness and understanding across cultures, may be the greatest hazard facing Americans today. To be shaken out of it may be traumatic but may also offer hope for the future. That willingness, to face and bear a confrontation with catastrophic change, is also likely the precondition for meaningful psychoanalytic work.

NOTE

1. This chapter is an amended version of a paper originally published as: Marilyn Charles, "*Falling Man*: Encounters with Catastrophic Change," *The Psychoanalytic Review* vol. 98, no. 4 (2011): pp. 425–50. Copyright Guilford Press. Reprinted with the permission of The Guilford Press. Excerpts from *Falling Man* by Don DeLillo. Copyright 2007 by Don DeLillo. Reprinted with the permission of Scribner Publishing Group, a division of Simon & Schuster, Inc. All rights reserved.

FOUR

Telling Trauma

The Wind-Up Bird Chronicle

> "I was in a printing house in Hell and saw the method in which knowledge is transmitted from generation to generation."
>
> —William Blake

Trauma brings us into the realm of psychotic experience. Psychosis tells a story that cannot otherwise be told. Much as DeLillo's novel, described in the previous chapter, enacted in form the experience of traumatic dislodging of meaning, working with psychotic experience poses particular challenges for the clinician, who is called upon to access psychotic aspects of personality while also keeping anchors in consensual reality. In a society in which psychosis is increasingly seen as a function of physiological anomaly and pathology, it can be particularly difficult for the psychoanalytic psychotherapist to maintain a respectful working relationship with the person designated psychotic. This dilemma is complicated when trauma has disrupted the integration of a coherent narrative. The story is then told through symptoms most clearly heard implicitly through the sensory registers of the less conscious mind.

As noted in chapter 3, we resist knowing the devastation that can be wreaked by encounters with life's adversities and have developed ways of fending off the common thread that might tie us to the severely traumatized individual. Thus barred from the common human discourse, the alienated Other then represents not only his or her personal narrative but also the narrative of exclusion in which we have become implicated. When working with an individual who has "lost" his or her mind, it is tempting to ascribe to this state an inevitable otherness, such as is found in DSM designations of schizophrenia or other psychotic illness. And yet, we know that the psychotic individual tells a story that has its own at times chilling coherence. In confronting an individual whose experience is of losing one's mind, the analyst is called to either enter spaces in which she must be willing to lose her own or, alternatively, turn a blind eye on the link with the traumatized other. At these times, the very theories that make our work possible can serve as additional defenses that falsely separate *us* from *them,* thus causing further harm. A brief case will be offered to illustrate some of the tensions involved in our work with severely traumatized individuals.

Trauma poses particular challenges because it is so difficult to take in. In offering us a traumatic narrative, the author can invite us into an engagement, not only with trauma, but also with psychotic experience. Although psychosis is often thought of as a genetic disorder, there is actually a strong etiological link between trauma and psychosis. Indeed, psychosis might best be conceptualized as a post-traumatic disorder marked by the incoherent narrative instability of self-experience that characterizes severely disrupted development (Main and Hess, 1990). Research into disrupted attachment processes has linked dissociative symptoms to the type of unresolved parental mourning that can make an otherwise good parent inaccessible to the child (Liotti, 2004). Parental failures to come to terms with their own losses create holes in memory that are passed along the generations (Charles, 2014a). Through these holes enter the ghosts in the nursery (Fraiberg, Adelson and Shapiro, 1975), the phantoms that come to haunt successive generations in the absence of recognition and repair (Abraham and Torok, 1994). In contrast to the medical model of psychosis seen in terms of aberrant signals, psychodynamic clinicians presume that symptoms are meaningful and try to understand the frame of reference of the psychotic patient. In a dangerous world, where potential caregivers may not be listening respectfully enough to be worthy of trust in spite of their best intentions, these signals may be seen as necessary distortions (Charles, 2008b) in a history that has become unspeakable (Davoine and Gaudillière, 2004).

Many novelists have spoken to these cultural forces that tear not only the social fabric but also psychic cohesion, thus helping us to relocate psychotic experience in the annals of a history that has gone terribly awry. In novels such as Piercy's *Woman on the Edge of Time* (1976), Murakami's *Wind-Up Bird Chronicle* (1997), and Nieh's *Mulberry and Peach* (1981), the authors characterize an uneasy negotiation between subjective truth and societal demands that push the individual into a disenfranchised and "crazy" place, leaving little room for them to grapple with the truths of their experience. In doing battle with madness as something to be exorcized or eradicated, *we* become part of a crazy system in which subjective reality is denied. From where, then, might such an individual speak? At the Austen Riggs Center, we see this type of dilemma playing out in our community program, where it is often the person designated psychotic who speaks most clearly and directly, nailing whatever dynamic is at play with uncanny acuity. We then see the rush to exorcise that voice from the room, to designate the person "crazy" who dares to speak such difficult truths. We also see these dynamics in the staff community, as well, when our heightened anxiety encourages reflexive action rather than reflective consideration.

At a certain level of intensity, heightened affect precludes reflective thought, impeding the cognitive functions so crucial to effective and cogent integration of experience. So, then, not only does trauma fragment history, destroying speech and leaving the subject estranged from self and other, it also invites our resistance, making it even more difficult for the communication to register and be recognized with respect. In our medicalized world, we have developed labels that organize our understanding of human distress and defense, but can also distance us from those so labeled. The label "psychotic," for example, tends to invite disrespect for the person's capacity to know herself sufficiently to take an active part in her own treatment (Charles, 2008b).

In spite of strong evidence to the contrary, psychosis tends to be equated with a lack of insight (Amador, Strauss, Yale, Flaum, and Gorman, 1993), so that psychotherapy is framed, not in terms of understanding or accommodating to painful realities, but rather, in McWilliams (2005) words: as attempts to "medicate, manage, reeducate, control, and correct the irrational behavior of people whose suffering is inconvenient to the larger culture" (p. 140). Our idealization of science obscures humanistic values (Peterson, 2004), reinforcing the stigma that impedes long-term recovery (Lysaker, Roe, and Yanos, 2007; Ritsher and Phelan, 2004), and furthering the mis-recognition at the core of the dilemma.

If we adhere to a trauma-driven model of psychosis, we find ourselves working outside of the realm of history, allowing the trauma to make itself known *as it reverberates* over time (Caruth, 1991), in the echoes that link us back into the realm of historical time (Davoine and Gaudillière, 2004; Lacan, 1972–1973). Much like Bion's (1967b) admonition to eschew memory or desire, setting aside our preconceptions helps the clinician to provide a space in which meaning might be made and perhaps to better tolerate experiencing a world in which thinking—in the sense of linking thoughts logically with one another—is not possible (Lacan, 1977e; Bion, 1992). In this pre-symbolic realm of primary process, the psychotic element in *us* is called forth and resisted in each encounter, as we are pulled toward the limits of what we can and cannot manage without feeling at risk of imminent collapse and fragmentation (Bion, 1967a).

It is through our ability to use these experiences as a template that the translation is made. As we begin to find words, we bridge the absolute chasm of otherness, moving from the *symbolic equation*, in which words are things rather than representations, toward *symbolization*, using words in a process of exchange, directly and consciously communicating with another such that meanings can be held, shared, and explored (Segal,

1957). When metaphor has been lost behind the dire pressure to survive, there is often a gap, as I will describe in my work with Leah, between what happens in the body or the mind, and what can be articulated in language.

Literature affords an as-if space in which to make contact with such experiences. In *The Wind-Up Bird Chronicle*, for example, Murakami (1997) takes us on a bizarre journey as Toru Okada tries to encounter exactly what he most resists, hoping to find his way beyond the impasse in which he finds himself. What initially seems to be an external limit can also be seen as an internal one, as the reader begins to recognize the blindness at the core of Toru Okada's troubles. As in other traumatic narratives, the story is offered in disjunctive fragments that both obscure and reveal the meanings we are seeking. Murakami juxtaposes fantasy and reality such that the reader cannot be entirely certain of where the lines between historical reality, narrative reality, and dream or fantasy might be drawn. In this way, he points to both the profound meanings that can be discovered through our attention to the primary process realm of dreams, phantasy, and free associations, and also the difficulty of coming to grips with whatever feels unassimilable.

As the novel opens, we encounter Toru Okada, whose cat and then his wife mysteriously go missing. Toru Okada is besieged by symbols, clues, puzzles, and characters he does not know how to make sense of, and is left to piece together the story of his life from the seemingly random fragments. Notably, in this novel, we are offered segments of history and pre-history such that meanings emerge subtly and precariously over time. Much like the dream, form becomes substance in a kaleidoscope of characters and settings, spaces and times, through which Toru Okada travels. Ultimately, he is drawn to the darkness of a deep and empty well, the well being a place marked by one character as a site within which meanings might be made. As Toru Okada sits in the well, he both loses and locates himself, losing the semblance that had covered over the deeper, more subtle and more various meanings to be discovered. Much as Bion (1990) suggests, at times we need to deepen the darkness to discover what we are seeking. For Toru Okada, it is in the deep darkness of the well that these more profound meanings finally come to light.

Toru Okada finds himself assailed by intimations of meanings that remain elusive and inscrutable, much as happens to my patient, Leah. In contrast to the apparent order displayed by Toru Okada at first meeting, however, my first encounter with Leah finds her caught in an impossible and relentless struggle to repair her "movements" so that she can leave behind the "disarray" and finally become the person she longs to be. In Leah's world, the dividing line between consensual and idiosyncratic reality is not clear and her observations range from uncannily acute—as when she describes the denied hostility underlying her mother's "good intentions"—to utterly mad, as when she describes with amazement how her father was able to project his face onto a movie screen and speak to her from that location. Even now, she is amazed, not at the capacity of her mind to produce such an experience, but by her father's uncanny ability to perform such a feat!

When anxious, Leah easily becomes derailed, whether by a chance movement that startles, or by her internal anxiety at the immanence of impossible meanings. During psychological testing, for example, she is asked to detail the blot elements she had used in a particular precept. When asked "what made it look like a bug?" her demeanor deadens and she responds, "Not really. Um . . . I don't know. I get overstimulated really easily—I react to people's movements. Five, six, seven, eight. I'll say it bluntly because it needs to be said. Six and one-third, five and a half, seven-fifty, eight point six, four point four. Thirty-six to fifty-two, sixteen to ten, kind of split. It's all in the second movement and centered."

In our sessions, we can be speaking about the most mundane of matters and then veer suddenly into territory inhabited by the magical numbers, colors, and sequences that organize her universe. In that universe, we are accompanied by the cacophony of the voices that may seem to come from benign and helpful gods or may turn mischievous and betray her by pretending, for example, to be the voice of her dead grandmother, eventually betraying themselves through the emptiness and vacuity of their routinized phrases. Although I cannot hear these voices or see the presences that accompany them, Leah is quite certain that I can. They are as real and present to her as my chair is to me.

References to numbers as powerful signs come up early in our work, as she tells me about the behavioral outbursts that threaten her treatment. I call them signs because they are indicators that seem packed with implicit meanings without being decipherable as symbols that can be reliably read. Much like Toru Okada, there is an intimation of meanings that are inevitably out of reach. Leah says that she has been working very hard to get the movements right, but that people would intrude and derail her efforts, such as one nurse who 'hit her with a five.' When I inquire into the meaning of the five, Leah pulls back, as though my question alerts her to some danger looming. Meaning seemed too precarious to withstand scrutiny. How we handle these disjunctions is crucial to the eventual course of the treatment. Such moments require our absolute presence, unbounded by desire or fear. As Davoine and Gaudilliére (2004) put it:

> The cognitive stakes are considerable, a prelude to the opening or the closing of the field of *logos*. A disingenuous reply or an embarrassed silence, when adamantly repeated, sends the subject into nonexistence on this point. He exiles himself, falls silent, goes crazy. Instead of speaking *to* him, people speak *of* him, as an aberration. (p. 70)

Inevitably, we will at times fail to catch the moment as it presents itself to us. Most often, however, our patients are gracious and offer other opportunities. As Leah tells me once again about her desire to be able to move properly, she refers to her dance class and the "five, six . . ." Suddenly, I have some thread of the meaning of "five" for her, which I communicate with excitement. Leah brightens and begins to tell me more about the five, linking it also to an open hand that might slap you.

Numbers, colors, objects, and events seem so laden with meaning that it is hard for us to explore them together, and yet meaning is everywhere, as she moves from association to association, becoming lucid and then retreating into more highly symbolized and abstract speech patterns that have idiosyncratic rather than consensual meanings. At times, she seems better able to let me into her world, whereas at others my questions seem dangerous, as though they would expose secrets best kept private.

During the projective testing, Leah's responses to subtle shadings in one Rorschach card reveal how even modest arousal can result in feelings of bodily disintegration, accompanied by an inability to determine what is coming from inside or out. "When I see it," she says, "it reminds me of a throat. It kind of makes me want to look at it and apply it to parts of my body . . . (she moves her hands to her own throat and applies pressure). If I put compression on it, would it work better? I don't know. That's what I was wondering."

This tension, and the vulnerability it marks, makes the thought of taking antipsychotic medication terrifying to Leah. Her previous experiences have not been positive. She describes it as "going unconscious . . . I feel like I can't even swallow . . . like it's all dark." This fear, of being swallowed by a darkness so deep she might drown in it, is reminiscent of the ambivalence with which Murakami's character, Toru Okada, goes down into the well of *his* history and *his* unconscious, trying to overcome the terrible dread that has kept him apparently safe but has also lost him what he loves best in life. Much like Leah's reality, in the novel we are offered bits and fragments of current and past history, interspersed with dream and phantasy, such that it is difficult to separate or catalogue the pieces. Rather, we are left with a dialogue in which conscious and unconscious exist side by side, interwoven into the type of fabric that has become Leah's own daydream nightmare from which she cannot escape. Much like Toru Okada, she is challenged to awaken from that nightmare into a deeper and more cogent engagement with facts of experience that seem too terrible to bear. The fear is such that she skims the surface and cannot penetrate either the darkness or the light that is blinding.

I try to understand Leah in her own context, to build a story in which the threads make sufficient sense that she can find a path that sustains her, rather than being so idiosyncratic and over-controlled that any intrusion disrupts her and sends her reeling. Like Toru Okada in the well, we create a space in which she might settle into her own thoughts and report about *her* universe, so that we can imagine a way to survive the disarray and move toward a more coherent and integrated order that won't be so easily crumbled by intrusions.

Leah begins to find anchors: "when I don't want to take the medication, and I think I'm just going to be ok, my Dad reminds me of the SWAT team." This guidepost helps Leah to remember how real it was when she was in Atlanta, trying to get rid of the bar codes, being attacked and ambushed by whatever was firing at her from every direction. It is a lived and living moment for her. As she covers her head with both arms and ducks as she talks, past, future, and fantasy seem to commingle in her being. "It's not enough to have the words!" she tells me. She needs to feel it in her body, from which she cuts herself off, desperately trying to find the lightness of being she was able to attain during her anorectic days.

It is easy to wish, along with Leah, for a magical solution to her problems, such as the medication prescribed by current medical standards, or the more elaborate solutions Leah prescribes for herself. And yet, I hear her telling me very clearly that medication does not offer salvation from the troubles that plague her. She says: "But the Geodon, I felt really sick—I was walking around outside barefoot, I thought I was in mourning because I thought my parents died, when I started taking Geodon." "So, that really made things much worse?" I say. "Yeah, every time," she replies. "Except it doesn't have increments, voice side effects—when I don't get the voices—but it wasn't any better . . . it's probably helpful to my doctor . . . I hate the smell of it. . . . I feel like there's another thing I want to tell you about my grandma. Every time she'd come to the door she'd always sit like this. She had two bathrooms and one had a rug like a hook rug almost, one was blue and one was red. So that was my Mom's mom. And I just wonder if . . . I don't think my grandmom was mentally ill, I think, I wonder if I was just destined to have this issue."

Toru Okada becomes confused and disillusioned by the various characters who purport to have answers for him but who seem also to have their own agendas, and descends into the well to consider meaning from his own perspective. So it is for Leah, who moves away from medication, the realm of doctors, and back toward considering the signs and symbols from her own life, desperately trying to fit them together into a picture that makes sense. I try to join her in this effort without enforcing my own point of view but rather reflecting back to her what I hear from her and also the meanings I have made from my experiences with her. In this way, I hope to help her to build a story in which her symptoms can be seen as reasonable attempts to solve a problem that no one has been able to help her with. If we think of self-development as grounded in and built upon the ability to make meaning from experience, this move toward developing a more cogent and coherent narrative is an essential one.

When Leah tells me her theory that what is really wrong with her is a learning disability, I agree that there has been ongoing difficulty putting information together to help her confront the obstacles she faced. This reading of the facts during a family meeting invites Leah's mother into a conversation that had been closed off by her frustration at not being able to be the mother she had hoped to be, one who could help her daughter to meet life's challenges rather than watch her become further and further derailed. Freed from the fear of being blamed, the mother can recall times when Leah's difficulties integrating information had come to the fore but then receded without finding any real assistance. The mother's engagement is something Leah has been longing for. In a further attempt to break through the parents' defensive withdrawal, I offer the family a model in which very bright young people can be uneven in their learning so that deficits can hide without being constructively addressed, resulting in greater and greater gaps as time goes by. In this model, neither Leah nor her parents are blamed for the dilemma they are in, and seem better able to join together to address some of the pragmatics of their current situation.

Perhaps the most difficult task is the one the family has explicitly charged me with, to offer a diagnosis that helps them to understand Leah's struggles in a way that points toward potential resolutions. My answer to their question is one that Leah has both offered and disavowed. In a recent experience at another treatment center, she found herself on a ward with psychotic individuals and had felt relieved—though also frightened—to be among people whose struggles were so similar to her own. In reading Jamison's book *An Unquiet Mind* (1995), she is similarly calmed and frightened by what she discovers there.

I realize that the diagnosis of "schizophrenia" is the one most descriptive of her psychotic symptoms but that the term has baggage in the society and in the minds of family members. And so, I give it carefully, pointing to the prevalence of cognitive symptoms over mood disregulation in Leah's dilemmas. Leah and her parents fight to re-impose the mood aspect, affirming their belief that I am giving Leah a diagnosis that has no hope or future, that I am imposing a psychic death sentence. To the contrary, I say, this diagnosis points to the difficulties in processing and integrating information that seem to be at the heart of Leah's difficulties. My experience is that this diagnosis, like any other, applies to a wide variety of individuals who may have very different capacities and life trajectories. It points to the types of symptoms and difficulties Leah might have to address as she tries to build a viable and satisfying life for herself.

We are living in an odd universe in which the very diagnoses that have evolved through our attempts to better define difficulties and offer more viable treatments have, at times, become so dehumanizing that they occlude the human being and obscure the struggles in which she is engaged and with which she could use some assistance. The diagnosis I offer, however, is no surprise for Leah, who has known that she is living in a psychotic universe and has been so frightened of what this might mean that she has tended to retreat into that place and wall herself up further within that prison. In acknowledging the extent of her difficulties and also believing in her capacity to face them and to work with them, I invite Leah to rejoin the rest of humanity, rather than accepting her belief that she would have to somehow look or be different in order to find a foothold. The little child who was bullied so mercilessly that not-eating became a way of being sufficiently light to float through her life without the burdens of disdain and isolation she had been carrying—that little child can perhaps stand aside from the elaborate chains of ritualized behaviors and cosmic connections in which she has armed herself. Perhaps she can begin to acknowledge the pain as an integrated part of her past rather than an irresolvable circuit she moves through repeatedly, relentlessly, in the magical hope of finally breaking through into that other dimension in which failure is not inevitable. At that point, she may be able to touch ground sufficiently to begin to discover herself, in process, as she makes her way in the world.

When social forces eliminate the subject, narrating the story becomes a way of affirming not merely one's being but also one's essential humanity (Davoine and Gaudilliére, 2004). Through her attempts at repair, Leah tries to eliminate herself as the flawed or unacceptable subject, to find the rhythm or pattern that might invite her back into a shared common humanity in which she is not constantly at risk of being rejected and discarded. In our work, I try to re-introduce her as the subject in her own drama that is unfolding, to hold both the wanted and unwanted elements together in ways that might help her to accept and integrate them over time into a story that is both coherent and congruent, and thereby learn to live more adaptively in this world rather than retreating into the other.

Leah is fortunate in that her parents have sufficient means to have found her a place where her meanings can be marked and held. In stark contrast to this story, in which we can find hope of a better future, stand stories such as those of Nieh and Piercy, in which the main characters' mourning goes unrecognized and unacknowledged, leading further and further into despair. As shame and guilt commingle with accusing eyes, it can seem like the right course of action to stop fighting the oppressive other and accept one's designation as impossibly impaired. In that process, one's own voice becomes distorted and silenced, her words 'written over' by the narrative of the other through which she becomes erased as a subjective being.

In Murakami's well, the darkness affords a space in which meanings can be integrated and difficulties transformed. This is not so different from Piercy's (1976) alternative universe, in which madness is a state that allows for reintegration through disintegration and a madhouse is a place in which one can allow oneself to go through this process, a place where: "people retreat when they want to go down into themselves—to collapse, carry on, see visions, hear voices of prophecy, bang on the walls, relive infancy—getting in touch with the buried self and the inner mind" (p. 58).

Struggling from the depths of this universe, the narrative form helps us to hold the richness of human experience, so that we can disentangle and look more closely at various threads while also having in mind the whole. In this way, literature has been one vehicle for exploring the human heart and mind, one way in which seemingly unassimilable experience can be brought into language, so that it can be shared, recognized, and assimilated into a history that can be known.

So, too, for Leah. The challenge she brings is a question she has been asking for a very long time: "is it possible to order my experience in such a way that I, as a unique subject, can go on living?" We both hope that the answers she discovers in our work will be in the affirmative, that I can keep in mind her needs, feelings, hopes, and fears sufficiently that we can work together to help her become more adept at living her life rather than my becoming one more person who speaks *over* her in my urgency to 'be helpful,' and loses her in the process. We hope that she can find, through the safety of the consulting room, her own well through which to make sense of her needs, feelings, and perceptions, and to begin to build a story of her life in which she is the active agent who can translate signs into meaningful symbols that help her find her way.

III

Dreams

FIVE

The Book of Intimate Grammar

Transgenerational Trauma

> "We are such stuff
> As dreams are made on; and our little life
> Is rounded with a sleep."
>
> —Shakespeare, *The Tempest*

Literature, because it affords glimpses from different vantage points, can allow the reader to have a view from behind the scenes and from alternate angles. In this way, it can allow us to recognize that what might appear to be a clear surface may actually be a composite made up of a multilayered palimpsest of personal and transgenerational meanings. In his later writings, Lacan (1974–1975, 1975–1976) grapples with this complexity through his writings on the oblique angle and his metaphor of the Borromean knot. The oblique angle recognizes that more may be seen from the side than if we are to look straight on. From the side, we might glimpse both the surface that is being presented and some of the effort that is going into that presentation. That effort reveals both character and intention. The Borromean knot metaphor recognizes that the three registers that Lacan elaborated, the Real (actual data as it exists in the world), the Imaginary (the individual perspective) and the Symbolic (consensual codings that structure social interaction), may be usefully seen as interlocking rings.

That structure recognizes the complex interpenetrability between these realms of meaning. Attention to these rings, as alluded to by Borges (1962), can reveal a great deal about the individual because, implicit in the way any particular experience is organized, we will find the underlying pattern of the organizational structure. While this may sound complex, it is only another way of talking about transference, but one that recognizes that each individual is caught between his experience at both the actual and social/structural level (the systems embedded in language and culture that prescribe meanings), and his ideas about the ways in which the world works and meanings are structured. Viewed in this way, each individual lives in his or her own particular universe that may be more or less consistent with those of others. This conceptualization is consistent with Borges' reading of Tennyson, that if we can understand a single flower, then that understanding will reveal to us something essential about being.

> Tennyson said that if we could understand a single flower we would know who we are and what the world is. Perhaps he meant that there is no deed, however so humble, which does not implicate universal history and the infinite concatenation of causes and effects. Perhaps he meant that the visible world is implicit, in its entirety, in each manifestation, just as, in the same way, will, according to Schopenhauer, is implicit, in its entirety, in each individual. (Borges, 1962, p. 163)

It is that presumption that underlies this book, in which we go back and forth between theory, literature, and a human life, to try to understand some essential patterns at the core of the dilemma of being human.

That dilemma is complicated by the ways in which we are embedded in and define ourselves in relation to culture. Bion (1970) notes the tension between what he terms the *Establishment* and the *mystic*, such that the group inevitably resists change but also needs the new idea in order to grow. In some ways, whoever stands even slightly outside the gates becomes a useful aid in being able to see more or other than can be seen from the inside. And yet, that outsider position can be a painful one. At times, in families, a child is positioned as the outsider because he or she is most sensitive to the traumas that have been carried along the generational lines without being resolved, the stories whose silent echoes take a terrible toll. Recent literature shows that unresolved parental mourning has a profound impact on children. Traumatic memory is spoken through the gaps, through what is missing rather than what is present. Children learn to tolerate those gaps by "going missing" themselves, learning to dissociate what cannot be recognized and worked through within the family system (Charles, 2014a).

The attachment literature shows ways in which trauma disrupts the parent's ability to develop a coherent narrative, thereby disrupting the ability of the child to develop the self-regulatory capacities so crucial to building a secure self (van Ijzendoorn, Schuengel, and Bakermans-Kranenburg, 1999). Pushing past mourning rather than facing it takes a toll. Turning a blind eye to one's own traumatic past leaves one less accessible to one's children, as well, so that the child registers the difficulty in the body, through the symptoms that mark the distress that cannot be spoken about (McDougall, 1989). Trauma that is passed along the generations in this way tends to speak in coded form, through those very symptoms that mark the distress (Charles, 2012).

Even with otherwise caring and attentive parents, unprocessed grief can result in disjunctive, frightening parental behaviors that are traumatic to the young child who needs to be able to approach the parent as a secure base during times of distress. Disjunctive behaviors of this sort create a break in continuity that the child must somehow manage, often leading to dissociated or encapsulated moments that are not easily confronted or worked through. Such experiences work against the important childhood task of developing organized and consistent strategies of affective self-regulation, leading these functions to break down, resulting in further disorganization (Main and Hesse, 1990). This type of disorganization is associated with a lack of coherence in autobiographical memory, resulting in conflicting narratives that are difficult to integrate into a cogent whole, the types of fragmenting foundations that we will see in the case to follow. Unverbalized memories can haunt a family, resulting in the types of *ghosts in the nursery* (Fraiberg, Adelson, and Shapiro, 1975) that can mark transgenerational trauma (Apprey, 1993). This type of discontinuity makes it difficult to recognize one's own strengths and weaknesses and, as such, to rely on and make use of internal resources with consistency.

To be able to mark the symptom as a sign of this type of intergenerational haunting may be crucial in working with someone who is caught in such circumstances. In such cases, if we can recognize the trauma that has not so much occurred but rather has *re*curred, then we may avoid developing hypotheses about the inherent vulnerability of the individual rather than recognizing the battle in which he or she is engaged. One metaphor that can be useful in conceptualizing these types of transgenerational traumas is that of the *archive* as discussed by Derrida (1995b), echoing an idea from Lacan, who talks about inhibition as an entanglement, as a symptom that is entombed, as though caught in a museum: "to be impeded is a symptom put into a museum," Lacan says (in Harari, 2001, p. 20). If we think about this issue of being caught in a museum that can become a crypt, then we are in a useful position from which to consider the dilemma of the person who stands outside the gates of the majority culture, for whatever reason, or of the person encrypted inside. Although the person standing outside can have a privileged vantage point, it can be difficult to believe in oneself from that position. That is where the psychoanalyst can be particularly helpful, in being able to take up the position of a Third perspective that can help us to struggle against the anxiety that can entomb and encrypt us if we cannot find a way to sustain the discourse. Notably, it is precisely the family's inability to speak together about the traumatic past that sustains the trauma.

David Grossman's novel *The Book of Intimate Grammar* (1991) brings us into the world of a childhood cut into by trauma, through the encapsulating transgenerational heritage that becomes a crypt for young Aron. As Grotstein (1995a, 1995b) discusses in his ideas regarding the *orphans of the Real,* being faced with life's difficulties too soon can be overwhelming and traumatizing to the child. As we see in Grossman's novel, this trauma can be passed along the generations so seamlessly that it is difficult to recognize the story being told, much less come to grips with it. Trauma leaves its marks upon the body, profoundly affecting our later experience and at times resulting in the types of inchoate experience that are well marked by Borges' allusions to implicit meanings and by Grossman's metaphor of an *intimate grammar* that holds meanings in a personal and uniquely embodied fashion.

In our work at the Austen Riggs Center, we take as complete a family history as possible, to help us to recognize the *trauma trails* (Atkinson, 2002) that are left behind in the wake of unresolved mourning. Atkinson conceptualizes these trails as *song lines,* melodies so fundamentally inscribed within us that we tend not to consciously notice them. Rather, they shape our movements and fundamentally proscribe our ability to move beyond their constraints. Often, it is the children who enact the untold story, in silent dialogue with the parent who must recognize the meanings in order for the crypt to open. This pattern marks the story told through Aron, who spends his time repeatedly trying to appear before his family in a way that will enable him to finally be recognized. The older generation's absorption in their own struggles, however, leaves them unable to recognize the needs of the child who, left to play out his dilemma, finally comes to an untimely end in his desperate search for recognition.

In this novel, the failure to thrive is marked quite literally. Like Oskar in *The Tin Drum* (Gräss, 1961), Aron does not grow, thereby signifying the failure of his family to provide sufficient sustenance to enable him to do so. "I'm beginning to think you are doing this to us deliberately," says the mother (p. 61). In contrast to Aron, Oskar tells us that he consciously decided not to grow up in order to avoid his father's pronouncement that Oskar should eventually take the place of the father, a position he refuses. The failure to find a father with whom he can sufficiently identify to be pulled into authentic adulthood leaves each of these children lost within the walls of childhood. Born with an adult capacity for thought, Oskar uses his gift—the ability to shatter glass with his piercing shrieks—to keep the demands of the world at bay. Although retaining the stature of a young child, Oskar survives to old age, attaining some of the milestones associated with adulthood.

In contrast, Aron seems fated not to grow up, in spite of his efforts to magically effect the changes that might resolve the impasse by reshaping the relationship between himself and his family. He becomes a magician, literally practicing appearing and reappearing before their eyes in the desperate hope of making sufficient impression to catalyze the needed change. Aron dies in the service of this impossible desire, whereas Oskar allows himself to be imprisoned for a crime he did not commit, in part, it seems, in atonement for those he did. In Oskar's drama, we see the difficult entanglements of the adult with responsibility and complicity, whereas Aron is deprived of this responsibility by virtue of his early death.

In juxtaposition to these two lives, we will look at the case of "Tom," who became caught as a young child in his position as the devalued younger son of a brilliant brother who was utterly incapable of finding his way into the social surround. Tom was eternally eclipsed by the brother's brilliance, making his successful efforts to find a place in the structures of peer relationships seem feeble in comparison. He was left longing for the position favored by the father, a position that had no foundation but yet took his father's complete attention. In relation to this early trauma, Tom was left feeling as though *he* had no foundation, as though even his high intelligence was a sham, a pretense.

As will be described more fully in chapter 10, the psychoanalyst is at times cast in the role of the magus, the omniscient Subject who is supposed to know our desires and destiny in ways we cannot. In this way, many individuals come to the consulting room seeking, not so much self-knowledge, but rather to be reimagined, reshaped into a form that better fits their ideas regarding who and how they should be. Whereas for some individuals, entry into psychoanalysis signals a quest for self-discovery, for others the self has been so devalued that development has already been foreclosed. The latter was the case in my work with Tom, whose ability to know his own thoughts and feelings had been fundamentally foreclosed, not only by transgenerational trauma but also by a personal trauma that he no longer consciously recognized had been endured.

Primary experience lodges in our bodies. We learn to make sense of our perceptions and apperceptions, telling ourselves stories that best fit the facts of our lives as we experience them. These stories are refined over time in ways that seem to work well enough but there are also moments when the story and lived experience become sufficiently disparate that we stumble. At such times, psychoanalytic psychotherapy offers a relational context in which we can recognize this stumbling as potentially meaningful, providing clues to information not easily accessible to the conscious mind (Charles, 2012; Lacan, 1977e). Such clues are often revealed through the dreams that mark the disparities between the story being told and the lived experience, helping us to recognize and begin to come to grips with some of the trauma trails of experiences that have not yet been encoded into language (Lippmann, 2000). The psychoanalyst takes a stand regarding the importance of the unconscious realm of dream, fantasy, and the primary understandings that we often ignore or disparagingly term *intuitions*. Dreams, much like symptoms, can mark important meanings not yet discovered, the territory of implicit understandings referred to by Borges (1962).

Dreams are particularly useful in this work because, like the myth, they can hold a great deal of complexity while also retaining their form. This capacity enables us to delve deeply into the components so that we can recognize the elements and their potential meanings while also attempting to orient ourselves within the multiple layerings. Notably, the language of dreams is largely not a matter of decoding the individual dream elements themselves but rather of recognizing the ways in which each particular individual structures his dreams to hide and reveal the information he is both seeking and avoiding. It is the press of that ambivalence that erupts into our sleep, where the unconscious mind can do its work, in Woolf's (1953) words, underground.

With some patients, the dream affords a useful way of translating symptoms that one might otherwise merely try to ameliorate without heeding the messages embedded there. In contrast, the psychoanalyst suspects that these symptoms are important internal communications that index meanings that have been inscribed in the individual by his own particular history in ways that might be unspeakable within the family or invisible because this is just *the way things are*. Thus, the dream affords a potential joining place for patient and clinician, an opportunity to find meaning together. Dreams can be particularly helpful in our work with individuals who read their own distress as a sign that something is wrong with them in ways that lead to despair rather than to working it through. That is the crucial juncture Bion points to between curiosity versus evasion. With problems that are unknown and seemingly unknowable, evasion can seem like the only answer.

For Tom, who came from a family in which intellectual pursuits had become a means for evading problems in living, his own difficulties finding his way into the world of social relationships marked him as doubly inferior, not only because of his failures but also because he cared. In addition, although his personal history included repeated traumatic experiences because of physical difficulties that plagued his childhood, the family's failure to recognize the impact had left Tom in some ways blind as well. His inability to recognize the meanings and ramifications of such events had left him increasingly uncertain about even basic facts. Tom came to me in search of the key that would unlock his own mysteries and reveal the treasure underneath without revealing the past from which that treasure has been manufactured. In this way, he comes searching for the magus who holds the magical key in opposition to, rather than in the service of, a desire that might be acknowledged or revealed. His inability to recognize the extent of the trauma he had suffered left him stumbling against its edges without understanding why. This stumbling then became further proof of his insufficiency, leaving him trying even harder to avoid recognizing the problem he was certain would mark him as both a failure and a fraud.

Tom was an intelligent and articulate professional man in his mid-fifties, who seemed to be at a stalemate in his career. He did not know that he had been traumatized, and so he brought the trauma into the consulting room in peripheral ways that eventually enabled us to encounter it together. Initially, Tom presented himself as very thoughtful, rational, and reasonable: a "real team player." He was frustrated at finding himself in a working environment in which he could not bring his ideas to bear to solve problems but rather was forced to sit in meetings in which the *pretense* of solution was favored over the actuality. Tom's frustration was mammoth and was resulting in great despair and agitation. His belief that he should be able to resolve this impasse, even though he was not in a position to do so, left him increasingly disregulated in ways that were alarming his wife and affecting his health.

As we continued to meet and deepen our understanding of Tom and the issues he was facing, it became clear that his internal experience was one of living in a complex and chaotic world in which paths were precarious and resources unreliable. In contrast to the denial of affective meanings in his family of origin, my careful tracking and interest in his experience helped to mark my assumption of its legitimacy, thereby providing anchors through which to locate ourselves in this ever-changing universe. My recognition of the intensely traumatic nature of his past helped him to recognize and be interested in the sequelae of that trauma as he experienced it in his life and as it surfaced in his dreams. Also important was my recognition of ways in which his early family environment had led him into the paradoxical situation of devaluing his internal resources while simultaneously holding a grandiose self-image he could neither believe in nor give up.

Important themes emerged in Tom's dreams. Early on, themes of *the jailer* and abandonment were coming to the fore. As Tom considered this notion of the jailer and the position this figure played in his life, I suggested to him that the jailer is dangerous because we believe in him, but he also provides a sense of safety because he keeps us from venturing out into forbidden territory. I said that perhaps the real danger is the prison yard, where we have the illusion of escape, but not the opportunity to engage around the real dilemma of being imprisoned by the jailer (our fears).

After an ischemic attack that marked the all-too real threat to his well-being of Tom's distress at work, he decided to take a leave of absence. During that time, he spoke about possibilities for better using his gifts and talents but, as time passed, it became clear that he was unable to move forward in any direction. His terror was marked by his experience of himself as though sitting in front of a blank page, trying very hard to tolerate the blankness so that he might leave room to discover himself rather than being paralyzed by his fear of what he will find. He reported the recurrent fear that surfaces when he contemplates taking on a challenge, the sense that the volume is missing or an ice floe is cracking. He linked his need to keep up appearances to reading deficits as a child and also to the panic associated with the chronic childhood pain that had begun at age three. The attendant themes of thickets and, in his words, "waylay" stations seemed to mark his confusion between rest and respite, and false reassurance and security, reminiscent of the metaphor of the jailer and the prison yard.

During this time, Tom's dreams seemed to mingle with fantasy but one particular dream helped us to recognize the extent and nature of the internal damage with which he was contending. This dream so vividly configured the precarious and dangerous nature of his internal world that I suggested he undergo a comprehensive psychological evaluation to help us to fix certain reality points. That evaluation helped him to discover that his intelligence was not a pretense but rather was real and extremely high, whereas his emotional and psychological resources were precarious. We could also recognize ways in which his ostensible comfort with self and others was a façade behind which hid the very frightened, isolated, and lonely child who could never quite find or hold a valued place in the interpersonal world.

Our journey together was a perilous one. Tom knew only too well the depths to which he could succumb during the episodes he termed "falling into the pit." His dreams provided a type of "waylay station" through which we were able to consider his dilemmas at a safe remove. Notably, at the point when he finally decided to quit his job, he dreamed that he was in a nursing home behind a locked door. In his associations, he recalled being a child behind a locked door. The dream was evocative of the vast, dark spaces into which he had fallen repeatedly. It was so vivid that it brought us both hard up against his terror of being alone in an impossible void, which parallels his fear of being engulfed by the trauma that haunts him increasingly as he struggles to avoid it.

This dream was followed two months later by the two dreams that together were to become the hallmark, cornerstone, and anchor of our treatment. In the first dream, he was trying to get somewhere but was caught in a labyrinthian morass. The building was Gothic, with arched and unreliable pathways. He described in great detail the complex series of elaborate arches and precarious paths that were fragmenting even as he attempted to traverse them. He evoked a vivid sense of a convoluted and impossible landscape in which there was no solid ground on which to stand. Nothing could be relied on. Pillars crumbled, paths were impeded, and the relationships between the structures were continually changing and eroding. In the second dream, he was once again in a complex structure and realized that he was bleeding and that he "had the same deadly syndrome as everyone else." The latter dream seemed to mark his utter terror at the damage already done and the disaster already in place. It also marked his conflicted fear and desire to be "like everyone else." I had the sense of the first dream as an Escher-type place, which he told me was a correct reading. I said that the paradox was that the path becomes precarious because he is afraid he doesn't have the resources to really *arrive* and be pleased with the accomplishment. Paradoxically, the complexity but lack of detail in terms of connecting links was precisely what made the path so precarious. His fear had impeded his ability to recognize these connecting links, which were exactly what we needed to discover in order to build a more secure foundation within. His avoidance was keeping him immobilized, unable to put his ideas into motion.

Over time, these dreams became guiding metaphors that we referred back to repeatedly, as we fleshed out his relationship to the goal that is out of reach because he does not believe he has the resources to arrive at it. *He* seemed to disappear when he couldn't get recognition and yet, in many ways, he was the only one who could take a stand regarding what did, indeed, have value for him. His inability to take this stand resulted in his recursive dilemma with his wife, in which he looked to her something she could not give precisely because she could not know *for* him what *he* needed to be able to discover for himself.

Notably, like Aron and Oskar, Tom needed a responsive other who could register his experience without becoming overwhelmed by it, someone who could recognize him sufficiently that he could use that reflective mirror as a means for beginning to better know himself. His parents had not been able to meet this challenge and his wife, too, had been failing. As Tom began to find, in me, someone who could register his experience without getting lost in it, we were able to recognize ways in which he was playing out the scenario of becoming lost and waiting to be found with his wife.

We anchored ourselves in the certainty of his intellectual capacity and moved from there to anchor ourselves, more precariously but with determination, in the facts of his isolation, his despair, and how valiantly he had worked to deny these. As we noted what had been accomplished through this denial, as well as the price, Tom began to feel a bit firmer in his foundations. But then we came to a difficult point in the treatment and Tom's distress worried his wife. Her worry threatened, once again, to spiral him down into the dark pit he dreaded. This time, however, he managed to pull through. In retrospect, he was able to recognize ways in which his wife's worry could become a pit he got lost in, precisely because it dovetailed so neatly with his own.

"It's like we care too much," he said. "It's like our concern for one another overlaps, leaving this space in the middle where we get lost." I said that perhaps this space in the middle was the result of the fear that the concern carried, which made it difficult for either person to work through the dilemma but rather each person's distress became exacerbated by the other's. Perhaps if Tom could recognize how the concern becomes fear that then reverberates between them, he could better stave off the fall.

He thought this over a bit, then his eyes lit up with delight. "One of the things I most remember you saying," he said, "was when I was telling you about my wife asking about our work and 'what was wrong?' I remember you saying: 'What is supposed to be wrong with you?' That just broke it open. I'll never forget that."

We work so hard, hoping to come up with what we expect to be brilliant interpretations that "put it all together." In the final analysis, however, what is left is the relatively innocent statement that breaks open the ostensible reality that has imprisoned the other. The vantage point of perspective affords a bit of respite, some solid ground that helps us to keep our bearings so that we can see the pit coming and perhaps stay clear of it this time, or at least catch ourselves and ease the fall.

It is often in our patient's dreams that we can find the most useful keys to the mysteries that have been eluding them, as we develop metaphors that are firmly anchored in the language of that person's unconscious. This is also the realm of Lacan's (1974–1975, 1975–1976) *sinthome*. Lacan describes the sinthome in terms of an idiosyncratic symptom. Because it is idiosyncratic, it can be comprehended only through empathic immersion in that person's experience. Much like the dream, in which the meanings can be elucidated only through the dreamer's associations, the sinthome marks the ways in which meanings have been configured for that individual such that the sinthome holds the key to the individual's mystery. To the extent that our discourse can be true to this idiosyncratic language, we have tapped into what Ehrenzweig (1967) calls the *hidden order* of the unconscious through which complex meanings can be anchored in a context so that they can be considered and re-considered over time. In the dreamwork, there is an interplay between the personal and the universal, such that universal feelings are brought into focus through their representation in images (Cassirer, 1957). Through the dream or sinthome, we can consider these symbolic forms in relation to one another, thereby preserving the possibility of exploring deeply while also holding the overall structure in mind.

As Tom and I continued to work on repairing his image of himself, his courage, determination, and remarkable acuity served us well. My belief in the possibility that he might integrate the fragments of his crumbling consciousness and be enriched and enlivened, rather than destroyed, helped him to traverse the difficult territory of traumatic dreams and dislocated memories that had merely haunted him previously. In these efforts, my refusal to play the part of the omniscient magus through whom he might be revealed, but rather to insist on Tom himself as the frame of reference, helped Tom to begin to stand on and thereby to strengthen his crumbling foundations. Grounded in the certainty of a meaning that could be anchored and marked *outside* of the analytic dyad, we were increasingly able to circle the pit and make our way through those labyrinthian dreamscapes so that he might better hold the fragments in mind as we made sense of them together. This collaborative engagement is part of the power of psychoanalysis, that someone who has been profoundly distanced from his own humanity, because his parents could not truly embrace the extent and the particularity of his experience, can be encountered in ways that help him to bring himself to life and into real and profound contact in his relationships.

SIX

Dreamscapes

Memoirs of a Survivor[1]

"We are such stuff as dreams are made on . . ."
—Shakespeare, *The Tempest*

Dreams, much like literature, can invite us into the realm of imagination. They are "filled with unwilled surprises, sudden focusing, unfocusings" (Lippmann, 2000), the realm of the type of startle that can invite reflection and growth. Dreams offer a succession of scenes through which condensed and compacted meanings are communicated, the very type of device Woolf (1976b) explicitly offered in her writing. In both literature and dreams, the elements and their relationships to one another can carry profound and multilayered meanings that may be unpacked over time and yet retain their mystery and, with that, the ongoing possibility of further exploration. In my own dreams, I often encounter rectangular spaces that seem to carry elusive meanings. These spaces have been tremendously evocative for me and have found their way into my poetry as recurrent allusive images, almost captured. As a result, I was particularly intrigued to encounter similar images in Doris Lessing's novel *Memoirs of a Survivor* (1974), in which both narrator and reader are tantalized by the imminence of meaning lurking in the hidden spaces within.

In this novel, set in a futuristic world in which the normal boundaries of civilized existence are breaking down, the narrator experiences the breaking down of her interior walls as well, as her reverie takes her beyond the walls of her actual domicile into the spaces beyond and within the wall, in which images of memories of self and other, and self-in-other, await. These experiences have the uncanny air of waking dreams. At times, entry into this realm is beyond the narrator's control, whereas at other times she appears able to move into it at will. However, even if she can imagine herself into this world, she has little control over the landscapes themselves, which seem to change according to their own rules and regularities.

In many ways, this novel takes the form of a dream within a dream, of a life that has been led by a woman who must both undream and redream herself in order to come to accounts with her life and its myriad meanings and possibilities. Multiplicity of meaning both obscures and reveals, enabling us to confront complexity without being entirely overwhelmed by it (Ricoeur, 1970). As we communicate through interactive metaphors, the distance of perspective is introduced, providing a potential space through which new thoughts and meanings might emerge (Bezoari and Ferro, 1999). The analytic space offers greater potential for the creation of new, consensual meanings that allow us to recapture archaic fantasies in ways that facilitate further elaboration (Ricoeur, 1970). In this way, dreams bring us into what I have termed the *lands of living metaphors* (Charles, 2002a), in which our internal realities become elaborated on a stage in which analyst and analysand may each play diverse roles.

Internal landscapes predominate in *Memoirs of a Survivor*, in which Lessing (1974) continues the explorations begun in her previous novels regarding the nature of the multiple realities we experience in inner and outer space (Lessing, 1972; Rubenstein, 1976). Within the multiple realities created within the novel, it becomes unclear as to the reality upon which any of these assumptive worlds is grounded. Concrete reality fragments into particles, as fantasy obtrudes its own reality. Within the worlds created in the novel, spatial relations come to carry meaning, much as in dreams there may be a strong proprioceptive sense of the meanings underlying how we locate our dream-objects in space and time. This directionality may relate to ways in which we have been located in relation to important objects and events in our lives, and meanings thus assigned. For example, in the novel, Lessing uses the term *behind* to locate whatever is elusive and cannot be seen. Rooms that are above others also seem to have meanings within the novel, being both safe spaces, from which one might have more control, and also spaces in which control is exercised. In this way, *above* seems to carry some of the meanings it might to a child, in which the grown-up world carries on its business set apart from the world of the child.

In the novel are revealed multiple layers of both inner and outer, from the inner world within the exterior walls of the flat shared by the narrator and her charges, to the inner world encountered through the interior walls of that same space. It is only the chaos of the external world that becomes the known, in contrast to the manifestly unknown world toward which the people of the city are continually migrating and thereby disappearing into the silent void. Each world is experienced, to some extent, as alien, and we are haunted by the danger that seems to lurk everywhere precisely because we cannot with any certainty locate it anywhere. The outer world beyond the flat—which is changing too rapidly to make sense of, and in which one can no longer rely upon those charged to translate the chaos—is countered by the inner world of a remote childhood, in which the world was changing too rapidly to make sense of it and there was no reliable authority upon whom one could depend to translate the chaos into meaningful bits. As the protective links of the reality imposed by civilization begin to give way, the links proscribing meaning collapse and larger truths behind the ostensible reality emerge. Without the protective coverings that can also be seen as dichotomizations of cause and effect, past and future, self and other, the dilemma of the motherless child becomes an eternal one, afflicting mother and daughter alike. There are no victims here; there are only victims here. There is no salvation; there is only salvation. As time fragments, ostensible meanings collapse, giving way to larger truths that are almost imponderable.

In Lessing's (1974) novel, the narrator introduces the world behind the wall in terms of her own incipient awareness. This

> consciousness of that other life, developing there so close to me, hidden from me, was a slow thing, coming precisely into the category of understanding we describe in the word "realise," with its connotation of a gradual opening into comprehension. Such an opening, a growing, may be an affair of weeks, months, years. And of course one can "know" something, and not "know" it." (p. 7)

Lessing depicts this growing awareness of the interior world in counterpoint to a growing awareness of external realities. The not-knowing of self and other are closely intertwined. The narrator becomes aware of a vitality behind the wall, which is patterned by the bare outline of leaves and fronds of old wallpaper, only partly obscured by a layer of paint. Then, one day, as she contemplates the reflected glow of sunlight upon it:

> I was through the wall and I knew what was there. I did not, that first time, achieve much more than that there were a set of rooms. The rooms were disused. . . . I did not go in, but stood there on the margin between the two worlds, my familiar flat and these rooms which had been quietly waiting there all this time. I stood and looked, feeling with my eyes. I felt the most vivid expectancy, a longing: this place held what I needed, knew what was there, had been waiting for—oh yes, all my life, all my life. I knew this place, recognised it. (pp. 12–13)

Later, the narrator distinguishes her original experiences through the wall from those she terms the *personal*. The personal is seen from the perspective of a child, in which the child's world becomes the frame and the adult world looms large, indistinct, and often ominous. As Lessing (1974) describes it, "The atmosphere was unmistakable always, as soon as I entered whatever scene it was. . . . the 'personal' was instantly to be recognised by the air that was its prison, and by the emotions that were its creatures" (p. 41). In that other realm there was the sense of freedom and possibilities, whereas in the realm of the personal there was no choice: "Nothing could happen but what one saw happening. . . . time was a strict and unalterable law and long—oh, my God it went on, and on and on, minute by decreed minute, with no escape but the slow wearing away of one after another" (pp. 41–42). Lessing's narrator seems to be caught between the dreams of fantasy—of purported escape from the past—and those of the path itself, through which she must move as though in a labyrinth, hoping without hope to come to terms with an impossible reality.

I encounter this novel with a sense of the uncanny, so familiar are these interior landscapes being portrayed. Closely intertwined with the hard-edged landscapes of my own dreams and those Lessing has created are the dreamscapes into which I am drawn with one particular patient, a young woman in her late twenties, whom I have referred to previously as "Nina" (Charles, 2002a). Nina seeks to escape the prison of her reality through dreams and altered states, and yet inexorably comes upon herself and those dilemmas that are yet to be resolved. Nina's internal world has been both refuge and prison. She nurtures her dreams and fantasies, and luxuriates within them, yet at times they turn on her and become traps from which she cannot escape. These repeated encounters with dream world configurations expose important patterns organizing her phenomenal world (Charles, 2002a; Stolorow and Atwood, 1993).

Nina's dreams seem to nest within one another, as meaning builds upon meaning, and the continuity of the dream spaces points us toward the idiosyncratic meanings she has built up in layer upon layer of dream experience. In Nina's dreams, there is a prevalent theme of rectangular spaces configured within a landscape in which the spatial relationships themselves have meaning. She describes to me, in some detail, how she moves from one space to another. Inside and outside, up and down, right and left. All of these directions carry meanings within the landscape of the dream. The images reflect the condensations of primary process, the symmetrizations Nina experiences between past and present, as she longs to move forward yet fears imminent destruction in the confusions between dichotomized representations of space and time, self and other.

The dream space has been likened to a theater, in which the setting is an important part of the drama being enacted (Resnik, 1987). I have noticed in my own dreams that location, in terms of the relationship of one thing to another and the apparent directionality of these objects, often seems to carry elusive meanings. These meanings are nascent, evoking similar configural experiences, stored as proprioceptive memories that may be elusive to conscious awareness and yet ineluctably familiar, intuitively and intimately known. In some of my dreams, there are rectangular spaces that carry implicit and often elusive meanings, much as we may recognize a familiar personage, even when he or she ostensibly looks nothing like that person in real life. In some dreams, these spaces border a pathway, much like walking through a film set, in which the adjacent spaces have been created as though for a drama yet to be enacted. In other dreams, these spaces appear to reside within a grid, almost like the configuration of a board game viewed from above. There are the spaces themselves and the spaces in between that become a grid or roadway, both connecting and separating. Alternatively, the spaces may be contiguous, more like the rooms of a house, whether or not the actual space is "inside" or "outside" within the dream. In dreams, we may walk across a field become ramp become stair landing, without any seeming discontinuity in these transformations, whereas at other times the discontinuity itself becomes meaningful.

Several of my female patients, in particular, also dream repeatedly of rectangular spaces, such as houses. They are inside, they are outside, they are wandering through rooms or passageways, shifting spaces that may become distorted or distended, or transform seamlessly into one another. Spaces become constricted or precarious, they enlarge and loom. In the realm of the dream, size, shape, and relationship of self to space all seem to carry important relational meanings. In Freud's (1900) view, rectangular spaces in dreams, such as boxes, chests, and tables, tend to represent women, the body as a whole often being "pictured by the dream-imagination as a house and the separate organs of the body by portions of a house" (p. 225), and the various ways in and out of hollow objects linked to their interiors. These rectangular spaces seem in many ways interchangeable, so that a house may represent a coffin and thereby a grave (Freud, 1900). These spaces may also represent the interior of self and (m)other, in the symmetrization of internal space with womb, birth, death, and destruction (see, for example, Klein, 1932, 1946).

Because this theme of rectangular spaces has been so evocative for me, I was struck by Doris Lessing's (1974) portrayal of just these types of dream landscapes in her novel *Memoirs of a Survivor*, which she calls in the dustjacket "an attempt at autobiography." In the book, there is a counterpoint between the *outside* world, as seen through the rectangular space created by the window through which the narrator gazes and the *inside* world, entered more directly through the rectangular wall that dissipates as she gazes into and moves through it. This interior space becomes the world of dreams, the landscape of the unconscious, in which the narrator is visited by her child self, displaced into the person of the child, Emily, who has been entrusted to her by a stranger.

Intertwining themes with this book she has never read, my patient talks to me of her own alter ego, a young woman she refers to by a name I will transpose to "Erin." Erin is at once innocent and capable of great violence. She is the voice in Nina's head that marks her own assaultive anger. Nina can enjoy Erin's antics within the safety of the displacement, as she writes in her own fiction the story of Erin's revenge on an unwelcoming world. Nina also brings onto the analytic stage her animals, most particularly one cat, whom she describes as singularly intelligent and devoted. In counterpoint, in the novel, the child Emily brings with her a great beast, Hugo. The two are singularly devoted to one another, a devotion that in some ways verifies and grounds their existence. When Emily is off in the external world, Hugo marks her space, watching for her through the rectangular space through which he views the world until the world's reciprocal capacity to view *him* becomes a danger. As the porousness of this window becomes apparent, the inner world becomes conspicuously vulnerable, a tension that Nina and I also encounter. It is dangerous to be seen.

In Nina's dreams, there are often rectangular spaces that are familiar and seem reminiscent of home but are not home. These rectangular spaces may be configured into rooms of a house or into passageways that link one space to another. Nina is often trying, with great difficulty, to leave a house in which she feels imprisoned. Escape is impeded by dangers lurking along the path toward freedom, in the form of people whom she is trying to elude or as corpses lying in her path. Similar to the dangers portrayed within the novel, the difficulties Nina encounters may be displaced onto her animals, as representations of her child self, who must be rescued and protected. In Nina's dreams, the rectangular spaces often become confining and restricting, like a cell or coffin. For example, in one dream, a corpse had been dug up and someone was describing to her every detail of the insides of the coffin. Nina said that it was terrible, she couldn't stop the person. I wondered silently in what ways I was this person and what I was both forcing and enabling her to see.

These coffin images were particularly striking to me in light of Nina's depiction of one particular aspect of a dream she had of my office. Her hands elaborating her words, Nina described a rectangular space, pointing to a place where my floor intersected the wall. This space has seemed to come to life, assuming a palpable identity within the analytic space, which has persisted over time. In my imagery, this space comes to represent a holding environment for the coffin of her deceased brother, which she keeps lodged for safekeeping until she is able to more overtly think about it and integrate it into her experience. Alternatively, perhaps, in the confusions between self and other, she creates an embryonic coffin from which she might someday emerge. In this way, Nina seems to evacuate both hopeful and troubling images into the analytic space until she can achieve sufficient distance from them that they might be used more freely as symbols (Segal, 1991). Until that time, she deposits them with me in their more concrete representations, signs rather than symbols, hoping that they may, in this way, be contained and transformed from annihilating images into more usable forms.

In the meantime, Nina speaks poignantly of the loss of the brother with whom she might have discussed their mother without such awful feelings of disloyalty, with whom she could say "You know how . . ." and he would know, terribly but empathically, their love softening the betrayal of recognizing the mother's failings. In her longings for the idealized other, whose very remoteness ensures safety, albeit unattainability, Nina affirms my insufficiency. Once again, dichotomization keeps her safe, stuck and alone, and yet, it is a victory to be able to call me to account for these failings and have me survive that assault.

Being in relation to real others continues to be elusive and dangerous. It is far easier for Nina to allow me into her dream world—where meanings are allusive and escape is more easily attained—than to engage me more directly. Her dreams are rich and evocative. As we talk about them, images from past dreams intrude themselves into her or my awareness and become part of the current process. Much as the narrator in Lessing's novel moves through the wall into layer upon layer of dream spaces, so, too, do Nina and I move through an associative trail of dream images that becomes a multilayered palimpsest of past and possible meanings. The intensity of Nina's affective experience encourages symmetrization, the collapse of the conceptual space through which distinctions are made (Matte-Blanco, 1975; Rayner, 1981). That collapse thrusts her more deeply into primary process, compounding her feelings of being overwhelmed to a degree that feels intolerable to her. At those times, she experiences symptoms of panic, which she often abates by smoking marijuana, thereby defensively occluding the unknowable. The dream space seems to offer Nina a means of representing her experience without being forced to know more than she can tolerate, so that we can work with issues that are of import to her while still protecting the privacy and fragility of her inner world. In this way, the dream offers Nina an appealing solution to her ambivalence over becoming known, in that it both illuminates and obscures.

In some ways, the dream is inherently a game of hide-and-seek between that which we would know and that which we would not. The dream brought into analysis introduces another layer to this game. As Pontalis (1993) points out, the gaps within the dream-as-expressed become affirmations of the dual inadequacies of the analysand to know (in the sense of being able to interpret) the dream, and of the analyst to know the experience of it. Nina becomes caught in the disjunction between my ability to be sensitive to her experience in ways that enable me to understand quite deeply versus my ability to be quite *insensible* to her allusions and intimations, which often become more obscure as they become more important. Occasionally, she becomes so enraged that she has left me a message saying that she has quit our work together, in order to clearly delineate the enormity of my transgression. Over time, she has been able to approach me a bit more directly, sitting silently enraged and punctuating her silence with hostile barbs regarding my incompetence. This more direct confrontation better enables us to come to some mutual understanding of whatever I had missed that needs to be put right.

For Nina, there is very little space, outside of her dreams or the novels she reads or writes, within which we can consider ideas. The capacity to move beyond the experience as such and to be able to play with ideas (Winnicott, 1971) is built upon sufficient dimensionality of experience to enable us to reflect on it. Matte-Blanco (1988) depicts dimensionality as an inherent aspect of unconscious processes, in that they operate "*in a space of a higher number of dimensions than that of our perceptions and conscious thinking*" (p. 91). These dimensions would seem to have meanings in and of themselves, in terms of their interrelationships with one another, which form the structure upon which the dream is built, creating a landscape within which position, order, and location come to carry meanings as well. In the realm of dreams, these meanings tend to be quite concrete, in terms of their representation, and yet may be highly abstract in their elaboration. At times, it is by immersing ourselves in the sensory experience of the dream, insofar as we can recreate it within our own sensibilities, that we can approach some of these more elusive meanings. If we can quiet the stumblings of the conscious mind sufficiently, the codings of nonverbal communication more easily reveal themselves.

Nina and I have worked together for several years. She comes in twice a week and, yet, after all this time, we are still in the process of negotiating her ability to enter into the space we are creating in my consulting room. There is always a disjunction for Nina in entering into this world. She comes to each session reluctantly, even when she has carried the relationship between us within her in a positive manner over the most recent interval and has even looked forward to our meeting. It may be at those times that the disjunction is most severe, as her fantasy of being together becomes assaulted by the reality of my actual presence.

For Nina, being-with has meant assault, intrusion, and often annihilation of self. She describes an extremely narcissistic mother who insists on being the only frame of reference within the household. Nina was never able to find a place for herself in her home or in the larger world, in which she felt tortured and tormented. She longed to fit in and finally managed to do so in college but only at a huge price to her sense of self, which became even more split than it had been previously. When I first met her, she was finishing a second degree and was devastated by her inability to accommodate well enough to the dictates of the professional world to make a home for herself there. She still mourns this failure, which was devastating for her. Nina now works at a job for which she is eminently overqualified, pouring her intelligence and creativity into reading and writing, and her yearnings for closeness into her relationships with her animals and, to a lesser extent, the two men with whom she shares her living space.

Nina's mother was very taken with psychic phenomena and floated from dogma to dogma in her search for some meaning that would leave her at its center. This lack of foundation has left Nina somewhat at odds with her own intuitive and grandiose aspects of self. She both relies on them and fears them as they threaten to symmetrize her sense of self with that of her mother, mirroring what she describes as her mother's confusion between self and daughter. It is difficult for Nina to rely on her own perceptions in this fluid and chaotic interpersonal space.

In contrast to the lack of clarity in her daily life, Nina has very vivid dreams, which she at times seems to prefer to her waking world. Her dreams are often of houses that are never quite her own. For example, in one dream she was to go to live in her brother's apartment, which was owned by her parents. It was unclear whether she was to replace the live brother or to become the dead one. Perhaps she was to exchange places with him, so that the "right" child—the favored child—might thereby be resurrected. In Nina's dreams, her brother is always alive but never seen. He has always just left, she has just missed him, much as she, in recurring dreams, tries against all obstacles to leave the home of her childhood, where she has felt as though she could never truly *be.*

In other recurrent dreams, Nina is trying to return home from some house in which she has been staying. For example, she recently reported what she described as a terrible dream, in which she had been on the grounds of the home of a childhood friend. The parents were friends of her own parents, and she had spent a good deal of time in that house as a child. It had been quite an old house, with secret passageways, and had been full of interesting things, such as coins, papers, and furniture, when the people had bought it. That house had been where her own piano had come from. The piano was old and intricately carved, and the names of the previous owners had been carved on the inside of the lid. She had described the piano previously, in reference to another dream, in which she had been in her elementary school and had been eager to show the other children the interior of the piano, the strings and hammers and how they worked. But a man had come in and angrily chased them all away. The children disappeared and only her mother was left, accusing her. Nina had tried to explain and pulled out my card, as if to say that this woman would back her up. But then she realized that would not do any good, anyway. Nina stood, inevitably alone, with the unrequited promise of a piano. This position seemed to carry, much as did the house, a sense of history overlain with multiple meanings that both intrigued and frightened her.

Intertwining themes of spoiling and envy recur repeatedly in Nina's dreams, as in her history. She reports that she had given up playing the piano because her mother had spoiled Nina's enjoyment via repeated envious interruptions of the daughter's playing. In the transference, I become the dangerous mother who will spoil her riches through either my envy or my stupidity. The stupidity is safer but leaves her alone again, without external resources and unable to bring her internal resources into the world without invoking this danger once again.

In another dream, Nina had initially been outside the house on the grounds, carrying two of her cats. One of the cats jumped down and ran away. She tried to catch it but it ran beyond the grounds and she could not follow it. She was concerned but then became distracted by a car pulling up and reassured herself that the cat would turn up at the picnic later. Nina then entered the house through the kitchen door and moved toward the stairway to the second floor. As she neared the stairs, the cellar door opened. The opening was black and gaping, and she was very frightened. As she started to go upstairs, there was a force, like a vacuum, pulling her back toward the cellar. She was terrified but managed to get herself up the stairs, into a room, and then to shut the door. She lay down in the bed and became aware that she was actually sleeping and could rouse herself if she tried. However, she was unable to awaken herself. She then decided that if she let herself fall deeper into sleep, she would be able to wake herself up. Nina tried out this plan several times. Each time she tried to awaken herself, she would open an eye and see details of her actual room but then the rest of the room would be just as it was in the dream and she would know that she had not managed to get out of it. She said that she kept trying but each time the same thing would happen.

Finally, there was a knock at the door. Nina's terror increased as the door opened and then abated as she saw her boyfriend standing there. She told him that she needed to get out of there and they went downstairs together, coming upon her mother and grandmother, who were standing in the open doorway. Her mother was wearing a flowered dress, "as though it was summer and they had just wandered in." As they stood there, Nina felt an urge to punch her mother. She said that she knew it was a dream, so she just punched her. It felt good and her mother did not respond, so she kept punching, with increasing energy. She was enjoying this a great deal and then realized that she could kick, too. As she was punching and kicking, her boyfriend and grandmother rather weakly told her to stop but she ignored them. Finally, she pushed her mother out the door and onto the ground and then ran off. In this way, the dream ended much as it had begun, with the vulnerable young kitten self escaping from the mother self. In this overlay, one can see Nina's struggle to dichotomize her experience as a way of affirming her disidentification with the evil mother she experiences within.

When I asked what the strangest part of the dream had been, Nina replied, "Not being able to wake up." She said, "It was pretty scary if you couldn't wake yourself up out of a dream. What if you just got stuck there?" I had the sense that she was frightened of the 'mad' part of herself that threatens to engulf her. She is afraid of getting stuck in the living nightmare she has been caught in. She said that it reminded her of "that other dream I had about a month ago, where I was trying to get away from someone and I got into that parked car but then it was locked and not being able to get out and the person coming nearer and nearer, and not being able to get out and not being able to wake up." Nina spoke quite intently about how frightening it is when that happens. Usually, she is able to make herself wake up when things get too bad, in some sense knowing that she is dreaming and that she needs to awaken herself in order to get away from the terror. In this instance, however, although she had tried, she could not manage to awaken and then, even when she thought she had managed to do so, she had awakened only within the dream, not into waking life.

When Nina went back to the current dream, she focused on the house, which had trap doors that led down to the cellar from various places. Her friend had said that there were rats down there and that she had seen one as big as a cat, just beyond the door in the bathroom that led to the cellar. This girl had been three years older than Nina. "She was brilliant," said Nina, and had been very interested in molds. The girl had samples of molds in various stages in her room and the girls traced their progress together.

The profusion of furniture in the house felt very imposing to Nina as a young girl. There was the sense that she had been both fascinated and terrified by it. There was a richness that carried an air of mystery and an almost sensuous pleasure but there was also extreme vigilance. In many ways, this dilemma seems to characterize Nina's experience of our work, which has a tantalizing quality for her and yet also seems very dangerous, perhaps by virtue of the strength of the appeal.

For Nina, the cellar has been an ongoing symbol for an as yet unknown, unnamable terror. It becomes a dark space she cannot enter, linked through her associations to her brother, some ten years older than she, who had drowned somewhat mysteriously when Nina was twelve. In regard to this particular cellar, Nina said that as children she and her friend had wanted to go down into it but had been prohibited because of the rats. Again, there is the theme of a tantalizing danger, which seems to be associated with some greater awareness, much like the mold, which grows according to a pattern that may not be known until it manifests itself.

Nina began to talk about the flowers on her mother's dress, which reminded her of a previous dream we had discussed, in which she had been in a basement and had fainted after pulling aside a shower curtain to reveal a huge, ghostlike woman, who began to walk right through her. Nina said she was reminded of the flowers she had noticed growing over the basement floor as she had fallen. She recalled the feeling of fainting and how distinct it was. She wondered how you could have so vivid a sense, while sleeping, of a physiological experience that you had never experienced while awake. It seemed to be frightening to her to imagine that the sleeping world could have such potential to it. This made the idea of becoming lost and locked within it more palpable and more terrifying.

In that particular dream, Nina had been in a house with a woman. Nina had been looking for secret passageways. The floor plans did not show the passageways but she thought she could find them and so went down into the basement. There was a bathroom with two doors, both of which were locked. Nina sought help but was unable to locate anyone. When she returned to the basement, one door was ajar. Nina walked into the bathroom, toward the shower curtain straight ahead, knowing that the passageway was beyond the curtain to the right. She pulled the curtain, revealing a huge woman staring at her. Terrified, Nina felt herself losing consciousness as the woman walked right through her. Nina's knees buckled and she fell to the floor, which was covered with flower petals. She knew that the people upstairs would not help her and so she called to her boyfriend, who eventually (in actuality) heard her and woke her up. As she retold this dream, she was reminded of "another dream I had when I was a kid with a curtain that was scary, too."

> We were at my grandparents—my father's parents—and we were all there, my parents, me, my brother. We sat down to dinner at a long table, and there was a curtain with scary noises coming from behind it, like the noises that scare you as a child. I was crawling around under the table—I used to like to do that when I was a kid—and I kept trying to get in someone's lap, but they were all real cold.

I said that there seemed to be a similarity between the secret passageways in the dream and crawling under the table, and a theme she had been talking about earlier, about flattening people—depersonalizing them—to make it more tolerable to be around them, as though she needed a safe inner space from which to contemplate being around them. When I asked about her associations to the height of the woman, she said she did not have any. I said that sometimes people seem big because *we're* smaller. She said, "Like my mother? I knew you were going to say that." I responded, "I'm predictably annoying." Nina laughed and said that she was not small in the other parts of the dream. When I asked about her associations to the woman walking through her, she shivered broadly and said she didn't have any—it was just scary. Then she added, somewhat dismissively: "The woman looked kind of like Glenn Close, and I haven't seen her in anything since *Fatal Attraction* [a film in which the character played by Close had stalked her ex-lover with murderous intent], so I don't know. She just walked right through me."

I said, "Sometimes it seems as though people just look through us like we're not there, and that is pretty scary for a kid. That seemed to happen to you a great deal when you were a kid—your parents treated you as though you were not there." Nina became infused with emotion. Because it was the end of the hour and I did not want her to leave overly disorganized, I said, "But you knew your boyfriend would be there." This reminder of her current self and capacities seemed sufficient to enable her to leave.

Notably, in this dream, Nina is under a table, which creates a rectangular space surrounded by people who are cold and unavailable. I wonder if some of her guilt and confusions come from having wished that the present (but cold and unavailable) mother could have been replaced by the absent (but, in memory, warm and available) brother. Certainly, in her dreams, there is this sense of imminence and replaceability in regard to her brother. Alternatively, one wonders if the mother's tremendous despair at the death of her son—which was coupled with her attempts to eradicate any trace of his presence in the house—made Nina feel as though her own presence was equally precarious, particularly in light of the mother's relative lack of awareness of (or interest in) Nina or her needs.

The disjunctions between dream and waking, past and present, self and other are often elusive lines for Nina. At times, she lives in a world in which the disjunctions are complete and I seem to be experienced as either a warm amniotic environment or an empty space with hard edges. Her preoccupation with, and terror of, being caught in a waking dream seem to carry questions as to whether she is being overtaken by a psychotic process. I noted to her the similarity between the theme of forces beyond her control in her dreams and a story she had been talking about, in which a warden had been trying to keep people out or in ("like the undead," she had said), and not being able to get out of the dream. I suggested that perhaps it had been important for her to not wake up out of the dream, that staying in the dream had enabled her to find her way through it. First, she had brought her boyfriend in to support her, and then she had found her own strength and had done battle with her mother.

Nina then associated to a dream that had occurred before she left her childhood home, in which she was trying, without success, to get out of her room. Although she beat on the glass of her window, it would not break. She was trapped within this world become prison and could not escape. Nina's memories of being in the empty space under the table and trapped behind the glass of her room seemed to interplay with the more recent dream of her mother, in which there was a lovely exterior with nothing underneath, much like the tall woman in the dream, who had no substance at all and had walked right through Nina, as though *she* had no substance as well. In both these dreams, there had been the pattern of flowers. The mother's flowered dress presented a pleasing cover, whereas in the other dream, the petals had covered the ground. I wondered if this image was linked with her brother's death and asked if there had been flowers at the grave. "No," she said, "no flowers, just donations."

No sentiment had been allowed. Her mother and grandmother had emptied out her brother's room immediately after his death. All trace of him had disappeared.

Nina said she had imagined for some time that her brother was not dead but merely had disappeared. He was off somewhere, which in her child's mind became "New York City." This lack of resolution helps to explain the coffin in my office, the empty space Nina wishes to neither see nor have described, and the empty feelings that brim over into tears at the approach of important occasions he will not attend.

Nina's fears keep her closed off from the world. Her failures become persecutors, keeping her locked inside herself, much as Klein (1946) depicts. Her fear of seeing the tall woman who could not see her brought to my mind the thought that, at times, when we have been humiliated by people, we do not want to look at them because they come to seem so powerful and even evil. Not-looking precludes the opportunity to see that they might merely be lost and not so terribly powerful. I said that it reminded me of the woman at work whom Nina had seen as evil and had described as her nemesis, until one day the woman had revealed her own vulnerability. Nina said, "Yes, but then I saw the pain, and that was just as bad, because it was so terrible to see." In that moment, I realized how caught she was between trying to keep others at bay by keeping them evil and dangerous, versus being engulfed by the terrible poignancy of the pain of the other, which threatens to suck her down into the void, like the blackness of the cellar in the dream. This impasse parallels the dilemma that has kept her tangled up with her mother all these years, and that also keeps her caught within the work, between the interstices of the internal and external spaces, in the dichotomized realm of disjunctive experiences.

Stolorow and Atwood's (1993) depiction of the dream as a concrete representation of important underlying themes is a useful rubric within which to consider the meanings of Nina's dreams. The subterranean world seems to represent a world of hidden meanings, which are important to discover and yet also to keep safe from. These hidden meanings stress the importance, for Nina, of being able to hide and not be known, an ongoing issue within our work, often having the feel of a thirsty person presented with scalding water. My efforts to offer her something are often at odds with Nina's experience. She needs, first and foremost, to be received. My role, thus far, would seem to be to create a space in which she can deposit her fantasies and fears, so that I might metabolize them without trying to transform them precipitously into some form she can neither recognize nor utilize. And so, we traverse these angular spaces, which are often hard-edged and assaultive, like the carnival rides in which we are always surprised by the abruptness of whatever intrusion has been lurking at the next turn. Even as the images become more and more familiar, we continue to be surprised, because that very sense of surprise is part of what is being created in order to remind us of all that we have yet to understand.

In Nina's dreams, passageways seem to carry the hope of transformation, the desire to evolve. This evolution depends on a movement from the concrete representation to the symbol that can be used toward understanding the salient themes in the dream, much as there is a transformation in Lessing's novel from the concrete (a wall that is merely a wall) toward the symbolic representation of an obstacle that must first become permeable in order to allow movement and interplay. Similarly, in Nina's elaborations of her dreams, she initially brings in concrete objects, such as the rectangular space she located within my office. At that time, she was not able to use the image any further than to merely deposit it within the space for safekeeping. That provision, however, has enabled me to integrate manifestations of that image into our elaborations of her material. In this way, bringing an intractable symbolic equation (Segal, 1957) into the analytic space facilitates the transformation of that image into representations that are mutually created by the analytic pair. Through reverie, the intractable element that could only be discharged is transformed into a symbol that can be used as a means for developing richer meanings and consensual understandings (Bion, 1977).

In her dreams and reverie, Nina idealizes past and present as a way of keeping at bay the necrotic ugliness that is always threatening to distort, distend, and destroy whatever she holds dear. Her obsessive thoughts and compulsive rituals help to keep at bay the imminent unknowable destruction that feels as though it has already happened (see Winnicott, 1963). Nina longs to find the secret that will release her from the prison that her life has become. She is relentless in her scanning for potential dangers and possible solutions to the ongoing enigma that has become her existence. In our sessions, she keeps close track of the time and tends to leave early. For some time, I had thought that this was because of her discomfort at being with me in this space and perhaps it is. But it is also her attempt to protect the space and appease the gods—to not overstay her welcome—to safeguard this space that has become a refuge for herself as well as her fantasies.

There have been times in Nina's dreams when she has tried to find my office but cannot. The buildings become confused in her mind. In one dream, she could not figure out whether our appointment was to take place in my new office (in which we have been working for four years) or in my previous office, which was located on the campus of the university she had attended. The confusions built upon one another, as the office became symmetrized with her college dormitory room, which then resolved into a building she associated with her elementary school years. My office had not been my current office but rather the one that takes its place in her dreams, which has long windows and a river running by. Although it seemed to be a familiar place, she had not run across it since she had begun dreaming about it. The windows remind me of the theme of glass barriers. The river seems to represent both the life that *might* be lived (yet is always beyond reach) and the musical themes that she runs through her head in ever-elusive solace. Nina said that at times, in her dreams, she has memories of dreams but is not able to remember the dream itself. All of these confusions between layers of experience and between past and present—as well as her uncertainty as to where she *should* be—made me wonder whether she is uncertain not only as regards her own bearings but also as to whether I can be helpful to her—whether she has found the "right place."

Nina enters our shared space jarred by the disjunction of these separate worlds. She often uses music like a transitional object, to soothe and settle her from her agitated preoccupations. In one session, the *Carnival of Venice* is running through her head. She hums it periodically. It is bright and cheery and, as I think of it later, wondering about the pattern of it, about the form, I think of the red shoes in the fairy tale of that name and how they took over the dancer, much as Nina had been describing having her thoughts take over. "They run away," she says, as she gestures towards the thoughts dispersing into space. They have a life of their own, they just go. "Where do they go?" I ask. "They go to the most murderous places," she says. As in her dreams, they assail her and attack her and I wonder what she is trying not to think of. I think of her dreams, in which she is being hunted, or haunted, by personages whose insistence she runs away from, much as she runs away from parts of herself that haunt her.

"I don't know how to stop it," she says. There is an irony in this statement. Often, if we are willing to stop running and face whatever it is, it transforms and we no longer need to run from it. Nina has to get away from whatever it is in the dream; she needs to get away from the dream. And yet, she cannot get out of the car, just as she cannot awaken from the dream and, even when she seems to awaken, she has awakened only within the dream. She cannot awaken into this life, where she believes she will have more control over what she thinks, but also fears what she cannot face.

Nina's inability to awaken sufficiently to control her thoughts leaves her feeling at the mercy of them and yet, in many ways, she works against being fully awake. For example, she believes that marijuana helps her to be less disturbed by the existence of others in her world, and also to maintain a greater equilibrium with self and other. In contrast, I suggest that the marijuana exacerbates her sense of otherness and causes her thoughts to turn on her, so that seemingly benign interactions become redolent with incipient dangers. Much as she longs to lose herself in the marijuana and in her books, which come to control her thoughts, she also attempts to lose herself in her music, which is now haunting her, deriding her: "You cannot play *me*," it says. "I am just beyond your grasp."

Nina is caught by the meanings she intuits and fears to encounter. Her fears are likely fed by the hatred she encountered in the mother, whose narcissism made her look right through Nina and whose greater love for the dead son invited Nina to derealize herself. The inability to clearly and comfortably find herself in her mother's eyes and to differentiate herself from mother leaves a profound confusion between self and other, and between inside and outside, that seems to be enacted in the rectangular spaces within Nina's dreams. We seem to be compiling the rudiments of the elements that must eventually be recognized and put together in relation to one another, as we also recognize and accept the conflicting and complicated feelings that arise in Nina in relation to this difficult work. There is the coffin deposited within the wall of my consulting room, much as Lessing's (1974) dreamscapes were located within the interstices between the surface of interior and exterior wall. There are windows for looking through, which become prisons entrapping Nina, much as her dreams become lovely prisons. Like the smoke trailing from her marijuana pipe, or the wisps of dreams that become allusive images, never quite captured, Nina becomes lost within her own fantasies as she loses herself out of her terror at finding herself not herself. She longs to find the secret passage that will show her the way to transmute herself into the self she had hoped to be, but her way is blocked by the mother self that intrudes into her, defining her in ways she must lose consciousness to avoid knowing.

In some ways, these rectangular spaces are evocative of the comforting outlines of a young child's drawing, in which the soothing lines of exterior space are framed to contain the interior rectangles of the welcoming or distancing house created there. There is something heartening in the frame itself, which tells us of the edges against which we might be buffeted and yet still find our house standing, just as it was before. Perhaps that is what Nina is building in my office: an edifice strong enough to withstand the opening of the coffin/womb and the description of the contents, so that she can begin to mourn that which must be left behind and move forward with whatever remains, in an interactive field in which she is not so terrifyingly alone.

NOTE

1. This chapter is an amended version of a paper originally published as: Marilyn Charles, "Dreamscapes: Portrayals of Rectangular Spaces in Doris Lessing's *Memoirs of a Survivor and in Dreams*," *The Psychoanalytic Review* vol. 90, no. 1 (2003): pp. 1–22. Copyright Guilford Press. Reprinted with the permission of The Guilford Press.

SEVEN

Reparation and Redemption

Nightmare and Memory in D. M. Thomas's Pictures at an Exhibition *and in Clinical Practice*[1]

"It didn't start as a nightmare but as a very pleasant dream."
—D. M. Thomas, *Pictures at an Exhibition*

In D. M. Thomas' novels, we see once again the form of the traumatic narrative as he struggles with nightmare and memory, reparation and redemption. In *Pictures at an Exhibition,* he plays and replays essential dilemmas in being human, casting and re-casting the parts until the figures blur and we wonder what characterizes a given individual. Whose voice are we hearing? How do we locate ourselves in time and space so as to make sense of the communication? This is the dilemma of traumatic experience, in which history and personal knowledge are disrupted and unknown. Into this chaos, Thomas entwines a mythic voice that warns us against believing our own lies, truths that are condoned by culture but become traumatizing to those deemed *other*. In looking at this novel, framed by the psychoanalytic universe, we can wonder what the writer is telling us about the psychoanalytic endeavor and about the perils we face as we enter into the domains of trauma and of truth. Bringing in a case in which the patient's narrative has become disrupted and meanings occluded by her own traumatic experiences, we can use these two points of reference as conceptual anchors that might aid us in thinking about how to work with patients for whom meanings are depicted chaotically and proto-symbolically.

As noted previously, literature endures, in part, because it brings us up against timeless truths that are easier to bear at this remove. Many authors have played with their fascination with analytic truth and with the place of psychoanalysis in the understanding and obfuscation of difficult truths, offering a different lens through which to view some of the challenges encountered in the consulting room. One author who has played with these themes repeatedly is D. M. Thomas. In his novels, we see him struggling with nightmare and memory, working and reworking these themes from various angles. In *Pictures at an Exhibition* (1993), he resurrects the themes of reparation and redemption that had been introduced previously in *The White Hotel* (1981). In this novel, we can find echoes of DeLillo's (2007) fragmented traumatic narrative but softened and smoothed over by the musicality, the weaving together of lyrical threads of meaning that we encountered in Woolf's *The Waves* (1931).

Pictures at an Exhibition is composed of a series of vignettes, its formal elements loosely based on Mussorgsky's piano pieces written in response to an exhibition of Victor Hartman's paintings in 1874. Thomas's exhibition, however, is configured around events many decades later, during and after the Holocaust, in a struggle to make sense of man's inhumanity to man. The work of art that most closely epitomizes *this* exhibition is Edvard Munch's famous painting "The Scream." In this novel, we are invited to view that image from several vantage points, to the accompaniment of music from Gustav Mahler, whose life, like that of Munch and the characters in the novel, was closely shadowed by illness, death, and tragedy.

The novel opens with a scene in which a doctor is suffering acutely and so another doctor is summoned to attend to him. This first scene is accompanied by descriptions of music from Wagner's *Tristan and Isolde*, which plays on themes of renunciation in the face of the inevitability of human suffering. Slowly, we learn that it is psychoanalytic treatment being sought in order to forestall the intolerable headaches experienced by Dr. Lorenz, the S.S. officer who holds dominion over life and death at the camp, and that the analyst, Galewski, is drawn from the inmates awaiting slaughter. Thus is set the stage in which life and death, virtue and evil are opposed and woven together, merging eerily like the ashes of burning bodies suffusing the sky surrounding the scene. That horror becomes the backdrop of our story, de-realized by the dissociation of Dr. Lorenz, who maintains control not only over life and death but also over what may or may not be known.

In this novel, dream opposes reality in a deadly dance in which life and meaning itself are continually at stake. Characters appear in one scene, only to ostensibly disappear in the next, though we feel their traces eerily, ominously, as we attempt to assemble some sense of coherence in linear time. In the first few pages, we are thrust directly into the timeless realm of the unconscious, in the form of a dream of the S.S. officer that configures the events in which he is mired but which makes no sense to him. The reader, however, anchored more firmly in time and space, can weave this story into a terrible narrative of atrocity whose very denial foretells our doom. Thrust into this uncanny position of being able to foretell a future as yet unknown to the participants, we watch with dread and horror as the story unfolds.

With no sense of irony, Lorenz laments his surroundings to his prisoner whose family has been devoured by the rats in the camp: "but–one has to put up with it," says Lorenz (p. 5). "True," says the prisoner, asked to commiserate with his jailer, who then recounts the dream:

> He had been trapped on the mountains, after a fall. Dragging his left leg, he had made his way down the moraine to the valley. He'd managed to reach a farmhouse, just before nightfall; a farm near a glade of birches. There was no one about, no one who answered his cries. He'd broken a window and got inside. Silence. An air of desertion. But food in the larder; he'd gorged himself on bread and sausage. At last he'd dragged himself up the stairs to bed.
>
> He saw the face of his mother, lying quiet, asleep, on the fresh pillow. He was surprised to see his mother in a farm under the mountain. He tried to rouse her but could not. He pulled the sheet down over her naked breasts, and further. And saw that the whole of the nether part of her body was being gnawed away, by rats. (pp. 5–6)

This novel, at times raw and grotesque, gnaws away at us but also eludes us, as meanings startle and then slip away. In shifting scenes—leaping across continents and generations—characters, names, and relationships change so enigmatically that we are never quite sure what epitomizes each character. The portraits are finely drawn and yet elusive. We wander through this gallery without the normal markings by which we might anchor ourselves in time and space and perhaps more clearly find our way. The titles for these portraits evoke emotional resonances that come to be our best guide in this particular journey, in which the normal guideposts seem markedly lacking or gone terribly awry. In this realm of primary process, meanings haunt us, providing urgency rather than relief.

We encounter the experience of disruption at various levels, a disruption that is in itself meaningful. From one frame, disruption is the fundamental dilemma of traumatic experience, in which communication and even knowledge itself is profoundly disrupted and unknown. The voice of traumatic experience is a voice of utter and terrible silence, timeless as the unconscious, echoing into eternity. From another frame, there is the disruption of these timeless truths, through a mythic voice that warns us against becoming too comfortable with the trappings of truth that beguile us into believing our own lies. At various turns, Thomas warns us explicitly against believing in the types of facile truths, condoned by culture, that become traumatizing to whomever is deemed *other* and thereby marked for vilification and demonization. In looking more pointedly at this novel, framed by the psychoanalytic universe, we can wonder what the writer is telling us about the psychoanalytic endeavor, its perils and its pitfalls, and about the very real and complex hazards we face as we enter into the domains of trauma and of truth.

In *Pictures at an Exhibition*, we are pulled out of our alliances with and allegiances to any particular character or story line and are forced to confront, rather, what may be most difficult in ourselves—our willingness to demonize others and to excuse ourselves in the process. In this novel, Thomas continually disrupts the narrative flow, pulling us in and out of any identification with form, ethnic affiliation, or historical context. By dislocating us in time and space and decontextualizing the anchors by which we might *believe* that we understand what distinguishes right from wrong, or one person from another, Thomas suggests that we must be laid bare in order to discover *ourselves* and that we should take care, as this discovery may be more than we can endure. At that outer edge of experience, he suggests, our choices are to go mad or to be blind, to not see whatever seems unknowable.

Using the frame of the traumatic past, and intertwining the search for understanding that past in the present (the realm of psychoanalysis) with the search for expression and recognition of the magnitude of the traumatic experience (which falls within the domain of art), Thomas puts us up against an essential lie embedded in our very humanness: our resistance to encountering difficult truths. Deftly, masterfully, he paints a vivid and complex portrait, a palimpsest that both obscures and instantiates the type of warning alluded to by Bion (1977), who pulls the Oedipal myth out of the relational space in which it had been cast. Extending Bion's vision, Steiner (1985) depicts the Oedipal myth as a dilemma, not between self and other, but rather one in which we are confronted with our own willful blindness, our desire to turn a blind eye and not know whatever seems too painful to encounter.

In reading this novel, we come up against our resistance to encountering our hidden vices: our greed, our envy, our willingness to do harm and even, at times, our sadistic pleasure. In a literary form that has the feel of fugue, Thomas puts before us story after story, voice after voice, and the instruments begin to have their own elusive yet distinctive sounds as they weave their own melodies, much as we found in *The Waves*. More implicitly, in this novel, we see emerging, elusively but relentlessly, the configural themes through which we come to know each voice, each character. We struggle to catch hold of these voices, to discern what distinguishes them and how we might know them, even as context, names, and conceptual anchors change. We come to accept that, even as we search to unravel the mystery, the dilemma goes beyond the mystery to its core: the tragedy of being human and of knowing that one at times may play destructive parts in this ongoing tragedy, even as one seeks to survive and perhaps even do some good.

This struggle parallels those we face in our work with people whose early relationships have been depriving and traumatic. These individuals often have no language through which to construct a coherent narrative and so the analyst finds herself caught between the need to resonate to what "Alice" calls the *silent scream* and the need to keep in mind what I call the *cost of crucifixion* (Charles, 2006b), a way of fixing in my own mind this dilemma in which we are called upon to acknowledge the pain without perpetuating a deadly enactment.

When there is no verbal language through which to express pain, it tends to be communicated through proto-symbolic sensory memories, in what I have called the *language of the body* (Charles, 2002a). When words fail (Farrell, 1995) and salvation seems possible only through external sources, one resolution is to invite the other in by marking (and often magnifying) the distress, lending an air of inauthenticity to what is, in fact, very real pain.

These patients bring us back to where they are stuck, to the point of rupture (Lacan, 1977f), where *possible* meanings intrude upon the *presumptions* of meaning that had occluded these possibilities (Lacan, 1977e). This point of rupture, or of *unlinking*, as Bion (1977) terms it, is the place of annihilation of mind and memory. It is only from this starting point that we can even imagine the journey we might be taking. At the nexus of traumatic memory, there are no words and so these patients demand that we attune to the proto-symbolic elements of the communications so that they can be assured that we might, truly, be reading *them*. This demand has its price for the analyst who works with those for whom need has signaled danger, as we find ourselves cast in the equally untenable roles of savior and persecutor.

When the price of engagement has been self-annihilation through intrusion or neglect, the question arises whether one can be fed without being destroyed and whether one can exist as a separate self. One is in the paradoxical and inherently unresolvable dilemma of needing to sacrifice the self as a way of creating one's life. In some sense, we have before us the story, not only of an ongoing crucifixion, but also of an immaculate conception—the Phoenix rising from the ashes—inviting us to consider questions such as how one might receive nourishment without being poisoned, taken over, or annihilated. These desperate issues are at times played out in the desire to abstain from eating altogether or, failing that, to disgorge whatever becomes toxic when taken in. The intensity of intolerable affect is itself traumatic and we find ourselves in a region in which narrative time is superseded. When rupture becomes an impossible point of annihilation, it is difficult to separate one moment from another or one person from another.

At this point of rupture, relational bonds are broken and become lost as a vehicle for meaningful interchange. Consensual language is built on the bedrock of relationships that are sufficiently attuned that we can learn to recognize self and other with some reliability. When parental attunement has been insufficient, however, it is difficult to build consensual meanings, or to clearly and adaptively distinguish self from other. When care has been purchased at the price of self, it is not at all clear that one can assert one's self at all. One cannot build a story in which one is the subject.

So then, in comes my patient, Alice, frightened and alone, isolated behind a façade that had become a desperate pretense at being a self. The mother who does not have sufficient boundaries to effectively mark distinctions between self and other is not well-equipped to help her child to develop her own boundaries and ego strength. Alice, then, tends to find herself at the mercy of either the withholding good or the actively bad object. This dilemma lends itself, in the treatment, to unstable relations in which the analyst is always in danger of being persecuted by the need to *be* the all-good object lest she be thrust into the abyss of becoming the murderous mother.

Melanie Klein, perhaps more than any other theorist, invites us into this dire realm of what she terms the *paranoid-schizoid position*, in which it is not the quality of life that is at issue but rather survival, itself. The paranoid-schizoid position is a way of characterizing a state of primitive anxiety in which there is a fear of disintegration or "falling into bits" (Klein, 1946, p. 4; see also Charles, 2004c). There is very little resilience or capacity for integration, so that affect is regulated through very early, primary defenses, such as splitting and denial, and relationships are split into dichotomized disjunctions of good and bad, persecutor and victim.

Klein (1946) helps us to locate ourselves in this disjunctive world through her descriptions of projective identification, in which whatever is vilified or causes excessive anxiety is not seen within the bounds of self but only outside, in the other. When the primary impulse is to harm or control, the other is felt, reciprocally, to be the persecutor. If the good parts are projected excessively, the other becomes the ego-ideal, resulting in over-dependence and a reciprocal weakening and impoverishment of the self.

Whereas Thomas characterizes this dilemma through the multiplicity of characters in his novel, Alice describes it through the multiplicity of characters in her dreams. One series of dreams, in particular, seems to be paradigmatic of the dilemma in which Alice and I find ourselves. In this dream, we can see the displaced aggression lurking behind its mask, waiting to destroy her and the treatment unless we can recognize it and contain both good and bad aspects of self and other. Her recounting is elusive, the dream a means of both revealing and obfuscating split-off aspects of self that she needs *me* to be able to integrate without destroying *her* in the process.

Alice tells me that she can't always distinguish between dream and reality, but reports one of a series of dreams having a theme of cats. She is not sure why she would dream of cats, she says, as she doesn't particularly like them. In the dream, she realized that she had a cat but that she had forgotten about it, and then realized that the cat would be needing things she had failed to provide. She went to see to it and "there was all this fur" and then she realized that there were lots of little kittens and she thought "Oh God, the cat was pregnant and had kittens." She then saw two big cats staring at her and they seemed menacing, a feeling that linked back to other cat dreams she had as an adolescent. In one, she had left a cat unattended in the bathroom because of a party. She needed to go see to it but was afraid. Once again, we encounter the sense of menace.

Alice's associations went to her brother, who was allergic to cats, and then to her father. She remembered him painting a room and needing to keep all the windows open because of the smell of the cat and her father being very angry over this. Alice seemed to think that the anger toward the "damned cat" was displaced.

Her associations then went to the room and the sense of place. She said she had never had a secure place in her home. Everyone else had a place but if someone was going to be displaced, it would be her. She described in detail the walls of her rooms and how they had been painted. She said that when she came in to our sessions she felt as though she painted a picture each time. There was always a new canvas, she said, and it depended on how she felt. Sometimes she had only three colors; sometimes she might have twenty.

Alice seemed to be telling me that she felt free to paint in her own way. She contrasted this freedom with her experience of her parents coming to town and trying to paint her apartment. Alice had mentioned wanting to paint one of the walls, and her mother had wanted to know "which color." Alice explained that she didn't want to paint it a *color*; she wanted to *paint* on it. Blatantly ignoring her, however, her mother kept searching for a color.

Alice contrasted this encounter with her mother with her experience of me, saying that this is the first time anyone has ever really listened to her. In the past, therapists had some protocol they were going through and it was like they could see only the tip of the iceberg and did not want to look beneath. I wondered what *I* was not seeing and referred to the kittens, wondering whether the kittens were a part of her that *she* was not willing to see and if I was perhaps colluding in ignoring important issues. I could sense the hazard of splitting off the aggression, such that Alice could not find her own agency or her separateness from me, and I tried to avoid colluding with this desire.

The dream helped us to mark Alice's aggression, affording a lens through which we could see how her hostility becomes displaced and masked by the forgotten cats whose needs make them menacing, and how I become responsible for marking the place of whatever is not being seen. Her abstention from need is an untenable resolution to an impossible dilemma (Charles, 2006b). Finding words helps to cast some light into the darkness (Bion, 1990). Although this light in some ways titrates our fear, for those caught between the need for food and the need to abstain or evacuate, there is a tension being played out between the words that might make the experience digestible and the terrible fear of knowing. This tension leaves us in a cat and mouse game in which good and bad cannot be so neatly nor so easily separated from one another but rather must be integrated into some coherent whole.

Much as Thomas paints and repaints word portraits of the various facets of a self he cannot quite integrate into an acceptable or coherent whole, we can wonder how Alice's willingness to paint a new picture masks her fear by painting a *pretty* picture while she unlinks one experience from the next. Her facility at splitting makes reality highly changeable, depending on the affect of the moment. Many colors may be needed to obfuscate and paper over the walls of a room that has become untenable, and windows may need to be opened to eradicate the smell of cat within. We are left with the ongoing dilemma of how we might position ourselves so that we can work our way toward a more stable and tolerable self-representation without splitting off the messier, more problematic aspects.

We find Alice stuck in much the same way as the characters in Thomas' novel, none of whom can free themselves from responsibility for their actions, however constrained their freedom might be. One of the sequelae of such trauma is profound difficulties in affect regulation that give rise to the somatic symptoms that plague Thomas' Dr. Lorenz, and the desperation that Alice experiences as inchoate feelings of panic or falling. Much as Lorenz and Galewski look to one another as a source of both persecution and salvation, Alice's difficulties in integrating good and bad aspects of self leave her caught in relationships in which she is inevitably persecuted by either the withholding good or the actively bad object. It is difficult to tell which is more dangerous, making it important that I try to withstand the persecutory invitation by neither rejecting my own badness nor accepting the role of the ideal good mother, who could *know* her without words. Otherwise, her avoidance of agency seems to become a passive-aggressive enactment through which she plays out the *pretense* of engagement without having to take the risks entailed in actual contact with another human being.

In the consulting room, we attempt to build a space in which the patient might think her own thoughts and dream her own dreams, in which the palimpsest can both hide and reveal the layerings so that we can contain and integrate them over time. We can see in the characters of Lorenz and Galewski, and their successive reiterations throughout the novel, an intertwining of self and other, perpetrator and victim. In Alice's dreams, we see hints of the obfuscative attempts to hide her own potency, an agency that has come to seem dangerous. The fear of *being* the deprecated object makes it difficult for Alice to even seek less destructive relationships, and yet, we cannot merely accept the dramatization in which Alice is cast as the menacing and forgotten kitten.

Much like the experience of reading Thomas' novel, trying to find Alice is like holding a Jacob's ladder and watching it change, endlessly. We see the split between the feared and the fantasied Alice, and how easily one becomes the other, as the grandiose Alice invites the devouring need of the annihilating other and the empty Alice invites deprecation and abandonment. The shadow of the murderous mother—emptying her of anything good and filling her intrusively and toxically—is always at our heels. Her avoidance tends to keep her in an as-if realm in which she can *pretend* to be but cannot actually *be*, in this way affirming her fears. My task, then, is to actively challenge these assumptions by finding and recognizing the hidden Alice, so that she might better locate herself. If she is to build a more viable and satisfying existence for herself, she will have to find a way of recognizing herself more fully so that she might move beyond the constraints of this terrible prison she has constructed.

Without faith in one's own value, the search for recognition becomes a search for misrecognition. Alice is so afraid that recognition would be deprecating that she cannot make any explicit demands. Her hostility is hidden behind her abdication of need, creating an alternate reality in which not-eating provides strength and refusal to ingest is an act of self-vindication. She acts out the fear that it is the Alice-who-knows who must be killed, lest the world shift once again and *she* becomes the bad object. Yet, clearly she cannot survive without her own potency, which is tightly entangled with her rage. If she would truly like to have a life, I tell her, she will need to make decisions based on values she chooses to assign rather than becoming lost in this treacherous universe that parodies her relationship with her mother, in which living is achieved through dying.

Alice struggles with these tensions between the terrors of growth and the devastation wrought by evasion. "I feel like this is a major problem that I can't just keep thinking is going to get better," she tells me. "Every day I get up and swear that it's going to be different, and every day I fail. I just don't know how to make it any better." I take this in and an image comes vividly to mind. "Adrienne Rich (1981, p. 59) has a poem called 'Turning the Wheel'," I say. "It begins:

> The road to the great canyon always feels
> like that road and no other . . .

but then she goes on:

> Today I turned the wheel, refused that journey . . .

"Sometimes we turn the wheel," I say. "We take a step sideways, in another direction. Sometimes it's almost the same direction, but not quite. It's a step."

In Thomas' novel, it is difficult to find our way. Reparation and redemption are offered, but always at a price. Ultimately, we are never quite sure who is the victim and who the persecutor. We slowly find our way through a world that confounds us, as he shakes the universe he is creating and it clouds once again, as though we were finding our way through a child's glass landscape.

We begin with the harsh counterpoint of a person in pain, trying to assuage that pain with sweet music, set against the ashes of burning bodies turning acrid in the wind. And we end, seeking solace once again but becoming caught, insidiously, by the secrets lurking in the silence:

> "Music is a great solace," says the patient, "I wondered if you'd mind my putting on a tape, very low? Thank you. The Goldberg Variations . . . Heavenly."
>
> "You'll start me off crying again," she continues, "That was wonderful! I wasn't imagining it, was I? You did lean over and kiss me on the forehead, didn't you? That's one of the most wonderful things anyone's ever done to me! You're such a kind man. I'm sure you're going to help me." (p. 274)

In my work with Alice, I am always perched at the edge of the split she so easily invokes between good and bad, between hopelessness and possibility, and between what may and may not be known in a given moment. My task is to acknowledge her current limits while also repudiating their inevitability, and to believe in her *viability* without leaving her at the mercy of her incapacity. There is always a choice, I tell her, and it is important to be able to make a better choice, to mark every success, no matter how small. For it is in the ability to mark meanings, to track experience, and to celebrate small successes upon which a life is built.

Moving back, then, into our novel, we are hoping to believe in salvation but are never quite clear whether we have found the kiss of the father or that of Judas, or which of these might be more deadly. So then, as we finish the novel, we are hoping for a thread to reveal, finally, the complexities we have encountered in this labyrinthian journey, and yet, we end as we began:

> "So how do we start?" writes Thomas, "With a dream?" (p. 274)

NOTE

1. The lines from "Turning the Wheel," from *A Wild Patience Has Taken Me This Far: Poems 1978–1981* by Adrienne Rich. Copyright © 1981 by Adrienne Rich. Used by permission of W. W. Norton & Company, Inc.

IV

Cultural Collisions

EIGHT

Collisions Between Conscious and Unconscious, East and West

Kafka on the Shore[1]

"Culture, the acquainting ourselves with the best that has been known and said in the world, and thus with the history of the human spirit."
—Matthew Arnold

Psychoanalysis thrives on paradox, which keeps us from settling on simplistic solutions to complex problems. And yet, in spite of increasing knowledge regarding the unconscious forces at work within the individual—and of the importance of culture in structuring individual experiences of self and other—we still expect to be *of one mind*. When we encounter collisions between conscious intentions and unconscious desires, we are often dismayed or appalled and seek to resolve the disparity, and yet, these collisions can make apparent some of the dualities that confront us in the clashes between our sense of self as an individual and also part of a collective. Psychoanalysis offers a means for encountering perspectives that might otherwise go unchallenged and for coming to terms with the multiplicity of the unconscious, including acceptance of desires and motives that are ego-dystonic. Psychoanalysis provides a lens that helps us to move beyond what appears to be true because of our embeddedness in the culture in which that truth has been defined. Through this process, we more fully encounter our humanity and, with it, our possibilities. Literature also provides this type of opportunity. As Haruki Murakami puts it, "symbols guide us to the roles we play" (2005, p. 375).

As we discovered in chapter 4, in his novels, we see Murakami struggling with otherness, weaving together conscious and unconscious forces while also trying to integrate Eastern and Western sensibilities. In looking at such works as *Kafka on the Shore* (2005), the Western reader is provided an external glimpse into his own culture and an internal glimpse into forbidden elements of the unconscious mind. In this chapter, I will use aspects of this novel along with fragments from my work with a young man of Indian descent to consider the universality and particularity of Oedipal themes from the disparate lenses of East and West; conscious waking mind and dream.

In our efforts to make sense of the impossible complexities of human experience, we run up against the limits of mind and imagination, and develop various systems for representing and communicating our experiences. Myth and literature have provided important means for such explorations. In developing models as ways of organizing and simplifying meanings within a conceptual frame, we create false dialectics such that we are always up against partial truths, and yet, through these enterprises, we are able to come up against these truths and perhaps more reflectively consider and attempt to integrate them. In the displacement, we are able to engage with territory that might be too treacherous if it seemed any more real.

Before the psychic exploration we call psychoanalysis, human beings pondered the imponderable through science, religion, and the arts. Literature has long provided a means through which we could consider ineffable aspects of lived experience, which is far more complex than we can ever fully comprehend. That complexity can be frustrating or liberating, depending on our ability to tolerate enigma. Murakami is one writer who explicitly enters the domain of psychoanalytic inquiry and explores territory such as the oedipal dilemma, intergenerational trauma, and the dream. For Murakami, enigma seems to be a divine playing field, in which he frolics relatively freely, offering up reality and fantasy, waking thought and dream, East and West in equal measure. In this process, he pulls the reader into considerations of the nature of meaning beyond the comfortable lines we tend to draw.

Freud's model of psychoanalysis is based on his insights regarding how meanings are conveyed through the dreamwork, much as anthropologists use myth and other narrative traditions as models through which to understand the work of culture. These models have in common the provision of a structural framework that helps to locate guideposts in configural space. Configural space is a useful rubric that provides a way of conceptualizing multiple relationships among elements, a strategy that is particularly important when investigating psychic reality. As we come up against the limits of our capacity to hold in mind complex webs of interrelationships, we need models that can assist us in reflectively considering not only the interplay between elements but also how these relationships change over time.

This is the type of model that Murakami (2005) employs in his novel *Kafka on the Shore,* in which he explores split-off elements of human experience, using literary devices that break apart those aspects that do not easily fit together. The novel is broken into alternating chapters that tell the stories of a fifteen-year-old runaway who has taken the name of "Kafka" and an aged man who has lost his memory but gained rare powers including the ability to communicate with cats. Kafka communicates with an alter ego named Crow (Kafka roughly translated in Czech). In this novel, dream and waking life coexist and we are often not certain which is which or exactly what the overlap might be. Murakami implicitly raises this dilemma through the form of the novel and explicitly raises it as well, as, for example, in his description of "The Tale of the Genji," in which the evil spirit of one of Prince Genji's lovers kills his wife. The lover has disturbing nightmares but no conscious knowledge of what her spirit has been up to.

From another angle, we are brought up against the forbidden as Kafka encounters a woman who may be his lost mother. Drawn to one another, they come up against both the attraction and the taboo. "We're not metaphors," says the mother figure. "I know," replies Kafka, "But metaphors help eliminate what separates you and me" (p. 294). Later in the same passage, Murakami reflects, through these characters, on the paradox between metaphorically approaching "actual" truth versus actually approaching metaphorical truth. In this passage, he presents us with an explicit statement regarding the importance of using alternate or even opposing methods in order to approach some more complex appreciation of truth. "Symbolism and meaning are two separate things. I think she found the right words by bypassing procedures like meaning and logic. She captured words in a dream, like delicately catching hold of a butterfly's wings as it flutters around" (p. 225).

Through these considerations, enacted through the displacement of characters within a novel, Murakami brings us into the arena of myth, through which human beings have for centuries contemplated complex truths of existence. "There's another world that parallels our own," he writes, "and to a certain degree you're able to step into that world and come back safely. As long as you're careful. But go past a certain point and you'll lose the path out. It's a labyrinth" (p. 326).

The myth provides a form and a forum for inquiring into unknown territory rather than foreclosing on this journey by imposing arbitrary limits. This territory is familiar to the psychoanalyst, who begins each journey relatively blind to the particulars of the other's individual experience but knows something of the path to be traversed. Much of what the analyst accesses in this work is stored in the unconscious—in implicit memory—rather than being more directly accessible to the conscious mind. The stories our patients tell us exist in dual registers between explicit and implicit, conscious and unconscious, known and unknown, and the analyst must be able to co-exist in present and past, actual and psychic realities, at one and the same time. As Murakami suggests, in our ability to tolerate the lack of clear distinction between metaphor and actuality, something is gained.

The psychoanalytic journey requires a facility that is not unlike being able to allow a fugue to play and replay, etching tracks upon our minds and beings, allowing the composer to affect us in ways neither she nor we can predict. So, too, the analysand narrates a story that is both more and other than whatever is consciously known, and we use the frame of the story as a means for locating various truths in relation to one another. Bion (1977) intuited the importance of moving to the level of configural structure as a tool for holding in mind complexities we cannot yet fathom. In his grid, he highlights ways in which it is the *function* to which a statement is put rather than the statement itself that should have our attention (Bion, 1989). This type of structure can help us to see beyond aspects of content that tend to obscure the functional relationships between elements.

In psychoanalysis, we come upon relational structures that seem to be common across cultures. Such is the case with the Oedipus complex, which can be seen as both universal in some respects and particular in others, as we note differences across cultures in terms of the force, potency, or valence of the dilemma (see for example Obeyesekere, 1990). This concept, marked notably in the Greek tragedies, has evolved from Freud's original focus on incest, to highlighting the confrontation with authority, to Bion's (1977) depiction of the oedipal tale as similar to other myths (such as the story of the Garden of Eden) in which it is willful blindness that is at issue, a willful blindness in which each individual can find him or herself implicated.

Looking across these stories, we see the importance of what has been termed the *Third* or the *Name of the Father* in locating knowledge or truth beyond either the individual or the dyadic perspectives, thus affirming the importance of Language as a symbolic function that anchors meanings (Lacan, 1977e). Such an external reference point helps distinguish between universal and particular aspects, thus better enabling us to encounter our own preconceptions and *pathological certainties*, and perhaps more reflectively consider the positions we take rather than presuming universality (Shapiro, 1982).

Preconceptions or received knowledge that has not been challenged by or integrated through personal experience can inhibit our ability to grapple with puzzles as they present themselves to us. Recall Bion's suggestion, introduced in chapter 3 (following Freud's 1916 statement to Lou Andreas-Salome), that there are some subjects that are merely further obscured when we attempt to illuminate them. In those moments, our efforts at understanding may foreclose on the issue rather than facilitating further discovery. Some inquiries, he suggests, require "a penetrating beam of darkness" (Bion, 1990, p. 20) in order that more information might be revealed. There is no substitute for the patience of the analyst who trusts in the process sufficiently to allow it to unfold.

This model encourages us to tolerate our ignorance rather than trying to immediately overcome it. Psychoanalysis requires humility. The psychoanalyst has reason, borne of his or her own experience, to trust in the process, whereas it is only the patient who has lived the story we are hoping to elaborate. We need one another in order to obtain sufficient perspective to enable us each to remain present and try to see beyond the limits that otherwise foreclose possibility. As we will see in the case example, the capacity to be present under duress can be a major factor in determining one's ability to learn from the experience of the moment in the service of development. As we become more present with one another, our nonverbal channels communicate in ways that help us each to tolerate what can be a terrible not-knowing, a distress that is tempered precisely because there are two of us suffering together.

Bion (1977) notes the utility of dual vantage points—*binocular vision*—in illuminating complex dilemmas. As we consider what becomes opaque when viewed through the lens of a given culture, a comparison of alternative mythic frameworks can be particularly useful in highlighting commonalities and differences. Lévi-Strauss (1984) stresses the importance of multiple vantage points in appreciating cultural differences, suggesting that in order to understand universal problems, one must be able to look from both inside and out, in order to see "what is peculiar to each culture in the form of myth, ritual and language—that is, in domains where the oppositions are both identifiable and unconscious" (p. 22).

Much as Bion (1990) points to the holes that can be discerned if we attend to the associative links, Lacan (1977f) picks up on a theme originally introduced by Freud (1924) to note that it is in the gap beyond what initially captures our attention that significance is revealed. Ricoeur (1970), conceptualizing the work of culture in line with the dreamwork, suggests that hidden desire can be located through the ways in which it is disguised within a given frame. From this framework, we use symbolic forms as ways of rendering more visible whatever is most difficult for us to tolerate knowing. For Ricoeur, being able to look across disciplines helps us to recognize common themes and relational elements. "Psychoanalysis is of value insofar as art, morality, and religion are analogous figures or variants of the oneiric mask. The entire drama of dreams is thus found to be generalized to the dimensions of a universal poetics" (p. 162). The mask helps to titrate the distress.

Adding insights from Melanie Klein to our understanding of the formal structures of the unconscious, Obeyesekere describes the unconscious as "inhabited by *beings*, and not just drives and wishes" (in Molino, 2005, p. 55), so that "narrativization, the very act of telling a story about illness may itself be part of the cure" (p. 58). In this way, he echoes Felman's (1995) remarks regarding the importance of telling one's story in order to literally realize it. Through the study of dreams, we see how meanings can be anchored in the positioning of subjects and objects in relation to one another. Narrative, then, provides a structure that helps us to track the transformations of these relationships across time. For Ricoeur (1984), as a "transcultural form of necessity . . . *time becomes human to the extent that it is articulated through a narrative mode, and narrative attains its full meaning when it becomes a condition of temporal existence*" (p. 52; italics in original).

From this framework, time is essential to meaning, providing an anchor in configural space for the primary perceptual elements that speak profoundly and directly, and thus *insist* on recognition. This is the realm of myth, in which universal truths are located in relation to an ethos framed by culture (Charles, 2004a). It may be most explicitly in those myths that have endured over time that we find the purest representations of symbolic form, in that "the world of mythical experience is grounded in experiences of pure expression rather than in representative or significative acts" (Cassirer, 1957, p. 68). Cassirer suggests that the myth has the form of a hologram, in which the parts contain the whole rather than the whole being capable of division into substantive parts. This is the actualization of affective meanings not yet consciously known, described in chapter 7 in relation to our discussion of *Pictures at an Exhibition*. Notably, Cassirer anchors meaning in affect, seeming to intuitively recognize the crucial organizing functions of affect in human memory. His suggestion that it is in the embodiment of affect that meanings can be perceived is affirmed by research that shows that such meanings are embedded in the prosody of visual and auditory manifestations of affect that are taken in directly without requiring conscious thought (Stern, 1985). In Cassirer's words, "the expressive meaning attaches to the perception itself, in which it is apprehended and immediately experienced" (p. 68).

The narrative form of myth provides a containing structure through which universal feelings might be comprehended by bringing them into, as Cassirer puts it, "a kind of spiritual focus, into the unity of an 'image'" (1957, p. 108). Because images arise directly from affect, they are by nature ephemeral and so it is the *representation* of the image that enables it to persist, both as a single instance and also as a symbol for something greater from which the instance emanates. These representations are then linked through the containing structure of the myth, which, like the dream work, derives meanings through spatial relations. Cassirer notes: "Myth arrives at spatial determinations . . . by lending a peculiar mythical accent to each 'region' in space, to the 'here' and 'there,' the rising and setting of the sun, the 'above' and 'below'" (p. 150) such that each region has definitive meanings, cloaked and vivified by their magical, mystical significance. Language then provides a structure through which these meanings persist and thus can be rediscovered. Language "provides that possibility of 'finding-again' and of recognition by virtue of which totally different, spatially and temporally separate, phenomena can be understood as manifestations of one and the same subject" (Cassirer, p. 108). What Cassirer is describing is the ability to detect patterns—or as Bion (1965) calls them *constant conjunctions*—and to build a narrative that makes sense within the meanings defined and proscribed within the frame of a given culture.

If we think of Cassirer's notion of the realm of myth as one in which meanings are defined and organized in terms of spatial relationships within a conceptual order, we can see how elusive it might be to attempt to define these meanings for one who is so deeply embedded in the culture that the road signs are implicit and thereby not easily noted. We can also imagine the complications for one who is *not* deeply embedded in the cultural order of his or her origins and yet is affected by meanings derived from that culture. Psychic reality is such that our conceptions of self, other, and universe are informed by the conceptions of those around us, even if these are not consciously known or communicated, as shown by the literature on the mirror neurons (Gallese, 2009) through which we are in touch vicariously with the experience of others.

In deference to the precarious nature of meaning, Bion (1977) developed his model of psychoanalytic inquiry using Poincaré's idea of the *selected fact* to reference the powerful effects of perspective on how we organize information. Coherence is always in relation to whatever selected facts are organizing the frame, and content can obstruct our ability to take note of whatever underlying factors are at play. Bion's grid (1989; Charles, 2002b) provides a structural model through which to view process, structure, and functional relationships abstracted from the obfuscating effects of content. If we see Freud's model of psychoanalysis as built on an enquiry into that which is explicitly not known but becomes revealed *because* it can be sufficiently displaced, disguised, or negated, then we can see that the grid anchors this task by pointing us toward the relationships themselves that can remain obscured when we focus on content.

Bion (1977, 1989) was acutely aware that any action could be used toward development or evasion and so, using his grid as a model of the analytic process, he locates a given statement or interaction in terms of the complexity of the thought, the sophistication of the thinking, and the function being served. In Bion's schema, myth holds a privileged position as a model that helps to anchor and give form to subtleties of experience. He was aware that facts are artifacts of the particular cultural and personal lenses though which they are viewed. By using the grid as a rubric through which to note constant conjunctions, he hoped "that the selected fact, that gives coherence and relatedness to the hitherto incontinent and unrelated, will emerge. Thus 'nominated,' 'bound,' the psycho-analytic object has emerged. It remains to discern its meaning" (1963, p. 103).

From another perspective, the meaning comes to our attention as we stumble over a gap that indicates that something is missing. For Lacan (1977c), the gap announces an absence that could be meaningful if we are able or willing to notice. He suggests that this gap does not merely signify a failure to attend but rather an alienation or denial of meaning, much as Bion (1967) describes in his ideas about *attacks on linking*. When meanings are too traumatic or painful to recognize, the associative links necessary for meaning-making may be denied, thereby de-signifying an element of experience that might otherwise carry significance. The gap, then, marks the place of something fundamentally important that cannot yet be integrated into the life narrative as it evolves.

If we think of culture as defining selected facts and of myth as a containing structure within which facts might reveal latent meanings through the use of symbols in relation to one another, we can begin to consider the plight of an individual whose history is located in two disparate cultures. To illustrate my topic, I will use the case of a young man whose reality is configured in relation to two mythic histories: one, his own native land and the other that of his parents' birth. His life journey has taken him back and forth between two continents with different underlying mythic structures. Our work together requires an inquiry into the overlay between cultures, as we try to understand the interplay between our shared culture and the underlying Hindu myths, symbols, and traditions that inform my patient's narrative. The transparency offered through these dual vantage points helps us to notice the configural elements rather than being blinded by the opaqueness of whatever remains unnoticed because it is too similar or too different from the cultural signposts we share.

If we also look through two lenses of theory, keeping in mind both Bion's grid and Cassirer's ideas regarding the "revolution" that takes place in the transformation from "action to schema, to the symbol, to representation" (p. 153), we see how each of these authors anchored thinking in perceptions embedded in primary affective experience. What I like about pairing these two minds is that, in the spirit of what Bion (1977) refers to as *binocular vision* and the *confluence of the senses*, we can see how each of these thinkers was working on a common dilemma, how a consideration of dream, myth, meaning, and culture can inform our understanding of this basic human process of utilizing configural, affectively driven meanings in the service of greater understanding or potency in our ability to navigate in our lives.

"Ravit" was born in the United States, but his parents' conceptions of culture and reality continue to be prescribed by and circumscribed within the myths, mores, and symbolic traditions of their native India. His "dual citizenship" affords the greater transparency of binocular vision through which to consider collisions between frames of reference and how these collisions may become more transparent so that we can better recognize ways in which we stumble into them and perhaps more effectively come to grips with our own preconceptions. The differences between Hindu and Western mythologies offer an opportunity to note the slightly different flavor of the confrontation with the Third between these two cultures, thus perhaps illuminating our larger enquiry.

For Ravit, the process of narrativization is obscured in conflicting veils of a palimpsest of intertwining cultures, further complicated by traumatic memories that distort his perceptions. An inquiry into his inner life, mind, and being is essentially an inquiry into the otherness that is an intrinsic fact of his reality from which he cannot escape. As he struggles with this issue of otherness, the twin poles of his reality twist and turn like a Mobius strip with two sides that can neither be clearly seen nor distinguished from one another. This blurring of edges in some ways offers respite from his fear of seeing more clearly exactly what he fears finding in himself. The failure to notice the gaps between meanings as represented by one culture versus the other has resulted in Ravit being unable to understand himself or to make sense of his relationships with others. Finding himself caught by others rather than being able to locate himself in relation to another has resulted in a stance in which he finds himself fighting off seemingly imminent destruction in the face of any approach. He finds himself jumping away from whatever seems treacherous or, alternatively, becoming so sleepy that he cannot consciously attend to the source of his discomfort. His defenses work so well that it is only by taking note of them in retrospect that he can begin to approach the subject of his unconscious desires.

In our work together, Ravit's dreams have anchored his dilemmas in ways I could not make sense of from the elaborate plethora of detail that he puts before me in our sessions. Analysts often find that patients offer up a dream that anchors the essential elements of the life story and, with it, of the dilemma at hand. I will begin by briefly describing the treatment. I then will offer a few snippets of dreams that afford a glimpse into his internal landscape before proceeding to describe and discuss the dream that seems to contain the essentials of this man's life story.

At the time being recounted, Ravit was a thirty-six-year-old man who had the appearance and demeanor of someone much younger. At the time, he was in his third year of medical school. Both parents are from southern India, each deeply embedded in the cultural traditions of their homeland. Ravit has unhappy memories of summers in India with his family, feeling constrained and bored, longing to return home. In many ways he is caught between two cultures, not comfortable in either, searching for home. In Indian culture, distinctions between parent and aunt or uncle, sibling and cousin, are not the same as in Western culture. His childhood narrative is peopled by an extensive network of relationships in which designations were not clear and boundaries were often transgressed. One maternal uncle, in particular, is marked as a predator in this family. Ravit experienced this uncle as so abusive that he became immersed in the discipline of Aikido as a way of denying and managing his feelings of vulnerability.

Ravit left home early, trying to find a place for himself in the country of his birth. A dark-skinned young man in urban middle America, he felt most at home with the rough and tumble youth from the inner city, who also felt themselves to be at the margins of society. As a late adolescent, Ravit's world was shaken by the attempted suicides of the two female cousins who appear in the dream reported here. In the wake of these events, he discovered that the same uncle who had tormented him was also implicated in his cousins' distress. These cousins each took their stand at the point at which a marriage had been arranged for them. As Ravit describes it, the family turned a blind eye to the various ways in which these young women had attempted to signify their pain, one shaving her head, the other running away. A third cousin did successfully complete suicide during the same year when Ravit's father was diagnosed with dementia and his college mentor (who had become like a father to Ravit) was diagnosed with cancer. These three events resulted in a tailspin that foreclosed Ravit's medical school dreams at that time. The reasons for the cousins' despair could not be discussed and the father would become enraged when Ravit tried to talk with him about his illness. Ravit felt even more alienated from his family as he attempted to grapple with these events alone. There seemed to be important meanings that could not be signified in this family, pain that could not be shared.

Ravit first sought treatment with me three years before the time being recounted, in the context of a failed love relationship with "Johanna," who continued to tantalize him, and the impending deaths of his father and his longtime college mentor who had become like a father to him. The mentor had recommended that he seek treatment, likely recognizing the tremendous vulnerability of this traumatized young man. Psychoanalytic treatment was an alien experience and yet Ravit entered in as fully as he could, coming in four to five times per week but at times holding on to the arms of his chair as though for dear life.

Ravit is extremely likeable. His ready smile and earnest attention invite a sense of engagement that is then belied by his descriptions of being ever at ready for the next attack. In the countertransference, one can easily mistake one's emotional responsiveness to the stories being told as marking Ravit's own ability to empathically engage with these traumatic memories. Ravit entered treatment believing that, somehow, he would tell a story that would serve whatever purpose had been defined and then quickly be on his way. What he encountered instead was some recognition, at the level of primary sensory experience, of the extent of the troubles he faced, including his desire to cut and run, to close up this hole he had created in his own story of seamless self-sufficiency.

In the first month of treatment, Ravit reported a series of dreams that proved to be important metaphors, reminding me that this young man, who represented himself as thoroughly embedded in our shared American culture, also had deep roots in his southwest Indian heritage. These dreams provided anchors in configural space that became more fully elaborated over time, guiding our work together. In the first dream, he was prodding a dust bunny with his toe, which turns into something living—a rodent, then a cry-baby lion cub, which reminds him of the Lion King dying to protect his son from the uncle—but then it is eaten by a hamster. He shows it to his mentor's wife and then it becomes a wet Kleenex, which reminds him of a toilet that links in turn to a sexual predator recalled from childhood, and then to being rescued when chased by wild dogs in the Himalayas.

The following day he goes back to this dream, associating to the comic books of his childhood, one, in particular, of Shiva's dreadlocks being cut and falling to the floor, becoming an army of demons. He then associates to his uncle ridiculing his tears, calling it "pissing through your eyes." From there, his thoughts go to having tried to talk to his cousin M as an adult, only to have her sister K bar the way, as though *he* were the predator.

Two weeks later, Ravit reports the dream that will anchor the treatment:

He describes being in a woods on a well-worn path, four feet across. There is dirty water, like a swamp on one side with trees growing out of it and there is a hill on the other side. There are three or four dilapidated barn-like structures in a series on the hill side of the path. On each end there is a structure. On one end there is a medical school, though he never quite sees it. He's walking to or from the other end, where there is a dilapidated wood building that he sees only once. There's a bird in a birdcage hanging over the path. The cage is rusty. The bird is a brilliant white blue and it is observing things. He never makes contact with anyone in the dream; the closest he can come is "nestling in the place where comfort has been," an allusion to his experience of nestling in his father's arms as a young child.

Ravit's dream reminds me of Murakami's (2005) story of the character Kafka in *Kafka on the Shore*. Kafka's story is an Oedipal tale, in which he runs away from the Oedipal curse only to find himself enacting it in alternate registers, through the dissociated stories of Satoru Nakata and the librarian/mother. This novel mirrors real life in that the riddles are not ultimately entirely resolvable and yet, in the process of struggling with them, knowledge is gained. For Murakami, the reverberation with mythic themes is a function of pondering essential dilemmas in human experience. His associative trails, much as happens in psychoanalysis, circle around the conceptual field. In this way, they deepen the darkness of our internal conflicts such that we can perhaps encounter them less blinded by the glare of our preconceptions. Similarly, aspects of Ravit's dream are so bright and vivid that we run the risk of missing the darkness hidden underneath.

> Ravit: "The colors are all grey except the bird. The only other person is my cousin M and her sister K—there's evidence that she is there. I'm staying in one of these barns—there's a dirt floor and I feel safe in the daytime. In the morning, I follow M to her med school class. As she's walking, she is wearing a vest and reaches down into the water. She takes a few sips, shrugs as though the water is dirty. I say 'isn't it dirty?' but she doesn't answer. Then she keeps going and I lose sight of her because she goes into the med school. I remember feeling very alone. I turn and walk down the path. Day is ending and it is getting darker. There's a sense of panic. I can't get to where I sleep. There's a lack of light—her place is absolutely uncomfortable, but it's closer. I find the place where she stays. It's creepy, an old barn with a dirt floor. I look down and our dog is next to me. I lock the door just in time. It's sunset. I see freshly raked dirt. There's a rusty bike covering one quarter of the freshly raked part—laying across on a diagonal. I can see the dog, so I feel better and I can feel that this is where K and M speak."

Ravit talks about lying nestled in the place where they had been. At a later point in time, we go back to this moment:

> MC: "I'm thinking of your dream again—the parrot, which seems to represent your Indian heritage, on the one side and the med school on the other—and the place where you nestle in between."
> Ravit: "Phillip [his mentor] knows a lot about Indian culture. Even in India, he's my comfort zone. He helps me become calm again."
> MC: "There was something in the dream about laying where comfort had been . . ."
> Ravit: "Yeah, it was warm, there was still the imprint of where her body had been and it was very comfortable. . . . This bird—It seems like there's a whole segment that occurs before I'm following M. I'm walking down the path and I see the bird—it's eerie—I'm not supposed to show it—something—I need to keep something hidden."

I ask him about his associations to the bird and he talks about a bird in his childhood home:

> Ravit: "He's old. Whenever someone didn't want their pet, we got him. This bird watches everything and if you're eating and he wants it, he makes a fuss until he gets some. Once I threw a pen at him and he didn't forgive me for ten years, but he has a close relationship to my dad and my uncle could trim his beak. I suspect it has something to do with that I was keeping things hidden from my dad and mom. It wasn't malicious, I just wanted them to ask me directly. The bird was hanging slightly over, so it could see the path. I feel like this has something to do with my dad. He's a doctor. Seeing down the path to the med school. Both K and M went to med school. I lost touch with them."

In the dream, Ravit points to enigmas that have plagued him for as long as he can remember, The dream affords just that space of enigma and transparency through which difficult truths might be revealed. Making use of this potential, Murakami locates the oedipal dilemma in the dream space. In this way, he enables the reader to encounter and confront taboos that seem impossible to engage with in the lived moment. In some ways, Murakami's exploration can be seen as the reverse of that undertaken by Ravit. Whereas Kafka lives out the Western oedipal dilemma in the Eastern world, Ravit confronts an Eastern oedipal dilemma in the Western world. In contrast to Ravit's conviction that both his feet are planted fully in American soil, in our work together, I have the strong sense that his life narrative is embedded in both his adopted and ancestral cultures, and that the meanings of the symbols he brings into our work are occluded by our joint difficulty in unpacking the meanings of these symbols and thereby anchoring them in the structure of his life. This sense is affirmed by the enactment in his current life of this very confusion. Ravit has found a non-Indian "family" who, through their entrenchment and deep interest in India and its religious and mythic structures, translate to him his underlying culture through the reassuring remoteness of the lens of the culture in which he was raised. In educating me about some of the meanings of these symbols and structures and his relationships to them, Ravit helps to build a conceptual map through which I can help him to locate himself. In counterpoint, I am able to view the complex interrelationships between the two cultures in a way that invites some transparency through which, as Bion (1990) terms it, I can begin to see the spaces that hold the net.

Ravit offered me a hint to the divergent paths of oedipal development in India—and to aspects of his own developmental dilemmas—when he left for me a small statue of Ganesha, often depicted as the remover of obstacles and the god of all beginnings. Apparently, as another patient who noticed the small statue later told me, Ganesha should never be procured directly for oneself but rather should be received only as a gift. In giving me this gift, Ravit both endorses me as a remover of obstacles and locates in my consulting room the otherness in which he is embedded.

Sudhir Kakar (1989), following Bose, suggests that the oedipal dilemma is not as strong in Indian culture as in Western culture, because the desire to be female is less ego dystonic. In Indian culture, according to Bose, "The Oedipus mother is very often a combined parental image" (in Kakar, 1989, p. 355), lending itself to greater "fluidity of . . . cross-sexual and generational identifications" (p. 355). The dominant narrative of Hindu culture, in terms of male development, is not that of Oedipus, but rather of "Devi, the great goddess, especially in her manifold expressions as mother in the inner world of the Hindu son" (p. 356).

One manifestation of Devi is as the mother of Ganesha and Skanda. Whereas Skanda is handsome and heroic, Ganesha, born solely of his mother, was beheaded by his father, who, realizing his mistake but unable to locate the boy's head, finds instead an elephant's head to place on the boy's body. I quote from Kakar: "Iconically represented as a potbellied toddler with an elephant head and one missing tusk, he is represented proportionately as a small child when portrayed in a family group with his mother Parvati and father Shiva" (1989, p. 358). For Kakar, "Skanda and Ganesha are personifications of the older child on the eve of the Oedipus complex. He is torn between a powerful push for independent and autonomous functioning and an equally strong pull toward surrender and re-immersion in the enveloping maternal fusion from which he has just emerged" (p. 359). Whereas in Western culture Skanda would be enviable, in Indian culture it is Ganesha who has the preferred position. At the price of remaining an infant, he does not have to feel the pain of separation from the mother.

In Ravit's culture of origin, parental ties are more complex and diffuse than in Western culture. He did not have merely two parents but rather grew up in a web of relationships with cousins and aunts and uncles whose roles were not clearly differentiated from those that Westerners would term the nuclear family. For example, the mother's brother lived with the family through much of Ravit's childhood. Whereas the father was experienced as warm and approachable to the young child, then receding painfully out of reach, this uncle was omnipresent as a harsh, critical and attacking figure. The mother's role, in my patient's mind, was to not-know what was not convenient to know, and to attempt to manipulate her son into whatever path or action she desired, in line with cultural traditions.

Going back, then, to the parrot dream, having in our minds both Skanda and Ganesha, we can locate Ravit on a journey from a resting place where warmth had been, on a road that had been foreclosed (he cannot go back to the place from where he had come yet never quite reaches the goal). He rests for a while in a place where there had been the yearned-for closeness from which he had felt barred (the world of his female cousins, which he describes as very intimate), and tries to follow his cousin but cannot. There is no resolution in the dream between the desire for a pre-oedipal union with the parent and the inability to go back to his origins or reunite with his cousins. In Ravit's associations, nestling occurs only in relation to a paternal figure: the maternal figure is alternatively engulfing or withholding.

The paternal function, in contrast, seems to offer greater hope, although it is still not clear how one would make the journey to adulthood. The bird seems to both point and bar the way, much as the road to med school had been pointed to by both his uncle and his father, his father as an expectation, his uncle in derision. There is no solid ground under

Ravit's feet; the earth as he treads it reminds him of an experience on a rain forest path, where he had felt a particular springiness to his step, as though the earth were not quite solid. In this image, one feels the layers of history in varying stages of decay yet each fragment retaining aspects of the former whole.

In this particular dream element, we find Ravit feeling through the layers of his history and pre-history, searching for tolerable meanings but fearing the intolerable. This hunger/fear bind is present throughout the dream, as he seeks out but never actually makes contact with another human being. This ambivalence between need and fear was particularly salient in the early months of our work together, as he moved back and forth between his longings for the father whose genes he carries and his reliance on the other father who had adopted not only him but his culture of origin, a professor of Indian studies, each of whose impending deaths were haunting him.

Ravit came to me so squeezed between these impossible longings that he could barely pause long enough to think. Much of our preliminary work entailed discovering the underlying fears such that they could be tolerated and explored, whereas later work required moving further into the configural aspects of the myths that underlie and prescribe meanings in this man's universe. The co-existence of two disparate cultures both complicates and eases our path, as the very complication forces us to look more explicitly at the myths themselves. As we stumble over the seamlessness of what is apparent, we are confronted with what has been omitted. As we recognize these gaps, we are more open to enquiring into whatever lies beyond the story being told. At that point, what has tended to recede as background and become invisible becomes more highly illuminated—or, in Bion's terms, darkened—such that we can begin to see the threads of meaning entangling Ravit.

These threads became an important metaphor as Ravit began more explicitly to take note of and to struggle with his tendency to jump—to become distracted and move forward. For example, in reading, if he hit something difficult to take in, he would jump ahead without realizing it, resulting in empty spaces or gaps in his knowledge. Eventually, it was the gaps that caught his attention, alerting him to his own defenses. In looking back at the spaces that had become gaps, he could see that these were emotionally laden and he could better catch his defenses in action. Together, we could form a metaphor of how he jumps over what seems too difficult, leaving, however, a thread behind. That metaphor of an entangling thread is culled from an early dream, in which he is trying to pull a sticky thread out from inside of him but there is no end to it. In trying to jump past something that seems alien but comes from inside of him, Ravit is caught in this paradox in which, as he continues to jump, the web of threads grows, like a spider web in which he gets caught again and again, becoming hopelessly entangled without any idea why. The ideas have been left behind in the spaces, as noted in his dream, where the affective meanings have nestled. He longs for these affective ties but so fears becoming entangled in them that he jumps as soon as the heat rises.

Behind him, as we are less blinded by the light he shines to ward off the recognition he fears will be vilifying, we begin to see the web closing in, choking and strangling him more and more tightly in the very moment of running away, as his defensive maneuvers elude any real intimacy with other human beings. He begins to see how he attempts to create longing in the other as a way of not being the one left longing. What he cannot yet do is tolerate meeting desire with desire. That still seems too treacherous. We come up against images of the engulfing mother and that is where we find Devi, who can create life and take it away and who, at some level, commands even the great god Shiva.

Early in Ravit's treatment, we could lay out the conceptual space of his childhood and understand that he had been terribly traumatized by the lack of empathic engagement by his parents and the relatively unchecked abusiveness of his uncle. What was less evident, however, but became clearer through his dreams on the one hand and the stories he would tell on the other, were the deeper meanings of this web of interrelationships and how these configured an idea of self in relation to others and to universe that were absolutely intolerable. In his dreams, we could better see how the myths of his parents' homeland that were consciously alien were also fundamentally entangled in his own worldview.

Perhaps most stunning in Ravit's seminal dream is the absolute isolation. The only person mentioned in the dream does not answer him when he speaks to her but rather disappears, leaving only an empty space where he nestles to find some warmth, some comfort. Even the bird does not speak to him but rather seems to guard a path that closes in as the dream progresses. In Ravit's depiction, there had been no one to help him make sense of all the bits of experience he could not usefully link. Together, we sit with the silence amid the multiplicity of words and try to build a narrative in which he can learn to sound the darkness and also encounter real others without such idealization, demonization, or terror that he must flee blindly, leaving larger and larger gaps where connections might have been.

A year later, Ravit describes another dream, in which there are cobblestone walls and a river splitting the town in half. There is a house on the other side of the river that belongs to a former girlfriend. He is going to live there. He sees Johanna in Indian clothes and then sees Phillip's daughter Sarah wearing a red dress. As he gives her a big hug, he senses Johanna in the distance. He got the news that someone is dying and that he needed to be there. He needed to go to the house across the river to get something but he never got there. He went to where someone was dying. Sarah was there and everything was ok.

In his associations to the dream, he reported that two images were salient; first that the city, as he was standing looking across the river, had a cobblestone wall undulating in a gentle curve, reminding him of Aix, where he had been with Sarah and her brother and father, before Phillip's illness. He said he couldn't figure out the bridge in the dream, that Johanna seemed to be walking across as though walking on water. The second image, he said, was of Sarah sitting on one of those undulating walls. As he gets closer, the background shifts from the city to sky blue. The person with Sarah disappears as Ravit gets closer. He is happy to see her and gives her a big hug. Regarding the red dress, Ravit thinks of the red sweater Sarah often wore around the time that Phillip was dying.

Ravit reports that he finds the river formidable and kind of scary—other people seem to be able to get across but he doesn't know how. This relationship seems very like his relationship to the medical school in the first dream, where other people disappear into the school but he cannot quite get there. There is also in this dream the imminence of death and loss and the elusiveness (and danger) of women. Of Phillip's wife, he says: "I imagine Linda with another little Linda inside just shaking until whatever she wanted done gets done and driving everyone else crazy. . . . Another part of Linda that bothers me is how she is constantly stating how selfless she is. . . . I can't state a desire because of a fear that I'm going to be imposing on her. I'm just sort of starting to realize what a sore spot this is on me."

Ravit talks about his fears as he continues in medical school and approaches his hopes and fears of being like his father, his terror of being yelled at by a father/surgeon for making a mistake, his urge to move toward a woman: "I can imagine the home she might make and I can slide right in . . . Man, this is freaking me out. I just want to go outside and jump up and down." "What would you be getting rid of?" I ask. "Feels like dust, dirt," he replies, "something that's caked on. . . . At night it feels like a war is going on in my head." We are back to the dust bunny in the early dream, which seems tied to an intolerable, insatiable female demand that is impossible to escape.

Ravit talks about potential partners as though they are interchangeable, listing their qualities as though he is buying a horse. We talk about how he becomes caught between a world in which people fall in love and get married (a path he cannot traverse easily because of his fear of falling into something dire and deadly) and a world in which marriages are arranged and qualities ordered rationally, as though one were selecting a home or a horse and discussing how the various qualities balance and compare (an idea he rejects consciously but enacts in his life). His universe is populated by relational elements that are insufficiently understood such that he approaches and withdraws without much clear notion of what he is reacting to or why.

Psychoanalysis has offered Ravit a frame within which to encounter himself in relation to others, and to also see the layers between dream and waking life and between the American culture he embraces and the Indian culture that underlies his dreams and conceptual framework. These worlds become less impossibly separate as we begin to see the connecting links. Through his dreams, he brings me up against the edge of what he consciously knows, and allows me glimpses of aspects of his experience that he cannot yet integrate. In coming up against this edge, I stumble over what appears familiar to me (looking for love) but is not (thinking about prospective partners as an amalgam of qualities one might consider in an arranged marriage). As I speak to him of this stumbling, he can, in turn, begin to glimpse the gap between what he consciously believes about himself and those factors lying underneath that have been hidden from view. Learning to keep in mind the *both/and* as opposed to the *either/or* of his experience helps him to appreciate these dual cultures that are each alive and well within him. This appreciation enriches his experience and affords him better grounding as he travels a path rife with layers of history and pre-history. As he learns to integrate disparate aspects of self, Ravit finds himself on a road increasingly peopled by individuals whose qualities he can better recognize and differentiate. Misunderstandings can be considered rather than requiring immediate defensive maneuvers, and problems can conceivably be worked through.

Dreams call to us, in part, because they lull us with their sense of intrigue and mystery. With our defenses thus softened, we can better tolerate knowing a bit more of what we fear and how we fend off the very understanding that might help us better make our way in the world. Ravit's dreams both obscure and reveal his dilemma. As one colleague suggested to me, in some ways Ravit's dreams become a version of Scheherazade's 1001 nights, as he fends off his own "beheading" at my hands by weaving for me beautiful, vibrant stories. And yet, the very vibrancy of his tales reminds me that his spirit is steeped in a tradition different than mine, one of vibrant colors and multiple gods. His flying carpet is both an evasion and a definitory statement, noting the ways in which he *evades* and *also tries to see*. For, just as surely as he is desperately trying to evade the intolerable, he is also working at trying to make it tolerable. Like all of those who seek psychoanalysis, I believe, what is needed is to encounter someone with sufficient faith in this possibility to enable the seeker to tolerate the journey required to achieve it.

NOTE

1. Portions of this chapter are taken from the article "When Cultures Collide: Myth, Meaning, and Configural Space," published in *Modern Psychoanalysis* 34 (2010): 26–47.

NINE

Cultural Chasms

Mulberry and Peach

"Life is not a problem to be solved but a reality to be experienced."
—Kierkegaard

Literature has become one way in which we can mark complex meanings in our current culture, as myths and religious symbols are increasingly overtaken by contemporary cultural tropes. As noted previously, traumatic experience is particularly difficult to put into words, such that it is often the gap that marks meaning in a story that is told and untold at the same time. Literature speaks through metaphor, holding complex meanings forward in such a way that we stumble into them and must pause to consider the possibilities, as in this passage from Nieh's novel of traumatic transformation, *Mulberry and Peach* (1981):

> Sang-wa sees our reflections in the pond. She says there's an attic made of water in the pond. In the water attic there are three people made of water. Their faces are covered with dirt, their eyes open wide in fright. The water people change shape when the wind blows. Their bodies gleam and sparkle. She throws in a pebble. The three water people shatter. The shards toss about on the ripples, then are reassembled into people again. (pp. 131–32)

There is a growing literature on trauma studies that shows how crucial it can be to re-contextualize an incoherent narrative within the annals of the history that has given rise to such disturbance. To explore some of the difficulties encountered in putting traumatic experience into language, I will offer case material through which we can explore ways in which personal trauma can be compounded when there have been disruptions in the family history. I will then use Nieh's novel, in which these same issues are explored, to highlight the more general problems encountered when cultural disruptions and collisions compound personal difficulties, and close with a story taken from the news media that further exposes the traumatic impact of these dilemmas.

Part of the adolescent passage entails being able to define oneself as a differentiated individual in relation to a deidealized other, and to come to terms with the inevitability of limits (Blos, 1979). That negotiation depends on the extent to which we have learned to effectively regulate our affective equilibrium within the context of a relationship in which one's own needs and desires at least can be recognized, even if not satisfied. Accomplishing these developmental milestones is further complicated when trauma has impeded their achievement in previous generations (Charles, 2000a). In the United States, we carry the burdens of a complicated legacy of a hopeful belief, endemic in American culture, that one might somehow move forward unfettered by complications of individual or sociocultural or economic difference. Implicit in this idea is a notion of unlimited possibilities that can invite us to fail to come to grips with internal and external constraints in ways that might give us greater traction. Effective action depends on having a road map with sufficiently clear guideposts to be able to find our way.

Also implicit in this American notion of universality is the idea of difference as either trivial or impossibly problematic, marking this nation's beginnings in relation to an irrevocable separation from the motherland. From that framework, difference itself becomes problematized, leaving us at times disrespectful of the cultural traditions that helped previous generations to negotiate difficult transitions (Akhtar, 1995; Apprey, 1993). Less visible, then, is how profoundly destabilizing immigration can be, and how taxing to the psychic organization of the individual. In turning a blind eye to real differences across cultures, we fail to appreciate both strengths and vulnerabilities in relation to cultural values and mores.

Cultures develop master narratives that encode and pass along abstracted information regarding values and standards (Fivush et al., 2011). Disjunctions encountered in relation to these values can be difficult to assimilate, particularly when the new, majority culture devalues aspects of the culture of origin (Charles, 2014b). Meaning itself is thus brought into question, particularly as the new generations struggle to locate themselves within the adopted culture, at times coming into direct conflict with parents whose values are more deeply embedded in the culture of origin. It is often difficult to express and explore these differences, much less work them through. For those immigrants who have been affected by trauma, the transmission of the master narratives that might engender pride in ethnic identity is further disrupted, creating ambivalence within the older generations, as well, particularly when mourning has been impeded.

The disregard or dissociation of difference has been particularly insidious for immigrants who became dislocated in relation to their cultural traditions, impeding mourning in ways that enhance particular vulnerabilities across the generations (Charles, 2000a, 2014b). What cannot be metabolized sufficiently by the parent leaves the child at greater risk for the type of overwhelming affective storm that itself can be experienced as traumatic. At the extreme, we find the type of dedifferentiation that obscures the signal functions of affect and impedes cognitive functions, as well (Krystal, 1988). This dedifferentiation can cause a rupture in the very possibility of meaning-making, as we see in the case of "Frances" to follow.

When the very cultural traditions that might ameliorate distress are marked as alien, the individual is not only deprived of potential external support but also is alienated from the disparaged aspects of identity as well. Failures in mourning arise in part from the wish that we could just 'move forward' without having to bear the distress we might encounter if we were to grieve more fully, a desire that is in keeping with the manic edge of current American culture. This evasive desire, however, may be seen as a function of a more general ambivalence we experience when we encounter major difficulties in living.

Although we may yearn for simple solutions, it is only when we consider behavior in context that we can discern and disentangle the threads of meaning in an individual life. Such a perspective is particularly important in our work with individuals who have been severely traumatized and thus in many ways stand outside of consensual discourse, commenting from the side. Speaking against a notion of the disturbed individual as inherently other or alien, psychoanalytic clinicians have stressed the importance of discovering the meanings embedded in seemingly meaningless symptoms. Bion (1967a), for example, left an important legacy in detailing his own process of trying to understand the frame of reference from which his psychotic patients were acting, a stance that opposes a medical model in which psychosis is seen in terms of aberrant signals to be normalized rather than meaningful behavior to be understood.

The medical view in some ways serves the needs of those individuals who have gone underground and send up distress calls that can seem maddeningly inchoate and unreadable. In a dangerous world, where potential caregivers may not be listening sufficiently respectfully to be worthy of trust in spite of their best intentions, these signals may be necessary distortions (Charles, 2008). And yet, if we see the symptom as an attempt to mark a meaning that is not otherwise capable of articulation, then we can recognize the importance of having some space within which those meanings can be marked and reflectively considered. The more dangerous it seems to mark those meanings, the more disorganizing this process can be for the therapist, who is called upon to bear witness to the articulation as an act in and of itself, and also as a symbol of something that cannot otherwise be articulated. We find ourselves in the uneasy territory of the yes and the no, the statement that is withdrawn in the very moment of its articulation.

This is difficult territory to traverse, to tolerate, and to articulate. In his early papers, Bion (1967a) attempts to describe the process of coming to make meaning from fragments that the individual cannot yet tolerate bringing together. Going back over the texts he had created as he tried to find his way through that difficult work, Bion then tries to discuss the experience itself, lest the reader be carried away by the details and fail to note and to begin to recognize, *from his or her own experience*, the process being described. Part of the dilemma, I think, is that we hope to find a way around madness. We label it, medicate it, manage it, and otherwise struggle with the ineluctable fact of it. Even our attempts at understanding are in part attempts to do away with the madness that—as many authors, Bion (1957) and Milner (1987) notable among them, affirm—is in some measure present in us all. This fear of acknowledging our own madness perhaps reflects a fear of moving into that treacherous territory and finding that the lifeline has left, that we are now through the looking glass, on the wrong side of the split between the sane self and our own mad one. That fear can keep us from being sufficiently present to recognize and witness the terrible pain the other person endures. That denial becomes a terrible betrayal that violates our ethical commitment to try to do no harm.

In opposition to this desired disavowal—that Freud marked as endemic to our species through his interest in the story of Oedipus, later reworked by Bion (1977) as a defense against knowing, a desire to turn a blind eye (Steiner, 1985)—the psychoanalyst is called upon to repair the humanity of both individuals by finding the common link. Linking with the world of one who has lost his or her own connecting links is precarious at best. And yet, we also know that the human mind, as resilient as it may be, can be pushed beyond its limits as experience becomes unmanageable and unbearable.

The ground of human understanding lies in the primary experience into which we are born and through which we find our way into the consensual language of verbal interactions. This consensual universe is complicated when the language of daily speech is not the language into which we were born. Each language has its own rhythms in which meanings are grounded. Adopting a new tongue brings us further away from those early prosodies of experience in which primary meanings and basic securities and insecurities are nestled, the realm of Bollas' (1987) *unthought known*. It may be that the transition from the rhythms of early nonverbal communication to verbal language may be more difficult for those whose parents' native tongue is alien and unknown to their children.

Consider, then, the case of Frances, a young, first generation Asian-American woman who sought treatment having become so ungrounded in her life and mind that she could not move forward. Although her parents were present and involved, neither had been able to effectively assist her in managing the challenges in living that faced her. Her parents were firmly ensconced in the values and traditions of their country of origin. Frances, the youngest child, was the only sibling who had no knowledge of her parents' mother tongue. She was thus alienated from those very rhythms of language that for her parents carried a sense of home. Displaced from the family history that might have cradled her, France was, rather, oppressed by the demands that made no sense in her current context and crippled her efforts to join into the world of her peers. These strictures, although ego-alien, inhibited her in ways that left her little access to her feelings or desires.

The family's unwillingness to recognize Frances' distress left her further depleted and pushed her toward the dissociative defenses that would eventually lead to the developmental impasse in which I encountered her. Psychosis can often best be conceptualized in terms of an identity problem, which marks the need for development of sufficient internal foundation to be able to build a life. When the life narrative is jarred by gaps and disjunctions, much as Nieh depicts in her image of the reflection that is shattered by the pebble in the water, building a narrative thread provides an essential framework for that secure foundation.

Frances' identity development was further complicated by disjunctions between standards she encountered inside and outside of her home. Her parents' values were firmly embedded in their culture of origin, in which men held the standards and were expected to make all of the decisions. Women were not expected to know their own minds or desires but rather to defer to the men in their lives, leaving Frances unable to turn to her mother for either assistance or positive role identification. She experienced her mother as kind but without backbone, unable to stand up to the father even when called upon to support the needs of her children. Her father was experienced as strict and controlling, rigid and unyielding, leaving little room for her developing autonomy. Both parents were more comfortable with reason than feeling. Emotional expression was frowned upon. Anger, in particular, seemed to be off limits, though her father's temper could flare unpredictably, marking his lack of resilience.

Much as there was no way to effectively make use of her parents to consolidate a competent, autonomous adult identity, Frances was similarly unable to make use of her extended family in that process. Rather, she tells a story of cultural dislocation, of a family that has lost its moorings, cutting off all ties with the grandparents back home, thereby delinking Frances from whatever historical data might have helped her to make sense of her current impasse. Notably, as we find in families in which there is unresolved mourning, depictions of family members lacked coherence, and stories in stark contradiction co-existed without any seeming recognition of their incompatibility. Frances' grandparents still resided in their native land and spoke no English. Unlike her siblings, she did not speak the family's mother tongue, leaving her parents and siblings able to converse with one another in a language she did not understand. The language Frances was most earnestly trying to understand, the language of feelings, held no interest for her family. She had no way of speaking about her struggles, leaving her feeling isolated and alien within her own family.

When I first met Frances, she appeared far younger than she was. In her early thirties at the time, although she had been successful academically, she had been unable to negotiate the tasks of young adulthood in terms of attaining greater autonomy from her parents and beginning to build a life for herself. Caught between needing to set herself free from the ego-dystonic demands of her parents and her dependence on them, she lamented how her father had made crucial decisions for her without taking into account Frances' needs, feelings, or interests. Perhaps more problematic for Frances, her mother would turn cold and withdraw when Frances marked a need that conflicted with those of the mother. Neither parent seemed able to recognize Frances as a unique individual with her own needs and desires.

Frances encountered a similar type of misrecognition in relation to the medical system in which she found herself embroiled. Like many others who have experienced trauma that has been insufficiently worked through, Frances' extreme symptoms had resulted in the diagnosis of schizophrenia. Although Frances could recognize the accuracy of the symptom picture that had given rise to the diagnosis, she felt utterly misunderstood by this label because it failed to take into account the facts of her existence. In contrast to the professionals, whose vision seems to be narrowed down to the diagnostic criteria themselves, Frances could recognize that there was a context within which those symptoms occurred that profoundly affected the trajectory of her development. In spite of her relative timidity, she was able to take a stand in relation to the importance of recognizing the impact of the abuse she had experienced in her childhood on her development. Frances's recognition is consistent with findings from studies that show a strong link between childhood abuse and the diagnosis of schizophrenia (Read, van Oss, Morrison, and Ross, 2005), and also with findings that link psychotic symptoms, particularly dissociative symptoms, with trauma and unresolved parental mourning (Main and Hesse, 1990; Liotti, 1992).

Consistent with the family values of stoicism, Frances described being told to just 'move on,' to not think about troubling events that had happened to her or about what was missing from her life in terms of warmth, affection, and the cultural ties that might have helped her to come to terms with what was present and absent in her family and in her life. She lamented not having been allowed to develop relationships with her grandparents, relationships that might have helped her to better understand and make sense of aspects of her cultural identity that were lost to her. She found herself caught between her parents' demand that she just grow up and her sense that to grow up would mean to lose her family forever. Her mother, in particular, seemed to equate the prospective individuation of and separation from her daughter as so disjunctive that it seemed like a type of death. Although Frances was angry at her mother, she had no way of expressing that anger without further alienating her mother and incurring further wrath and distancing from her family. More concerning however, was how profoundly she could lose touch with herself in response to the lack of recognition by the other, ways in which she would lose touch with her feelings and with meaning itself. This is the type of dissociative response that we see in those who have disorganized attachments to caregivers, a response that can appear psychotic but can be tied more directly to an extreme—and adaptive—response to unresolved trauma (Liotti, 2004).

Through psychoanalytic treatment, major shifts occurred in Frances' reflective function that enabled her to attain greater internal stability under stress. Frances' greater capacity for reflective function helped her to think through difficulties she encountered in her relationships with friends and colleagues, to consider ways in which they affect one another and to take responsibility for her part in relationships without becoming lost in them. She became more competent at holding her own with her parents, and sustaining her own perspective when it was countered by their own very different vantage point. Increasingly, their denial of her reality no longer utterly confused and immobilized her. Rather, she was able to attain sufficient perspective to recognize the disjunctions between perspectives and to be sad about the gaps she encountered in her relationships with family members. In turn, her greater capacity to hold her ground helped her parents to be able to locate her as a separate and autonomous person who could also, still, be part of the family such that it no longer seemed to them as though she would either have to capitulate or be lost to them. Although Frances was able to attain a much stronger sense of self and identity, she still could become derailed emotionally by her parents' lack of recognition. Her relief at being able to hold her own was tempered by her bitterness that they would ask for proof rather than merely accepting her word. She could mark the gap between the type of respectful acceptance she would like to have and the reluctance she still encountered in her parents.

In trying to understand Frances's dilemma, we find ourselves up against the edges of what Lacan terms the *Real*. For Lacan, the Real represents that which is both necessary to accept but also impossible to fully understand, the limits we encounter and must come to grips with in spite of our inevitable failures to fully comprehend their nature and scope. Although it is unarticulated, the Real is nonetheless marked, becoming that which "doesn't stop not being written" but rather remains outside space and time, intruding upon us in its own ways (Lacan, 1972–1973, p. 59). This element would seem to be what Bion (1977) refers to as *O*, his way of characterizing a truth that can be sought but never entirely achieved, in part because it is always in process.

Salient to this dilemma, if I am understanding Lacan and Bion correctly, is that trauma, by definition, brings us into contact with a Real that is uncontainable and unassimilable. From that perspective, the traumatized individual becomes what Grotstein (1995a, 1995b) terms an *orphan of the Real*, denoting the state in which we are cut off from the social fabric by the extent of a trauma that occurs too soon or is insufficiently moderated to be endured and assimilated. Trying to depict that experience brings the teller and the listener toward something that eludes words and invites resistance by its very nature. We resist getting closer to the psychotic element present in each of us that is called forth in the face of intolerable frustration or pain, which Bion (1957) characterizes in terms of a preponderance of destructive impulses as well as a fear of imminent annihilation. This perspective is lodged in a model of trauma in which the individual is at the limits of what can and cannot be managed or integrated without feeling at risk of imminent collapse and fragmentation.

Even in therapy, Frances found it difficult to imagine that she would encounter someone who would not judge her in the ways in which she had felt judged by her family. Over time, she was able to describe the difficulties she had encountered in our work together, noting ways in which speech had been impeded. She spoke of having found it difficult to speak into the void she had encountered in the early days in which she could anticipate only that I would respond similarly to her mother or father. She had been afraid that I would devalue her efforts, that I would tell her she was not "doing it right" or not trying hard enough. She had also come up against the family values of stoicism that inhibited her from recognizing or expressing her feelings. She was so accustomed to holding back that it had become reflexive and it took a great deal of time and effort to begin to bring the buried feelings forward.

In spite of her concerns about being judged and misunderstood, Frances had appreciated having the opportunity to talk about herself that therapy had afforded. She had enjoyed being able to have a space in which she could talk about whatever was on her mind, and to be able to be curious about and to explore her feelings. She could recognize the importance of both having room to find her own way into the process and also to having me invite her to share more without insisting that she do more or be more than she could manage. That had, at times, been a difficult balance for us to negotiate and likely it was in the context of those very skirmishes that Frances was able to recognize the disjunctions between her analyst and the parental transferences she imposed on me. These skirmishes also helped to mark for her my interest in and care about her as a separate and unique person, entitled to her own needs and desires.

During our time together, Frances became increasingly able to explore her needs and feelings but was also aware of ways in which she was inhibited and held back. Although she was not sure what made her hold back, she was increasingly aware that she was doing so and that her inhibition marked a problem she had not yet been able to work through in the therapeutic relationship. She recognized that part of the difficulty lay in talking at all, particularly talking about feeling-laden material, the type of communication that had been deplored and inhibited in her family of origin. She had become so accustomed to holding back that it was reflexive. Her therapy, however, had enabled her to build sufficient reflective capacities that she was able to recognize her own internal limits and motivations and to be able to put these into context. Even though she could still encounter impediments, she did not become utterly lost to the degree that originally brought her into treatment.

Part of what was transformative for Frances in the therapy process was her experience of being engaged at the level of person rather than at the level of diagnostic categories. When I first met her, Frances had learned to load much of her problems and symptoms into a diagnostic label that marked her as ill rather than in distress, even though she knew, at some level, that her life experience opposed that very diagnosis. Speaking with someone who could recognize the symptoms of schizophrenia without losing touch with her personhood helped Frances to move out of that medicalized view toward a more reflective and respectful stance. When approached from the perspective in which her symptoms, like daydreaming, having trouble concentrating and not functioning as well as her parents expected, could be read as signs of strain rather than psychosis, Frances was better able to consider her own perspective on this matter. In this way, my insistence on addressing her as the legitimate subject of the conversation invited reflective function, in part through the recognition that a symptom may be read in different ways by different people. Given the invitation to offer her own perspective, her own point of view, Frances could consider her position. She could feel sad because of the ways in which she is marked as a failure in the family context, particularly in relation to her siblings. She also, however, could recognize that her problems occurred within the context of a troubled family system that affected all family members.

Countering the family view, Frances could recognize her accomplishment in addressing her problems in ways no one else in her family had managed to achieve. Within the consulting room, we could recognize the strength it had taken to acknowledge and work through her problems, and Frances could feel proud of her work. Even though she could verbalize this stance, her internalization of herself as defective still persisted. In her life outside the consulting room, she struggled to sustain a sense of possibility when she would once again become preoccupied with the fears of judgment and deprecation that threatened to move her back toward the daydreaming and other escapes from reality that had proved so debilitating. Her depictions of her struggles to resist moving back into these destructive defenses highlighted the virulent impact of these types of internalizations and how profoundly parental criticism and neglect can affect character development. Increasingly, however, Frances' ability to recognize the link between her deep longing for connection, and her vulnerability to becoming so caught up in her fantasies that they begin to take the place of reality, helped her to think about how to build stronger connections with others that would sustain her.

In the context of a respectful interpersonal engagement that recognizes that there can be two valid, albeit different, perspectives, Frances could explicitly link her symptoms to abuse. She spoke of having tried to talk with her mother and having her mother brush off Frances' concerns. Frances was thus caught within a void in which her troubles could not be recognized, spoken about, or worked through. In that context, she had learned to distance herself from her feelings and to dissociate rather than standing up for herself and saying no. Within this context, we can track the emergence of the symptoms that were later to result in the diagnosis of schizophrenia that Frances at first accepted but later, in the context of intensive, reflective experience in psychotherapy, learned to question.

Being able to connect her experiences with one another helped Frances to develop a narrative thread through which she could be respectful of her own efforts to manage unmanageable experiences. She could also recognize ways in which her parents' inability to move beyond their own limits had made them inaccessible to their daughter as a source of support or repair. From the vantage point of her newly gained perspective, Frances could recognize that other members of the family had known about the abuse but did nothing, neither overtly recognizing the abuse nor helping Frances to deal with the sequelae. That type of recognition can be a critical factor in putting together the pieces of traumatic narrative and thereby reducing the symptoms that have marked the gap between what one has experienced and what can be known within the family context. Notably, Frances highlights the profound impact of being able to put together one's own narrative with cogency when she describes the abrupt ending of her flashbacks in the context of finally confronting her brother.

Over time, Frances' story began to have greater coherence. Being being able to tell her story as she experienced it enabled her to have better and fuller access to her own mind. Memories that had been inaccessible began to become available, further enabling her to make sense of her own experience. She was increasingly able to draw a narrative thread in which she could recognize some of the shifts that had occurred over time. Her story was no longer one of a person becoming increasingly impaired by illness, but rather of a relatively happy and engaged young child who became distant, remote, and preoccupied in the context of very real problems in living that were unresolvable at the time. As the details emerged, Frances was able to draw a narrative thread that included a time before and after the abuse and, with that, to draw a sharp distinction between then and now. That capacity helped her to keep the trauma in the past, where it belongs, rather than as an ever-present danger that could intrude in any given moment.

Poignantly, Frances described the extreme disjunction between life before and after the abuse. In that context, there emerged a picture, not of someone who somehow failed to flourish, but rather of a young girl whose development became disrupted by abuse and whose parents failed to sufficiently mark her distress to be able to come to her aid. Subsequent to the onset of the abuse, Frances found transitions difficult but there was no one to register why she was having difficulties. When she began to encounter academic difficulties, no one asked why. Similarly, no one seemed to remark on her sudden turn inward, away from the activities she had previously enjoyed into a fantasy world in which she became increasingly isolated.

The type of massive denial encountered by Frances in her family impedes the development of reflective function. In the histories of individuals with psychotic disorders, we often find histories of trauma along with just the type of stance toward thinking described by Frances, in which certain issues are just not thought about. This type of enforced denial can be literally crazy-making, as we can see in Frances' struggle to piece together her history. The re-emergence of narrative, once the pieces can be put together, highlights the difficulties Lysaker and Lysaker (2011) discuss regarding the disruption in self-experience that is often attendant to psychosis. From that perspective, recovery from psychosis is facilitated by encouraging the self-reflectivity that is an important facet of metacognition. Lysaker and his colleagues (2011) note the importance of actively introducing and modeling reflective thought in interactions with individuals for whom the reflective space has shut down.

This is the type of modeling of a curiosity and openness to possible meanings that occurs during psychoanalytic psychotherapy. We can see the impact of this potential space in Frances' increasingly cogent reflections, as respectful engagement establishes the basis for coherence and self-reflection. Whereas, when we first met, she had little motivation or interest in any activities, over time Frances' interests and even passions emerged and she was able to stake a claim for these. Rather than the empty fantasying described by Winnicott (1971), Frances was able to have productive dreams in which she could envision herself engaged in enjoyable and enriching activities. She was also able to engage in learning that helped her to develop a conceptual framework within which she could recognize and make sense of some of the ways in which her family had foundered. She could see, for example, the lack of boundaries that had made it difficult for her to separate and individuate, to know her own mind and feelings. She could also recognize the ways in which the dissociation of disturbing feelings or events had made it impossible for her to work through her difficulties. Rather, as the one "with the problem," she had become the family scapegoat, the target of family members' frustration and anger.

Further, Frances could recognize that there were ways in which culture had complicated the family dilemmas. As the youngest child, with the least connection to the culture of origin, Frances had felt profoundly cut off from the rest of her family. As a young child, that gap had felt impossible and intolerable, something she desperately needed to cross. As an adult, however, with the perspective afforded by her work in therapy, France could consider to what extent she truly would desire to measure up to those familial standards. On the one hand, she felt that the distance marked her as unworthy, as though she was being left behind. On the other hand, however, she could recognize that that feeling was countered by other, equally compelling desires to pursue her own dreams and to live by her own values.

Across time, we could see progress in terms of Frances' ability to talk about her relationships in a more cogent, reflective, and reciprocal manner. Unlike when she first sought treatment, she clearly had developed a theory of mind and could reflect on what the other person might be thinking or feeling. She was also able to be empathic and to recognize the difference between another person's needs, desires, and interests versus her own. With her mother, she encountered precisely the point of impossibility we find in the literature on disorganized attachment, that terrible emptiness encountered in the absence of the mother's loving gaze. Initially, Frances struggled to locate herself and her emotions within the context of relationships in which she felt as though important aspects of herself were forbidden and, more profoundly, as though her very existence might be denied. Increasingly, however, she could think about the mother's difficulties letting go as her mother's problem rather than taking it on as the forced choice her mother imposed.

Part of the challenge for Frances was to be able to represent and articulate traumatic truths that were not acknowledged in her family system. Psychoanalysis provided a means for this process to occur. Literature, too, has provided a means for making sense of these types of complexities of human experience, and immersion in literature or other forms of art helps the psychoanalyst to be receptive to primary process meanings that may be less accessible through the conscious mind. Bion (1977) notes the importance of myth and other forms of cultural narratives that serve as structures that hold complex meanings in manageable form (Charles, 2010). These structures help us to recognize our common humanity even when that humanity is being tested seemingly beyond human endurance. Crucial to coming to grips with this dilemma may be our willingness to encounter one another across whatever divides we might face, prepared to bear together whatever seems most unbearable if confronted alone. In these moments when we have before us the choice of joining with another human being who is unbearably present in his or her misery or, alternatively, turning a blind eye to our common humanity, what may be at stake "is precisely the coming into being of the subject, the subject of a history not so much censored as erased, reduced to nothing, and yet inevitably existing" (Davoine and Gaudillière, 2004, p. 47).

These are inherently impossible, intractable moments. Part of what is elusive in psychoanalysis is the very real difficulty of attuning our receptors to precisely what is unspoken and seemingly cannot be apprehended. Much like the psychoanalyst, novelists have attempted to offer up statements that invite the reader to perhaps develop a greater respect for the dilemma of one caught between self and culture such that the articulation of the dilemma is difficult for others to hear or make sense of. Although psychoanalysis has in some ways marked the psychotic experience as outside the realm of analyzability, some theorists, notably Kleinian and Lacanian clinicians, eschew this desire to split off our primal terrors into the other in that way. Davoine and Gaudillière (2004), for example, contextualize madness in the annals of a *history* that has become unspeakable, noting that "people said to be crazy, in the ordinary sense of the term, show us what it was necessary to do in order to survive. . . . In our experience, the successive shocks that constitute the rhythm of an analysis of madness always lead back to the same region, the field of historical and social traumas" (pp. xxii–xxiii).

This is the realm of the nonverbal—the uncanny—in which communication is made at the level of the body, through affect that is displaced or through other somatic experiences. Novelists at times attempt to enter this realm of the uncanny, to speak to something vitally true that seems somehow beyond words. Such efforts can be terrifying, as Virginia Woolf (1953) describes, "moments of such intensity and intoxication that I seemed only to stumble after my own voice, or almost, after some sort of speaker (as when I was mad) I was almost afraid, remembering the voices that used to fly ahead" (p. 169). In pushing past the comfortable symbols and signposts of consensual reality, Woolf was able to speak to the reader poetically through the nonverbal aspects of the text. This is also the endeavor Milner (1969) undertook in the clinical work chronicled in *The Hands of the Living God,* in which she uses her patient's words and drawings as mediums through which to enter into the world of the other. Milner finds that it is through her attempts to vicariously enter into the other's experience that she comes closest to understanding her patient's dilemmas. She discovers that while theory at times augments or supports her understanding, it cannot replace this more primary exploration of the material.

Much as Milner found, art, like the dream, can provide a means for representing truths that we are repressing. Unlike the dream, however, art often transcends the personal, thereby elucidating cultural truths that may be vitally important but that we are having difficulty integrating into our waking understanding (Charles, 2011; Lawrence, 2004). As we have seen, in novels such as Doris Lessing's *Memoirs of a Survivor* (1974) and Haruki Murakami's *The Wind-Up Bird Chronicle* (1997), there is an attempt to chronicle ways in which the individual may be driven mad by cultural constraints that are alienating and dehumanizing. From that polarized position, truth can be articulated only to the extent that it is couched as "crazy." That designation, itself, then becomes the unsaying that allows difficult truths to be revealed, much as Bion (1967b) reminds us that we must be willing to not-know in order to learn.

Psychoanalysts are in a position to know something of how trauma fragments history, destroying speech and leaving the subject estranged and alienated from self and experience (Charles, 2007). However, as Bion (1977) reminds us, knowing *about* something is not the same as being willing to know it from one's own experience. Whatever we are not willing to know does not cease to exist but rather goes underground, symbolized in ways in which the knowing and not-knowing can continue until such time as the meaning can be recognized without such imminent danger of annihilation. Bion (1967a) terms this type of desymbolization process an *attack on linking,* as the individual de-signifies an element of experience that might otherwise carry significance. This type of designification is a way of keeping at bay overwhelming affect (Krystal, 1988), leaving the fragmented meanings to mark the gaps in our understanding. Just as Krystal notes the adaptive aspects of this type of defensive denial, Lacan (1977d) notes that these gaps are of essence meaningful in that they do not merely signify a failure of attention but rather an alienation or denial of meaning that paradoxically points to the meaning beyond the gap. If this gap is not recognized by the individual, the fragmentation and alienation may then be passed along the generations,

> transmitted to whichever of the person's descendants try, in some outburst of madness, to communicate and demonstrate the deafening screams that were left in a state of suspension, until they find someone . . . to accompany them to those places that no one wants to look at anymore, so that they can begin a transmission. (Davoine and Gaudillière, 2004, p. xxviii)

Through that type of transmission, a process is begun where translation might take place, as meanings register and are acknowledged, from one person to another. At best, that is the possibility afforded by psychoanalysis, much as Frances discovered, through which such gaps can be marked directly but are also marked indirectly, as in the empty speech that covers over a pocket of meaning that is not being articulated. The empty speech itself then becomes a marker of the impossibility of speaking that missing truth, while also drawing our attention to it (Charles, 2012).

Literature, too, affords an "as-if" space in which to attempt to make contact with such experiences. In novels such as *Mulberry and Peach* (Nieh, 1981), the author can juxtapose fantasy and reality in such a way that the reader cannot be entirely certain of where the lines between historical reality, narrative reality, and dream or fantasy might be drawn. In this way, the reader encounters the difficulty of coming to grips with whatever feels unassimilable and is put into the position of the individual who has lost her moorings and feels driven mad by experience. The traumatic narrative invites the reader into this experience through the structure of the novel itself, characterized in part by the types of disruptions that typify traumatic memory (see chapter 5). In this way, the structure breaks through the armament of defensive barriers we erect in our efforts to distance ourselves from traumatic experience. These barriers include pathologizing diagnostic labels, such as *psychosis.*

In *Mulberry and Peach,* for example, it is difficult even to know which character is speaking. Nieh (1981) frames the narrative against the backdrop of serial revolutions in China by offering a dialogue between a U.S. immigrations officer and a woman who may or may not be the person he is seeking. This woman insists that she can tell the story he seeks only in the third person, as though it were a narrative of some other person's life. She will talk to the agent, she says, but "only on one condition. You can't call me Mulberry" (p. 3). In this way, the author explicitly and implicitly considers the difficulty of knowing oneself when the context provides no stable anchors through which such continuity of being and experiencing might be known. The agent tries to trick Peach into revealing herself to be Mulberry but she will not be thus engaged.

> Mr. Dark, don't try to be so smart! You think that I'm going to tell you that I was born in Nanking on 26 November 1929 so you can prove I'm Mulberry? Well, you're wrong, Mr. Dark. I was born in a valley when heaven split from the earth. The goddess Nüwa plucked a branch of wild flowers and threw it to the earth. Where the flowers fell, people sprang up. That's how I was born. (p. 5)

Lessing (1974), Murakami (1997), and Nieh (1981) each describe a universe in which the standards in place leave little room for the individual to grapple with the truths of his or her existence. To some extent, that dilemma is a function of our current medicalized world, in which we tend to do battle with madness itself as something to be exorcized from the individual. In taking that stance, however, we become part of a crazy system in which the individual's reality is denied. From where, then, might such an individual speak? Davoine and Gaudilliére (2004) note that disruption, itself, marks the need for language. The gap marks the point at which the realm of the symbolic might enter into human relations. We need to be able to share words in order to bridge the gaps and to make sense of our experience, and yet, in our interactions with traumatized patients, we are confronted with the absence of words, often in conjunction with an inability to feel the distress from which they have lost touch. In such an encounter, we must be able to tolerate co-existing at the level of primary process, so that the psychoanalyst,

> like a photographic plate, receives the impressions of what is shown there. . . . What we say on these occasions is that we are feeling, imagining, and dreaming in the patient's place, and that we have to tell him about it; otherwise we would be experimentally continuing the excision of otherness that was perpetrated on him. (p. 76)

Notably, each of the novelists mentioned offers a multiplicity of perspectives through which the reader can consider whatever is being spoken about. This stance offers a reflective space in which truth might resound and form a space within the receptive reader's mind, a truth that can be told implicitly rather than explicitly. This reflective space is similar to that which the psychoanalyst hopes to invite in the consulting room, a hope that becomes further problematized in relation to the traumatized individual, who by definition has been disturbed, shocked, shaken. Such an individual both tells a story and asks a question regarding how—or whether—he or she might make sense of that story. In such a narrative, what is told and what is omitted may be equally important, as may be our confusion as we try to understand. As Bion (1992) notes, the very act of trying to understand can impede our ability to register what is being told, as we impose order and transform the bits into elements that are more easily digested or less terrible to bear, such that what we term *understanding* at times may be more accurately termed *mis*understanding.

Frances' dilemma resonates profoundly with the dilemma described by Nieh in her novel *Mulberry and Peach*. Nieh recounts the story of a young woman repeatedly dislocated in time and culture, until the character Mulberry can no longer contain all of the disparities. It is at that point that Peach, our narrator, enters the scene. She refuses to be confined within the character who had become so impossibly constrained and insists on their absolute discontinuity:

> You're wrong. Mulberry is Mulberry and Peach is Peach. They're not the same at all. Their thoughts, manners, interests, and even the way they look are completely different. . . . Sometimes Mulberry wanted to die, sometimes she wanted to live. In the end she gave up. I'd never do that. Mulberry was full of illusions; I don't have any. People and things

> I can't see don't exist as far as I'm concerned. Even if the sky fell and the world turned upside down, I still wouldn't give up. (pp. 5–6)

Through the these disjunctive yet entwined characters of Mulberry and Peach, the novelist asks questions about how much trauma can be endured and what is the cost of survival when one's roots—one's ties with history and with meaning—have been cut and cannot easily be known any longer. Nieh creates an alternate universe in which the main character can only begin to locate herself as she moves beyond however she is being designated by the society in which she lives. Using this literary device, the author can comment on the society's demands and their impact on the individual's developing identity, thus inviting us to consider more empathically the plight of the individual who from one angle disappears behind whatever designation obscures her complexity and her particularity.

Nieh begins her novel with the main character's refusal to identify herself in accordance with the demand of the other. "I'm not Mulberry," she says, "Mulberry is dead!" (p. 3). In this way, Nieh designates at the outset that the subject cannot be encountered directly. To seek her is not only not sufficient, it in some way creates the very conditions under which she cannot be found. This invitation to view a character from more than one perspective is in line with the stance of the psychodynamic clinician who assumes that patients' problems can be best understood in the context of the life narrative in which they are embedded. This perspective demands that we listen respectfully and carefully to the story being told through the symptom as much as through the word, coming up against our own internal resistance and also against current ideas regarding standards of care that might demand a very different way of viewing patients and of attending to their distress (Charles, 2008b).

This dilemma is particularly problematic when working with patients labeled psychotic, a label that tends to invite disrespect for the person's capacity to know him or herself and thus to take an important role in any ongoing negotiation regarding his or her care or well-being. Such labels can also invite the clinician to dissociate him or herself from the enormity of the pain of the individual thus designated. Dissociation, as we know, is a primary defense against the onslaught of overwhelming trauma. We are always up against our own and also our patients' ambivalence over what it means to encounter this distress, for us as well as for them. In such cases, it is easy for the Jacob's ladder of self and other protection to form a bubble that keeps us from encountering precisely what must be known in order for development to proceed.

In spite of findings that level of insight is not correlated with severity of psychosis, there is a tendency to equate psychosis with a lack of insight (Amador, Strauss, Yale, Flaum, and Gorman, 1993). David (1990) suggests that insight is not unidimensional but rather includes recognition that one has a mental illness, the ability to label unusual events as pathological, and compliance with treatment. Clearly, these standards are lodged firmly within a model in which the assignation of *insight* depends on the extent to which the individual's self-assessment would agree with that of a health-care provider (Transulis, Corin, and Kirmayer, 2008). These types of standards work directly against an alternative model in which the traumatized individual is seen as fighting to find ways of speaking whatever has become unspeakable.

The psychotic individual can be seen as lost outside of history in the realm outside of symbolization referred to by Lacan as the Real. Nieh vividly portrays the type of chaotic turbulence that ensues when there is no home to go home to, when even the facts of our basic existence are called into question. This territory can become the land of the living dead, in which the person lives outside of time, "in a certain sense . . . no longer part of the world of the living. Hypersensitive or unable to feel, they are beset by images that are too vivid or, on the contrary, ghostly though not always frightening . . . they are in exile in our world" (Davoine and Gaudillière, p. 115). The analytic task, then, is to work with the individual, "in search of an echo" (p. 11), attempting to be sufficiently present with the other that we might form a link, such that together we might begin to narrate the history that has been carried alone. As portrayed so vividly by Nieh, this dilemma is further problematized by the cultural upheaval that forced emigration from their homelands for many Americans.

Davoine and Gaudillière (2004) note how social forces "tend to eliminate the subject" (p. 25), such that narrating the story becomes a way of not only affirming one's being but also one's essential humanity. This elimination of the self as subject can be complicated when multiple subjectivities—and multiple vertices through which to recognize or misrecognize these subjectivities—are at play. Consider, for example, the case of Xiu Ping Jiang, a woman in Florida who was brought into court because of suspicions that she did not have a visa. In chilling parallel to the dilemma portrayed in *Mulberry and Peach,* this young woman was chided by the judge for giving her name before the court interpreter had translated the judge's question. As reported in the *Times,* the judge said: "Ma'am, we're going to do this one more time, and then I'm going to treat you as though you were not here." When the judge said "The respondent, after proper notice, failed to appear," Xiu Ping Jiang replied, "I'm going to die now" (*New York Times,* May 4, 2009). She was put in jail and quickly decompensated.

Xiu Ping Jiang's actual story, as told by her sisters, was of being a very young mother who hid from the authorities when pregnant with her second child so that she would not be forced to have an abortion under China's one-child policy. When caught, she was fined and sterilized. She came to the United States, hoping to find political asylum and then be joined by her two sons. Instead, she became increasingly despondent, and her attempt to bring over her younger child through Canada failed. The child was caught by Canadian officials, placed in foster care, and eventually adopted. The elision of the facts in which Xiu Ping Jiang's story can be located and recognized—her utter and basic desire to care for her children—is chilling.

In May of 2010, in part because of the notoriety that had ensued when a *New York Times* reporter had come upon this case while looking for another woman of the same name, Xiu Ping Jiang was finally granted asylum by the U.S. government. In the meantime, the notoriety helped to bring to public attention the larger problem of ways in which immigrants can become casualties of an oppressive bureaucracy. In some ways, an external threat can be easier to deal with than an internal one. As in the case of Frances, when a negative self-image has been internalized, it can be extremely resistant, particularly when social forces reinforce that negative self-image. There is also the damage done. Xiu Ping Jiang's identity is confirmed but her children still have been taken away.

Consideration of the case of Xiu Ping Jiang shows the additional vulnerability that can be experienced by the immigrant who does not have sufficient social support. Immigration, even at its best, is an anxiety-producing experience because of the disruptions experienced and the challenges posed (Grinberg and Grinberg, 1989). When the immigration has occurred in previous generations, it may be difficult to recognize the cultural factors complicating the individual's development (Charles, 2010). And yet, the lack of coherence ensuing from failures to fully integrate the culture of origin with the current culture can be a clue alerting the clinician to the need to pay attention to historical and cultural as well as individual factors in order to develop a narrative within which seemingly disparate facts might attain coherence.

The case of Xiu Ping Jiang shows how an individual may literally be driven mad, not only by the exigencies of circumstance, but also by others' failures to recognize the very real difficulties that do exist. Adaptation requires sufficient solid ground under our feet to be able to take a step without feeling as though we are walking further into chaos. Recognition of a difficulty may not solve the problem, but at least provides a meeting ground that affords some scaffolding within which problems can be recognized and possible solutions explored.

When I initially encountered Frances, she was at a crossroads. She had been given the diagnosis of schizophrenia, which marked an internal difficulty in making sense of self and world. In opposition to this diagnosis, however, she was able to mark the particularities of her experience that made this designation false. Likely, that ability to mark such a fundamentally important meaning became a cornerstone on which a new sense of self could be built and a more cogent and reparative narrative constructed. Indeed, over the course of her treatment, Frances was able to contextualize her experience such that she could create a world for herself in which she could be competent both in terms of work and also in terms of forming reciprocal relationships in which there is room for two separate individuals who can respect their differences even when they do not agree. At its best, psychoanalytic treatment can offer a space in which two minds can grapple with difference such that each can enhance the capacities for self-reflection from which resilience is built. It is within such a context that even disparate aspects of identity can be integrated such that development can proceed.

V

The Hero's Quest: Identity and Relatedness

TEN

Journeys into the Labyrinth, Part I

The Magus

"I fled Him, down the arches of the years;
I fled Him, down the labyrinthine ways
Of my own mind . . ."

—Francis Thompson

Fiction provides a means for understanding experience that lies outside of our own personal realm, in that way introducing cultural objects and symbols that can be shared, discussed, elaborated, and integrated (Oatley, 1999). The labyrinth is one of the oldest and most mysterious representations of life, death, and the human spirit. It has been found across cultures, suggesting that it relates to something profound and essential in the inner life (Bloos and O'Connor, 2002). It seems to be one of those essential patterns referred to by Campbell (1949), a symbol for the transformative quest through which we attempt to ferret out the truths of human existence.

The labyrinth has become a trope that marks the enigmatic challenge of the hero's quest. In this way, it stands as a metaphor for literature that serves the function described by Burke (1957) in terms of an enterprise that better equips the reader for the challenges encountered in living. The labyrinthian novel invites the reader on a journey of self-discovery of a particular kind, a journey that parallels the encounter with self that occurs in the course of psychoanalytic psychotherapy, as the individual discovers herself through the transference (Savitz, 1991). Traditionally, the labyrinth has referred to the place in which the darker side of man's nature might be held and captured but also to a path to God or divine wisdom. In some ways, it is another manifestation of the apple eaten from the tree, the dangerous wisdom we seek that might hold the key to salvation or the seeds of destruction. In that way, the labyrinth marks the oedipal challenge as described by Bion (1977) in terms of the tendency to turn a blind eye or even the perceived admonition to do so, to remain a child deferring to an external authority rather than facing the challenge and standing on our own.

The labyrinth is one way of conceptualizing the human journey. Marcel Marceau (1965) frames it thus: "I have designed my style pantomimes as white ink drawings on black backgrounds, so that man's destiny appears as a thread lost in an endless labyrinth. I have tried to shed some gleams of light on the shadow of man startled by his anguish." The labyrinth is also a profound metaphor for the inherent dialectic between order and confusion that is a function of being human. "It holds a tension between order and chaos, pattern and disarray, clarity and confusion, depending on the perspective of the viewer; how we experience the maze depends on where we stand" (Savitz, 1991, p. 462). From inside the labyrinth, only the individual bends and turns along the way are visible but not the whole. It is only from the outside that the overall pattern can be seen.

In classical Greek mythology, the labyrinth stood at the threshold of the underworld, at the edge of potential transformation or annihilation. In the Greek myth, it is love in the form of Ariadne's thread that leads the youth safely through the confrontation with the Minotaur. Importantly, however, Ariadne is betrayed in the process. Perhaps one cannot solve for another the dilemma of the confrontation with whatever waits at the core of darkness within the labyrinth. At some level, more profoundly, there is no solution to the maze. The yearning for ultimate transformation seeks something that cannot be attained in life. Even though we may be able to undergo transformative experiences, we are still human and therefore subject to the perils, paradoxes, and difficulties of daily existence, including the inevitability of that final transformation into death.

Grotstein (1997) suggests that the motif of the labyrinth and the Minotaur can be seen as an allegory in relation to the development of "courage—in the sense of an energy of the developing ego aimed at bearing action, exploration and thinking" (p. 590). One hazard inherent in the metaphor of the labyrinth is the possibility of a defensive withdrawal in which one might become embroiled and unable to face the challenges that living brings. According to Grotstein, the magus in the Greek myth is Ariadne, who stands as the guide through the maze of the labyrinth, a guide who may perform a positive, shepherding function or, alternatively, may lure the hero into danger.

Through its characterizations in Greek mythology, the labyrinth came to represent a hero's quest and has come to carry echoes of transformation and transcendence, the allure of the uncanny and godly. However, as Murillo (1959) notes, the "Cretan labyrinth is an artifice, an ingenious creation of intelligence and of art, and as a corollary, the way to its center (and the way out) is easily accessible to its author, or to anyone who has the 'key,' the right directions" (p. 260). From that perspective, the labyrinth is that which excites by virtue of the illusion at its core, an illusion inextricably entangled with its authorship as a creation by the hand of man, not God.

In the writings of Jorge Luis Borges (1962), the labyrinth is a salient metaphor. In his fictions, the labyrinth is both form and process, and the creator of the labyrinth is also its victim, caught in the web of experience as it evolves over and within time. "Time is the substance I am made of. Time is a river which sweeps me along, but I am the river; it is a tiger which destroys me, but I am the tiger; it is a fire which consumes me, but I am the fire" (Borges, 1962, p. 234). From this perspective, we can imagine that the labyrinth is a way of investing mystery around aspects of reality that are difficult to confront, and also of recognizing that the mystery holds the key. Murillo (1959) suggests that Borges' labyrinths symbolize the consciousness and challenges of man in our time; his fears, anxiety, helplessness and, above all, his despair. Although the labyrinth can take many forms, and can lead to death and even rebirth and transformation, an even more perplexing labyrinth awaits as we anticipate what lies beyond this life.

In Danielewski's (2000) novel *House of Leaves*, the labyrinth is both form and substance, a metaphor that is elaborated not only in the content but also in the structure of the novel itself. Like Borges, Danielewski creates and decreates a narrative. His characters construct a reading of a story while also effacing and erasing it. In this way, the gaps, too, have meanings, inviting us to attend to the ellipses, to what is missing from the discourse, much as Lacan (1977c) suggests in relation to narratives as they unfold in the consulting room. Danielewski's novel is layered and enigmatic. A couple moves into a home that houses a labyrinth. Their discoveries there are narrated by an old man, the fragments of which are recovered by a young man who is searching for an understanding of his relationship with his mother. "The uncanny atmosphere of walking the labyrinth is reproduced in the narrative, where protagonists are altered by the text, leading to the suggestion that the reader is similarly altered" (Cox, 2006, p. 8). There is something about the enticement of such a text, in which the reader is positioned in relation to a mystery waiting to be solved, that is inherently compelling.

At times, however, the mystery can be too compelling and occlude the experience. John Fowles (1977), for example, rewrote *The Magus* in an attempt to resolve some of the mysterious elements he had devised. In that novel, we find exemplified the theme of the labyrinthian nature of life and art. For Fowles, mystery is energy, a vitality that infuses the text and enlivens the reader. In the first version of *The Magus*, however, he appears to have erred on the side of mystification. Although there is greater clarity in the elaboration of the narrative in the second version, it, too, ends with mystery. We do not know what Nicholas' fate will be, only that he has come to accept enigma as a part of life and is better able to live more fully in that present moment that accepts the limits of what can be known. In the novel, our protagonist hopes to be initiated into the alluring mysteries that surround and entice him but is more often chastised for his inability to engage sufficiently in his experience to be able to begin to comprehend. Ultimately, it is this lack of engagement with his own desire and his failure to take a stand that leaves him standing by the roadside in relation to a life that has, in some ways, passed him by.

The psychoanalyst has, at times, been cast in the role of the magus, who tantalizes us with the idea that our mysteries might be known. The history of psychoanalysis, itself, has been a paradoxical one in which Freud learned by exploring his own internal experience but then this exploration was passed along from master to pupil in ways that threatened to foreclose on the very process that gave rise to the desired knowledge. Bion seemed to oppose this trend by highlighting the value of passion and intuition, as did Lacan, in his admonition to not subvert one's own becoming by taking a master rather than facing and acting in accordance with one's own desires. Whereas for some individuals, entry into psychoanalysis signals a quest for self-discovery, for others the self has already been so devalued that development has already been foreclosed.

The latter was the case in my work with "Nikolai," whose ability to know his own thoughts and feelings had been fundamentally foreclosed by the family dynamics that skewed him toward mystification rather than exploration. That tension, between the possibility of being able to be curious about that which one does not know versus the need to turn away from the narcissistic injury of not-knowing, was a crucial juncture pointed to by Bion (1967b) when describing the essential preconditions for analytic inquiry. For Nikolai, having been positioned by the mother as the oedipal victor in relation to the derogated and disrespected father had left him trying in vain to recapture the favored position without having a male model with whom to identify. His failure to find his way into the social matrix left him further alienated and alone, and his autistic defenses assuaged his bruised ego but in ways that left him further and further estranged from the people he needed for self-validation. Eventually, predictably, his defenses failed and he entered treatment. That treatment, however, faced him with the dilemma of needing to accept his limits in order to be able to make use of another mind.

Nikolai stumbled repeatedly in his efforts to take whatever might be of value from our conversations without allowing any real dialogue. Rather, he would "accept" my offerings by taking them over and reworking them according to the story he had already built regarding the reasons for his failures. He was most comfortable in the role of the-one-who-knows and would become deflated quite easily when his performance failed to produce the desired effect. Because I hoped to help him be able to bump into precisely that performative aspect that seemed to seal him off from the actual engagement with others he purported to desire, this pattern played out repeatedly in the consulting room. Too easily, I became the maternal tyrant who held (or withheld) his value in her hands.

Much like Lily de Seitas in *The Magus*, I find myself faced with a man who is so caught in the web of appearance and idealizations that my words often have little or no meaning for him. He points to the disparity between his culture of origin and the culture in which we are living to locate reasons for this confusion of tongues but that discrepancy does not seem to be the source of his problems. Rather, it seems like an evasive movement through which he can discharge his hostility by disparaging the otherness with which he is faced. In his universe, in which the failure to be adored and admired leaves him feeling impotent, weak, and devalued, we struggle to come to grips with his own self-devaluation at the core of his dilemma. Although he can hear me speak about these things, he has no way of making sense of words that force him into the place of his father, a place where castration and impotence have been so effectively loaded that truly thinking about himself in relation to his father is effectively closed off.

In Fowles' novel, the problem of what will be revealed is a fundamental one, such that the magus can reveal answers only to the extent that one is willing to see them. This desire/fear dilemma is a profound one for Nikolai that makes precisely what he is seeking most inaccessible to him. In our work together, I have encountered many of the challenges described by contemporary Kleinians in terms of difficulties working with individuals who rely heavily on projective identification for self-regulation. The transference and countertransference are powerful, and I too easily find myself in the place of the intrusive, overbearing, castrating mother who Nikolai then fends off either by sarcastically or masochistically ostensibly bending over and taking it, or by engaging in the types of mind games he finds so energizing. I have learned to notice when he veers off into what I term "philosophizing" and increasingly am able to mark and speak to this turn in a way that helps us to recognize the territory we are in rather than merely repeating the sadomasochistic engagement.

As the time neared for Nikolai to discharge from treatment, he became preoccupied with what he might learn from his peers before leaving. He wanted to know how to frame his question to them. I asked him to tell me what his question was about, what he wanted to know. As he explained his question to me, it seemed to be a moebius strip in which the question he seemed to be asking did not lead to the answer he said he was seeking. He was ostensibly asking to hear more about his vulnerabilities, but with the idea in mind that he would be hearing people's misperceptions that he could then correct.

I tried to relate back what I was hearing, which seemed to invite further philosophizing that easily turned to self-blame when challenged. I then told him that he seemed to turn to those two defenses to avoid knowing about something that he said he wanted to know about but did not appear to actually want to know. He said that he did not want to face any ignorance on his part because ignorance was not acceptable in his view. I said that taking that position left him in the unfortunate position of not being able to learn anything about precisely what he said he had come to learn about. In not wanting to see or to face his ignorance, he was sustaining it.

Rereading *The Magus,* I am struck by the closing scenes, in which there is the possibility of engagement with a real, living, loving human being. Nicholas, however, finds himself so preoccupied with the fantasy of the magus, the omniscient god who holds the strings regarding to what extent he is to be valued, that he cannot locate himself or Alison in real time. Much like Nicholas, Nikolai is so preoccupied by the "godgame," by his narcissistic investment in playing out the fantasied role that would affirm his value, that he is not free to engage, in the moment, with anyone. Nicholas finds himself so absorbed in his reliance on the magus who might absolve him by seeing him differently that his focus keeps him from being able to really reflect on the words he has been offered that, perhaps, afford some key to the mystery.

At the core, suggests Fowles, *eleutheria,* freedom, was that crucial word.

> The final truth came to me, as we stood there, trembling, searching, between all our past and all our future; at a moment when the difference between fission and fusion lay in a nothing, a tiniest movement, betrayal, further misunderstanding.
> There were not watching eyes. The windows were as blank as they looked. The theatre was empty. It was not a theatre. . . . Perhaps it had all been to bring me to this, to give me my last lesson and final ordeal . . . the task, as in *L'Astrée,* of turning lions and unicorns and magi and other mythical monsters into stone statues. (pp. 654–55)

In the absence of the ostensible gods who controlled meanings and thereby controlled his behavior, Nicholas was left with the ineluctability of his own freedom, constrained perhaps, but his. In Borges' terms, "With relief, with humiliation, with terror, he understood that he too was a mere appearance, dreamt by another" (1962, p. 50). If we take this scene from the novel and transpose it to the situation in which we find Nikolai, we see how Nikolai cannot yet locate himself in the arena in which he is positioned in relation to an imagined panoply through which he is judged, in each moment, as the victor or the vanquished. Even learning something from me thrusts him uncomfortably into that vanquished role, eliciting his defenses such that he begins to use words as instruments in a duel rather than as a medium of exchange.

In psychoanalysis, our words often become weapons that are turned back on us. Nikolai tells me innocently of his love of the game, particularly of winning the wars with words. I then take notice when he seems to be engaged in a game in which words are the medium of exchange, and suggest that this enterprise keeps him from having to think about the very things he says he is here to learn. My words, then, in cutting off his pleasure in his game, castrate and humiliate him, and we find ourselves once again in the familiar enactment of the parental pair, the mother who is always waiting in the wings to castrate whoever dares to defy her, and the humiliated father whose efforts inevitably fail.

In Nikolai's dreams, there is often a couple and he is on the outside, looking in, aware of the desirability of the woman. The focus, however, is rarely on any yearning on his part. Rather, the yearning is actively denied: "I can't recall a sense of loss that this was something I've never had," he says. The focus turns toward the other man who does not deserve the attention he is receiving. It is as though Nikolai tries to preserve some space for the excitement of the attraction and some distance from the possibility of being actively rejected by focusing on the dyad, of which he is an observer, from a safe distance. There is an absence of difficulty in this triangle in which he describes the sense of "great familiarity between me and her—we seem very close as if I'd known her for a long time," although there does seem to be some nascent awareness of the part that denial plays in his lack of discomfort: "I don't know if in some way I had given up where my own efforts are concerned," he muses. There is something in the staging of these dreams, as though the couple becomes a performance that allows him to play with his desire without being tested in any way, that is reminiscent of the staging in *The Magus*, through which Nicholas is able to become so caught up in his fantasies about the play that his ability to engage in his life is utterly threatened without his being able to recognize what is at stake.

That is precisely the issue that plays out in my work with Nikolai, as I try to make visible for him this staging and empty rhetoric in which he becomes so entangled that it is hard for him to recognize that he is actively allowing his life to continue to slip away. At times, however, he is able to catch hold of a bit of this pattern, as when he came in and began to talk about his addictive relationship with food and with sweets, in particular. He talks as though to impress upon me the physiological nature of this desire, the fact that it is obviously not psychological. I try to meet him in that place and invite him to think about the dual aspects of hunger and desire, the difference between the desire that is born of hunger itself versus the desire that is about some deeper distress that one has learned to assuage through food. We talk back and forth through our metaphors. He offers the pregnant woman whose desire must be satisfied in a particular way, and I counter with the difference between the desire for the beef that provides particular nutrients versus the steak that fulfills a different order of desire.

I wonder with Nikolai about the urgency, for him, of focusing in the direction he does, and invite him to consider what he may find more difficult to think about regarding his own unfulfilled hungers. The underlying question that lurks in these discussions is what these hungers mark, for him, about his perceived deficits that keep him bouncing back and forth between the desire to fulfill his fantasies and his self-derogation for failing to do so. In this circle he gets caught in, we can see the addictive tangle Lacan (1988) refers to in his view of perversion as a desire that becomes satisfied in a way that precludes growth. Continuing to struggle toward the unattainable goal keeps Nikolai from having to face his own limits. The price of this failure has been his inability to build a satisfying life, relationship or even career, and yet, giving up on the fantasy would puncture his grandiosity and leave him utterly deflated, conflated with the castrated father. Somehow, failing to achieve greatness has become less onerous than being satisfied with something less.

This impossible dilemma, we can see, was set up in his childhood, in repeated failures to be included by his peers while receiving solace from his mother's accolades. His tendency to resort to the sour grapes resolution left him increasingly isolated and alone, armored by his grandiosity. Even now, using anything I offer feels tenuous, as though it might upset the precarious balance he has created. Terribly isolated and alone, he so longs to be admired that it is difficult for him to engage in any real way with others, leading to further rejections. We consider together whether this desire for engagement rather than relationship serves in part to keep him out of what feels as though it would be a regressive entanglement with the mother. That line of inquiry is fed by fears of becoming emasculated, feminized, if he were to become too close to a woman. It is as though the relationship itself would be emasculating, leading him to further fantasies of conquest. We can wonder whether his desire to be admired is to be engaged in an absorbing experience rather than a relationship. That position seems to entail essentially an autistic and therefore a perverse pleasure in that the other becomes both a signifier of his virility and a vehicle for the satisfaction of his own desires.

Seen from that perspective, his current dilemma is etched sharply in the form of his childhood dilemma, in which he was cast as the oedipal victor in the war between the mother and the father. The difficulty of growing up in a household in which no one's opinion or preference could stand unless it mirrored the mother's own left Nikolai utterly dependent on the idealization by the idealized other, and caught in the dichotomization between the powerful female and the deprecated and emasculated male. The price of the mutual idealization between mother and son was to be utterly unable to identify with the father and thereby to have no direct path toward manhood.

The impossible dilemma in which Nikolai found himself was fed by the family's isolation and interdependence in the wake of their forced emigration from their homeland when Nikolai was thirteen. Following Lacan, Derrida (1995b) writes of the archive that is a mausoleum of memory. There are ways in which the unrecognized grief within the family becomes a trap that has left Nikolai foundering, with no clear path toward manhood. His story, then, is one of an utterly constricted entanglement, that speaks to the entrenchment of his symptoms and defenses but leaves little room for actual development. "To be impeded is a symptom put into a museum," says Lacan (in Harari, 2001, p. 20). In my work with Nikolai, I can see how strongly etched is the transgenerational trauma of this family who left the political oppression of their homeland only to act it out within the dynamics of their very troubled and enmeshed family. My hope in our work together is that my interpretations, rather than being experienced as impossibly shaming and thereby denied, devalued, and ignored, will provide the type of encounter described by Fowles in *The Magus,* so that Nikolai might be able to recognize his own dilemma sufficiently to be able to learn to find his way out of the museum, to face his limits and, with them, his possibilities, and so begin living his life.

ELEVEN

Through the Unknown, Remembered Gate: Journeys into the Labyrinth, Part II

The Glass Bead Game[1]

> "If the doors of perception were cleansed, everything would appear to man as it is, infinite."
>
> —William Blake

The labyrinth, as a trope, has framed the human quest for meaning for generations. "And why wander in these labyrinths," asks André Maurois (1962). "Once more, for aesthetic reasons; because this present infinity, these 'vertiginous symmetries,' have their tragic beauty. The form is more important than the content" (p. xiii). The metaphor of the journey into the labyrinth is a poignant and powerful one for the analyst. Each new individual—each new encounter—takes us further into reciprocal journeys as the path of the other intersects our own. This interplay often has the feel of a multi-dimensional palimpsest, in which I am continually reworking the enigmas encountered by my patients through my own being. Experientially, this is often quite perplexing, as I find myself traveling some familiar path, long since taken, and wonder at the re-finding of myself within it. Hadn't I already traveled this road, some time back? As I have tried to find my bearings within the layered workings of patient-in-analyst and analyst-in-patient, the initial feel of this recursiveness, for me, was of an endless circle—a heavy image, with little room for play. Each image evokes its own metaphors, consigning meanings and proscribing possibilities. It was only as I began to notice the disjunctions between the current journey and the ones before that the path came to seem more like a spiral, in which the recurrent sense of familiarity was both true and illusory. It was never quite the same path and I was never quite the same person. The role of analyst adds further dimension to these representations, as we travel our own experiences of the roads depicted by our patients on their journeys.

As I have become more familiar with this particular peculiarity of the analytic process, I have felt a growing comfort at this odd affirmation of the unconscious at work, duly performing its own tasks, much as Bion describes in *Cogitations* (1992). These recursive beginnings and re-beginnings are a part of becoming engaged by the narratives being created via our patients' and our own attempts to understand whatever has not been understood. The image of the Native American storyteller comes to mind: the seated doll, with arms and legs outstretched, as tiny figures perch upon them, entranced by the outpourings emanating from the open mouth. In similar form, we carry our analysands with us, processing, in myriad aspects of our beings, the stories being created, re-created, re-digested, and thereby transformed into new beginnings, new possible narratives. These are the possibilities described by Borges (1962) in terms of the perennial *fork in the road*, knowing we can never divine the outcome but only follow somewhat blindly, with eyes open, to learn whatever we might from this particular go-round. "Time forks perpetually toward innumerable futures," writes Borges (p. 28). Our challenge, then, is to continue to choose, to relinquish, and to choose again.

The ongoing reverie that is captured in the frozen moment of the storyteller image is an important—perhaps essential—part of the work going well. Recurrently, as I continue this work, I become aware of bits of myself occupied in digesting some bit of experience in the life of a patient. It is almost like catching sight of one's self in some cosmic mirror that reflects an aspect of becoming that is being processed by patient and analyst in some remote aspect of their being. I sometimes describe this feeling in terms of finding one's self in the midst of several novels being read at recurrent intervals but digested simultaneously, at varying levels of consciousness. We may not recall the particulars when we think about it but when we once again pick up the novel and begin to read, as we become absorbed once again in the narrative, the details come flooding in, along with whatever refinements ensue from the processing that has occurred.

Bion (1992) suggests that it is through the unconscious that our most important processing occurs. This deeper level of processing enables us to take in and metabolize the facts of our experience, rather than more explicitly thinking about them through the relatively less efficient rational mode. This less conscious metabolization occurs in the realm of primary process, facilitating what Matte-Blanco (1975) refers to as *symmetrical* processing, whereby the basic experience is transformed in relation to its similarities and dissimilarities to previous experience, without the excessive use of categorical imperatives that encourage disjunction. The unconscious mind knows the patterns whereby material is sorted and metabolized, whereas the conscious mind is a relatively poor player at these games.

This move toward the basic patterned form seems to be at the heart of Hesse's novel *The Glass Bead Game* (1969), in which the players' immersion in their particular field helps them to discern underlying patterns in ways that cross disciplines. This metaphor presumes basic truths underlying all experience. Notably, in this novel Hesse highlights the hazard of becoming lost in the game, whatever it might be, and failing to recognize the basic truths that underlie ethical living. As we search for these basic truths, translating the transactional patterns into rational language enables us to communicate with one another but there is also a destructive element to that translation process through which much of the meaning, richness, and subtlety of the experience may be lost. The analyst tries to stay in the both-and of primary and secondary process so that she can hold the complexity, the sense and the non-sense.

Borges (1962) speaks of this layered traveling in his fictions, in which space, time, and meanings tend to be symmetrized such that we can never be quite certain at which point we stand, nor with whom. That territory is much like the dream space, in which all may be true and not true simultaneously, a perfect model for the analytic process, as for life itself. There is a perennial shifting of time, place, personae, that leaves us further "in." Our growing awareness leaves us ever more aware of the disparity between the known and the unknown, even as the patterns emerge ever clearer. Those of us who do this type of psychoanalytic exploration take up our armament of images on our journeys, taking heart from those who have come before, who become our beacons and signposts along the way. At times, in holding forth our own particular beacons, we become so for others as well. For me, such a beacon has been James Grotstein, who shines the beacon of his intellect and finely tuned unconscious on the words of such luminaries as Bion, Klein, and Matte-Blanco, reminding us of the incredible richness of paths yet to be taken or re-taken.

Much of Grotstein's writing has focused on trying to expand our collective consciousness (and unconscious). He points out our tendency, as analysts, to constrain ourselves within the extremely rich beginnings of the analytic journey, as described by Freud, rather than taking our hearts into our own hands and forging our own paths. In this endeavor, he follows hard in the footsteps of Bion (1963), who attempts to show something more in the oedipal myth by bringing in other myths in which inhere the same constant conjunctions—invariant themes—that structure them and give them life. Always attentive to the patterns underlying the analytic process, Bion (1965) brings to our attention the constant conjunctions that come to have meaning, whether or not we can articulate them.

This view is resonant with Jung's (1919) depiction of the archetypes as *typical modes of apprehension* that carry meanings that transcend the personal. By moving more deeply into the realms of myth and meaning, Grotstein brings to life the rich wealth of meanings undergirding myths that have endured by virtue of their deeply etched universality, in this way also enriching the Freudian tradition with the work of Jung, which had largely been lost in the Freudian line of transmission. Notable among Grotstein's (1997a) attempts to enlarge our armament beyond the oedipal myth to include the greater diversity of archetypal idioms carried in our collective histories have been his reflections on the labyrinth as a *myth of mastery*.

Mastery is a primary aspect of the hero's quest. Much as Hesse describes through the character of Magister Ludi, the urge toward mastery and transcendence can become compelling. Extending Bion's essential affirmation of the individual's inherent capacity to know, Grotstein (1996) describes a *transcendent position* in which one moves beyond the conflictual dialectic of Klein's (1946) paranoid-schizoid and depressive positions to achieve a state of greater serenity with one's becoming. In *The Glass Bead Game,* this transcendence is sought through a reliance on meditation as a means for self-mastery. From that place of internal grounding, one is better able to resonate with what is, rather than defensively de-creating or un-knowing it. Integral to the achievement of the transcendent position is the capacity to reach a consensus between one's own experience and that of others. Grotstein (1996) notes that Bion includes in his notion of *common sense* not only one's actual sense impressions and the extent to which one could confirm them to be in common with those of another but also: "the 'verdict' of intuition, the 'seventh servant,' the sense organ responsive to internal events" (p. 111). It is through the fine-tuning of this organ that Magister Ludi is able to eventually leave his post and accede to a higher call of duty that leads him further toward his own transcendence.

In this struggle, the character of Magister Ludi dramatizes the struggle Bion and Grotstein describe. In his finely grained focus on "how man seeks and hides from the ineffable" (Grotstein, 1996, p. 126), Bion struggles with the frustrations inherent in our attempts to move toward knowing, rather than merely knowing *about,* affirming our inherent ambivalence. Bion's approach invariably turns away from the more common ways of arriving at knowledge and moves, instead, toward a more idiosyncratic common sense, in which the variability of perspective helps to ensure that one does not become too mired in one's own defensive unknowing.

In line with Hesse's portrayal, along with the more abstract modes of understanding, such as mathematics and science, Bion (1977) affirms the importance of three further realms of meaning. He notes that the *mythical* illuminates the constant conjunctions, or patterned themes of experience;

the *aesthetic* affirms the value of the gestalt; and the *mystical* incorporates the notion of an intimate, personal relationship with the Ultimate. Our ability to learn, to think, or to know in any real sense is constrained by our ability to encounter what might be known and to tolerate this encounter without un-knowing or defensively occluding it from our experience (Grotstein, 1996). Real learning, for Bion, comes through experience, so that our knowing bears the stamp of our individuality, as well as the conviction born from personal engagement. Because human experience is inevitably personal, Bion (1963) warns against engaging in irresolvable debates regarding the nature of reality, highlighting instead the *universality* of the underlying truths inherent in myriad manifestations of similar myths. He uses as an example the Garden of Eden, Oedipus, and the Tower of Babel, each of which points to the hazard of turning a blind eye to experience rather than learning from it.

Inevitably, the knowledge we seek is never entirely attainable but rather is filtered through our experience and our characters as they evolve over time. Our only real access to the transcendent occurs in moments of resonance to what Bion (1977) terms *O* and Lacan (1977b) calls *the Real*. Bion's conception of *O* would seem to be in line with Jung's depictions of the collective unconscious, in that both allude to a reality beyond the constraints of any individual consciousness, an essentially incommunicable and unknowable reality. In his explications of the transcendent position, Grotstein (1996) encourages the type of knowing that moves toward continually and reiteratively becoming, incorporating our diverse understandings into the ongoing search for the unattainable, which becomes the more fully lived life. Through the following case illustration, I explore how this willingness to both know and not-know becomes an ongoing point of entry into the enigmatic labyrinths of the analytic journey, as we move into layers that allow us to reveal further truths while retaining the hope, illusion, and fear of remaining hidden.

My work with one young woman, in particular, has had the frustrating and challenging feel of the labyrinth, as we have twisted and turned into blind alleys, luminous landscapes, and dark corners, trying to fathom the unfathomable, together, alone. There has been an integral interplay between our reciprocal journeys, as we each come to know more fully both self and other. The twists and turns come, in part, from "Kate's" variable ability to know. I am often the carrier for what has been but cannot currently be known between us. In this way, as she hits a blind alley, her not-knowing becomes a wall for me, as well, and I must know alone what cannot be known together until such time as it can be further metabolized.

What cannot be known between us often emerges in Kate's dreams, many of which have a mythic quality to them. Oftentimes, we each have the sense that something important, something uncanny, something archetypal is being played out in them. In some of the dreams, it is the personages who have this quality of timelessness, invoked as god, demon, temptress, or crone. In others, it is the configuration of the dream itself as it plays out over time that seems most important. One pattern that has been prevalent has been that of a journey into a mystery of labyrinthian quality and proportions. This configuration is often associated with the hero, portrayed in fairy tales as the young man who would slay the dragons, win the princess, and live happily ever after. However, even though there is a part of Kate that longs to be rescued in such a way, there is that very Shakespearean "Kate" quality to her that defies anyone to tame or rescue this princess. For better and for worse, Kate is determined to be the hero in her own mythic journey to the center of her soul.

I have become, in many ways, the other self against whom Kate struggles to find and define herself, taking me in, spitting me out, annihilating, digesting, and transforming me into whatever she needs at the time. In her dreams, Kate moves through spaces that are both familiar and unfamiliar, internal and external. There is an intricate interplay of within and without, as she fends off intruders or stands outside, herself, cast out or repudiated. She alternates between taking the position of the victim and projectively identifying with the aggressor, thereby participating in her own victimization, which leaves her further depleted and bereft. This theme of depletion has been a recurrent one for Kate. Her interiors are in many ways unknown and unknowable. These interior spaces appear to be inextricably entwined with the feminine and with mother (Charles, 2000b; Freud, 1900), aspects of self that terrorize her with fears of symmetrization with or engulfment by the mother, too awful to contemplate. Nevertheless, it became increasingly clear that one of the labyrinthian twists toward finding herself leads, inevitably, through a reconnaissance with aspects of the mother/self (Charles, 2001).

From one perspective, the labyrinth becomes a place in which safety might be found, the "right" direction may be known. However, another facet of the labyrinth myth is the Minotaur, who may be waiting around any corner or hiding in plain sight. In Kate's dreams, the dangers are often displaced, as the cast-off brother/self—not she—falls prey to them. Grotstein (1997b, 1998) marks the importance of affirming those aspects of the monster that are related to the individual's ongoing creation of chimeric beasts from the dichotomous realm of the paranoid-schizoid mode of being. Otherwise, it is difficult to discern the wizard behind the curtain and to mourn the loss of the idealized other that also represents the self.

The Minotaur would seem to represent both the horror of knowing self and the wish to *be* truly horrible, to have the teeth to scare away whatever monsters lurk in the darkness. Kate prefers to create of me an old, ineffectual witch with no teeth—those problematic teeth she had disposed of in an earlier dream of disjunctively shifting scenes. In that dream, she had floated regally down a river through lush landscapes, followed by creatures in pairs. When the creatures showed their monster selves, the scene switched to a laboratory, in which she was putting some old teeth on the top shelf "for safekeeping." Perhaps she can accept the existence of the teeth only to the extent that they are other. They are not only not-hers, they are also not dangerous but merely "interesting specimens" to be considered dispassionately (for a further elaboration of this dream, see Charles, 2001).

Grotstein (1997b) points out the hazard in accepting what he depicts as a *myth of innocence* without the complementary myth of essential and absolute culpability, which he terms *autochthony*. It is the self as creator that must ultimately come to terms with the forms into which Kate's characters are cast. Grotstein (personal communication, September 1999) posits O, itself, as "the ultimate innocent demon" that tortures and tantalizes us, pulling us toward both the knowing and disowning of self, confusing and confabulating self with other and other with self, in the creation of our own personal Minotaur. When the curtain pans and the wizard is revealed, we are left for the moment with the self and the myth standing separate and apart, without the web of illusion to weave them together again. Much like Nicholas in *The Magus*, we have the opportunity to recognize our own hand in the drama we are creating *if* we can tolerate this knowledge.

The spaces Kate inhabits in her dreams are both known and unknown, inviting her further and further into the labyrinth. For example, in one dream, she returns to her childhood home and realizes that "everyone had known" that she had been abused, a fact that she alone had not been allowed to know. In this depiction, she highlights her puzzlement over what could possibly have gone wrong to have left her in such trouble, unable to manage her feelings or move forward in her life. She offers herself a further opportunity to come to know what had been hidden by the forced dichotomizations between what might and might not be known and still allow inclusion in the family, as well as what might and might not be known without rupturing her sense of self.

In another dream, Kate was in her own apartment, suffused with a sense of foreboding, as though someone was after her. Then she was at a large affair of some sort and needed to leave but was not safe alone. The person who was supposed to transport her had not arrived and she was trying to figure out how to get to her destination. Just as she was arranging to be driven by a group of people, her friend showed up. She got into the friend's car and then, suddenly, Kate was at the wheel, driving through the streets of her hometown. Although the streets were familiar, there were many obstacles; things were different, distorted, altered, or made difficult. Then, it was as though she was in a kiddie car, driving onto someone's lawn, and there were objects under her wheels being crunched. What had seemed like debris turned out to be children's toys and things that belonged to Kate, like her quilting tools, even though this was not her house and the people who came out on the porch were strangers. She described having left somewhat sheepishly, an intruder once again, in her tiny toy car.

In the next segment of the dream, Kate was at her mother's house. We encounter the familiar trope, in which there is the sense of being at home in a place that is no longer home. There is a loss in the leaving and yet there is also the sense of a different way of seeing that could not be validated in her family of origin. An event had brought all her brothers together, even the eldest, who had not been at a family gathering for many years. She was not sure what the occasion had been. It may have been a death but no one seemed sad. Her mother was in one room with her own friends and they seemed to be making things—quilts perhaps—and there was a rug under Kate's feet that reminded her of her childhood room. She had the sense that many of the paraphernalia of her childhood were in that room.

Kate went into the kitchen, where her brothers were all together, talking. Her brother "Dave" had brought two packages of meat. Kate opened them and noticed, with some repugnance, that there was fat all around them. She would have to trim them extensively to get rid of the excess. People were talking in a generally good-humored way, and Kate said something to Dave about having brought the meat to make up for not having given her a Christmas present. This joke seemed to fall flat and she realized that she had "better just go along with things." After a while, her brothers went upstairs to get the bedrooms ready and Kate went back into the living room, where her mother was. Kate was trying, with some urgency, to relate to her mother some information that seemed to be very important for her mother to understand. Kate tried to help her mother by telling her what she was seeing but the mother was very resistant. When the mother's friend tried to say something in aid of Kate's efforts, the mother took two pillows and smothered the friend with them, making the friend disappear. As Kate continued to try to talk to her mother, the mother became increasingly angry, remote, and distant, and then her face became that of a cloth bunny with glassy eyes. The deadly hatred was chilling. Kate knew that her mother wanted to destroy her, as well. Kate said that she thought that she needed to make the face that of a stuffed animal because she could not have tolerated, even in sleep, seeing that expression on her mother's face.

Kate associated to the pieces of childhood in the dream. Her parents' unwillingness to speak or acknowledge truth had always been a source of distress but she was particularly distressed by her own similarities to her mother and with how she seemed to become her mother in certain ways. Her boyfriend had remarked as he listened to Kate recording the dream into her tape recorder that the resemblance to her mother's voice as she spoke the mother's parts had been uncanny. Kate is terrified of becoming like—which for her is equivalent to becoming—her mother. At times, she has noticed, when writing in her diary, that her writing becomes like that of her mother. I suggested that being like her mother is a way of trying to understand her. As a child, she had needed to understand her mother in order to save her and to try to save herself in the process. However, there comes a point when the knowing becomes a means for separating and for giving up on the hope of saving, and also requires a distancing and a willingness to survive even in the face of the other's imminent destruction, which is horrible in its own way. Kate asked me how I know all of this, if I have a crazy mother inside, as well. "Perhaps a lost one," I said. "I know," she replied, "That was just the poet in me." I said that I think that we all have crazy mothers in us and it is more a matter of the extent to which we are willing to know this and grapple with it, or prefer to become "normal" in denial.

In Kate's dreams, there is often a sense of evil. Over time, we have watched the opposing forces change from male to female and from dangerously evil to merely "the opposition," as there has been less urgency to dichotomize these parts of herself. In this way, evil is increasingly allowed to be present in both self and other, and thereby can be more fully known, calculated, and slain (dealt with). In one dream, Kate wandered into the lair of a man who was in charge of the fate of the innocents there. She described a person,

> like Jeffrey Dahmer, or the serial killer in the movie *Silence of the Lambs*. I was in his lair, walking through a room with cots attached to the walls, like in a prison, row after row. He seemed to be doing experiments on whoever was in the cots. There was flesh and limbs, mutilation; the eyes were silent, tortured; some were living, some were dead. They looked like seals; one was empty, rotted out. It was awful. Just the skin was left, like the chapter in *Women Who Run with the Wolves* about "seal skin/soul skin." One seemed to be empty, as though the soul had gone. There were huge barrels of flesh and men were moving them. There was no story line; it was just being there.

Kate recalled a story she had seen on the news several years previous, in which men had been clubbing seals to death. She said that she could not understand how people could do that. There was something about the willingness to assault a poor, dumb animal that was chilling to her. When I asked her how she had felt in the dream, she responded, "frightened. But it feels like 'other.' I can't talk about it and be there at the same time. It's like when I try to bring myself in, the other gets pushed out; we can't occupy the same space at the same time." Later in the hour, Kate was talking about a new relationship with a man in which she was feeling very present, which made her realize how not present she had been during the two years previous. She becomes the other, the disowned, dead, empty self that could tolerate the inhumanity within the dream, much as she has had to be not-herself in order to tolerate the terrible isolation and assaultiveness she has experienced in the world.

At that turn in the labyrinth, there are only dead-ends. However, at other turns there are intimations of immortality, as Kate plays with omnipotence in the face of this terrible sense of non-being. In one dream, Neptune figured prominently. He was both powerful and playful. She was a mermaid and enjoyed feeling her own power, which had a transformative, emergent quality to it. In another dream, in which individuals from all different stages of her life (yet all at her current age) were mixed together, there was an old man who gave her a gift. It was a thick, heavy, mahogany game board, with a hundred indentations for dice of varying hues. She did not know how to play the game and he had promised to teach her. It seemed to be some sort of game of chance but you needed to know the rules in order to be able to play. She followed the man around, waiting for him to teach her, but she never found out how to play. Like Plonius in *The Glass Bead Game,* she remains the outsider, looking on enviously at the Master of the Game.

In her daily life, Kate has tended to rely upon the other to translate for her the rules whereby this game she is playing can be brought to some end that is not disappointing. However, in her dreams, she explores a universe in which no one else seems to be able to hand her the keys. More often, she cannot even prevail upon them to follow her. Just as she was unable to save her family, Kate is unable to lead the other toward the intended destination. She often has a sense of rightness, an inevitability and purpose about her movements, an urgency that is not shared by the other. She is willing to attempt to save the other, though not at the price of herself, as before.

Kate's dreams show an ongoing struggle to know and to see, an important theme in her family, in which she had been vilified for knowing how ill clad were both the emperor and his wife. In many ways, she seems to have been used by her brothers to project their own uncontained rage, from which safe distance they could revile and vilify her (see Charles, 2001). In one dream, Kate was with a boyfriend, who became her older brother, Dave. They were in a water-treatment plant and she was aware of some danger there. They came to a diverging path and she knew that it was important that they go to the right, that the other way led to danger. But her brother wandered off to the left, in spite of her warnings, and fell into some water there. She heard the splash, sensed danger, and ran to find him. Kate said that a shower type thing came out of the wall. Some spray got in her eyes and she "knew it was bad." Dave was screaming and someone helped Kate to get him out of the water. Then they were in a locker room and she knew that things were very bad, that he was going to be blind. She sat sobbing, with grief. Her brother was on the other side of the wall of lockers. As she went over to him, he kept saying "no, no." She knew that he still could see her but that his eyesight was fading and that he did not want the last thing he saw to be her crying. So she took his face in her hands, composed herself, and looked calmly at him. He kept saying that he was sorry, as she told him that it was all right.

Kate said that the water-treatment plant reminded her of therapy. Dave had decided to go into therapy after a stint in an anger management program. Much like their mother, Dave would go into rages and be completely unapproachable. Kate's associations to locker rooms led her to swimming pools. She said that her father had had a swimming pool, and then stopped abruptly. "What are you thinking of?" she asked. I said that the locker rooms made me think of boys' and girls' facilities being separate and of how she had felt closed off from her father and brothers. Kate said that when she was around seven, shortly after her parents had divorced, her uncle had been divorced as well. Because their children were the same age, her father and uncle would plan activities together. Her brothers had companions but Kate, being the only girl, was alone. She particularly hated going into the locker room alone. She wanted to be with her father, with whom she felt cared for but never quite secure.

In a second dream that same night, Kate had been waiting to see me but I informed her that she would have to wait half an hour, as I had to go to my own doctor and would have to wait half an hour there. This brought to my mind her distress in the previous session. She had said that a comment of mine bothered her a great deal (I had said that, at some level, it could be either one of us sitting in either chair). That comment made her anxious because she needed me to know more and to be more than she. I had burdened her and she did not understand why I would do such a thing, much as in the dream I gave her a very large check to hold for me with writing on it that she could not decipher. At first, she had thought it might be German or Dutch, but then she realized that it was South African. It was very large and cumbersome. She wanted to make it smaller and so had folded it.

In the dream, I stood in the doorway of my office talking to her, explaining something. This image brought to my mind a criticism from the previous session, in which she referred to my talking too much in the session previous to that. She said that it seemed as though I was talking from my own needs, rather than from responsiveness to her, though that had not bothered her but rather made her see me as more human. In the dream, I was talking differently than I usually do, "with the accent they have in South Africa." There was an African man there with me, whom Kate found very interesting and attractive. I was telling her a story about him but then let him tell his own story, which was about atrocities in his country (which set me thinking how uncanny she is sometimes; I had been reading a book about Rwanda. Although she had no way of knowing that, her depiction of the story was in extraordinary synchronicity with that book). Kate wanted to get closer to this man, with whom she felt a bond, but realized she had spent the previous night with the other African man who was present, and regretted this. The man she had slept with tried to comfort her but she said that she did not want his comfort. That was not what she was needing. She did not remember what had happened the night before and so he began to tell her. When she asked where I had been, he answered that I had been with the African woman, who was also present. Kate was feeling left out and unincluded, as though she could not quite enter into my world. I wondered about her feelings at my abandoning her in that way but she said that she had felt more as though the way was open but she just did not fit. It was not my barring her way, but rather her inability to enter, that precluded passage.

Kate then said that she had been thinking about joining the Peace Corps. She had always wanted to do that but had thought that she had nothing to offer. I said that although she may not have many of the accoutrements that in our culture signal that a person has anything of value within, the final image of the dream in the water-treatment plant clearly showed her awareness that she has a great deal to offer. She said that in the following dream she had been aware of how much more there was to me than she had imagined. I wondered aloud whether I represented the part of *herself* that had much more than she had been aware of previously. There seemed to be, in both dreams, elements from a book she had brought me (Alice Walker's *By the Light of My Father's Smile* [1998]), which seemed to be, very profoundly, about *being* and whether one can be true to one's self and one's principles and not get lost.

As Kate comes to better appreciate her own strength and comes to a greater equilibrium within herself, she is faced with a new dilemma. She finds that she had been working so hard toward survival that many of her gifts had been languishing. It is as though pieces of her life have been on hold and are sitting in boxes, waiting to be sorted through. She is not sure which ones she wants to pull out or what she will make of them. She is not sure she has what she needs or can figure out what to do. She said that she feels as though, on the one hand, she is on the edge of a great journey and yet the way seems so difficult that it is almost as though there is a disjunction between the two. I smiled and suggested that both could be true, thereby acknowledging both the difficulty and her tremendous capacity. She said "that's easy for you to say," and I laughed and agreed with her. Relinquishing the hope of a savior leaves us at a difficult precipice, from which we might make the most exciting, and yet oft-times terrifying, journey of all.

In her dream, Kate felt as though she were being invited into my space. I had left the waiting room door open so that she was able to participate in the gathering that was taking place in my office but she was not sure whether she should or could be there or not. There was an unfamiliar language being spoken and I seemed to be unaware of the plight she was experiencing. This is a familiar theme, this question of whether I know her and hold a place for her, or whether I merely imagine her in a way that can never be realized, but rather must bring inevitable disappointment.

In *the Glass Bead Game,* Magister Ludi dies to leave way for his pupil to discover himself. In Kate's dream, she is trying to find her own place, her own language, trying to make sense of that which I cannot make sense of for her. She is also trying to see herself in a new way, as though she would need a new language in which to speak of a self that had become too saturated by the old words even to be able to envision alternative possibilities. That would seem to be a higher-level working through, when we have the sense of the subtle ways in which we become confined and proscribed by our conceptions of ourselves, irrevocably tied to the languages in which we have learned to define ourselves. In much the same way, the analytic language, too, can become a way of constraining and proscribing, as well as a way of freeing us up and creating alternative possibilities.

I wonder if the check I give her to hold for me in the dream represents, in some measure, the burden I give her in return for helping her. This theme of her indebtedness to me comes up periodically, as she wonders what she has given to me during our years together. She has watched me grow, as well, and would like to affirm that she has played a part in that process but is afraid that this cannot be acknowledged. She finds herself in me and also finds myself in her, as she becomes aware of turns of phrase or ideas she has taken in. Have they become her own? Does this represent a finding or losing of self? Our reciprocal transformations become entwined, as we hold a place for one another, metabolizing the transformation of both self and other yet also encountering the ostensibly unmetabolizable bits or the "lies" (Bion, 1963) that must also become known sufficiently to be able to struggle with them more consciously.

Kate attempts to disentangle our various selves, as she moves through the labyrinth that has become her identifications and disidentifications with aspects of me as mother, lover, analyst, and destroyer. In one dream, there is a party at my house. Kate is in attendance. I was spending a great deal of time cooking and Kate was getting hungry. When the meal finally came, it did not seem to warrant the extensive preparation time but seemed to be a rather paltry offering. Kate was very curious about my life and wandered through my house. She noticed that my mother had the same physical anomaly as Kate, herself, does: a crookedness, of sorts. I had a young son who appeared to have some sort of birth defect and Kate identified with him. He seemed to be crooked in some way, as well. She noted that I seemed to be relatively unconcerned about his condition and it was not clear whether this was a good or a bad thing. Am I sufficiently aware of the crookedness within her to help her come to terms with it or am I merely oblivious and need her complicity in this? I too easily become the idealized other, or ego ideal, against whom she tests herself and tries to come to know herself, as she tries to find a place in my life and also tries to find herself in that place. In identifying with both my idealized self and my insufficient child, she moves closer toward my own insufficiency and humanity, and thereby closer toward freeing herself from her bondage to me.

Late in our work together, Kate brought in two dreams of old ladies in successive sessions. In the first dream, Kate had been getting married and was waiting at the church for people to arrive. No one came and it was getting later and later. Kate was feeling very irritated at having been left to arrange everything and having no one even bother to arrive on time. At one point, the groom was there but was just hanging out with his friends. Kate's irritation reached a peak and she just decided to leave. As she was going down the steps of the church, she came upon a group of old ladies who were talking about her in a judgmental kind of way. At one particularly snide remark, Kate stopped to "flick the woman off." Kate said that she was surprised at herself and also surprised at this depiction of an old lady. In her dreams, the old lady is usually the crone, a sign of wisdom, of knowing. However, in this dream, *she* had known better.

In the second dream, there was another old lady, this time a "kind of funky-looking woman with big hoop earrings and odd clothes." This time, Kate had told the old woman to "fuck off." Kate was surprised and somewhat distressed by the disparity between the soothing solace of the wise old woman she generally encounters and this new personage, who was so easily discounted. When I asked her about her associations to this woman, Kate responded that she reminded her of her paternal grandmother, "Lena," now deceased, who had worn outrageous hats and had enjoyed flaunting her individuality. Lena had been thwarted in her own creative strivings and had seemed to enjoy Kate's spirit and individuality. In contrast to Kate's discomfort, I was enjoying her irreverence in the dreams, a fact she became aware of. She beamed, saying: "You're enjoying this," and wondered what I was thinking. I said that I had two associations to this part of the dreams. First, I thought of her current boyfriend, who in many ways did not want her to be her bawdy and irreverent "Lena" self. Second, I thought of her relationship with idealized aspects of me, which she was needing to move beyond, as well. My enjoyment of her irreverence seemed to help her to enjoy it as well and to help her to find the self that was getting lost beneath her boyfriend's (and her own) needs for reassurance that she could be the good girl and dutiful wife.

Another prevalent theme in Kate's dreams is of waiting for someone who never comes, reminiscent of her experiences with her father, who would often forget his promises to meet her, even for important occasions. As she settles into the familiarity of being left at the altar of her anticipation, she recalls waiting for hours, hope dwindling into despair. In this image are configured, quite strongly, the elements of the recent dream, in which Kate is left once again at an altar but this time she can decide, not only whether she will wait, but also what sense she is to make of the waiting. She no longer needs to accept the old view of herself as abandoned and therefore insufficient and is thereby released from the urgency of finding the "right" man, who will lift the spell by altering the end of the story. This freedom from the archaic images of mother and self enhances her ability to acknowledge the positive and negative poles of her legacy from her grandmother, without the positive becoming engulfed in the negative. In this way, her grandmother's and mother's inability to successfully negotiate the search for self are transformed from a curse that becomes an injunction to do the same, to the more facilitative image of the grandmother, in fantasy, enjoying Kate's more successful negotiation of the labyrinth from beyond the grave. Encased within this image, too, is the affirmation of her ability to keep me present, in a positive sense, without needing to idealize me into some form that would become ultimately self-defeating.

One important facet of our work together has been the interplay of our reciprocal developments. When I began working with Kate, I was a novice therapist, at which point my heart made up for whatever my head may have lacked. In the early days, Kate had very little resiliency, which required a great deal of pliancy from both myself and the frame. That pliancy may very well have kept her alive, however, it also left us to accommodate to the layers of ripples in the intervening spaces.

Kate had very little sense of self when she first entered my door. When asked about herself, she would cast about in her mind and then tell me how some other might see her. Over the years, she has 'tried me on for size,' much as I have done with her, trying to understand her experience from within the confines of my own sensoria. In reciprocal fashion, we have shaped the journey of the other, setting up challenges, bridges, and roadblocks, as we attempt to negotiate the difficult process of transformation.

Kate has commented periodically on the fact of our mutual and reciprocal growth in this journey. It seems to be important to her to affirm that she has given me something, to help balance her sense of having taken. Now, as we come to the end of this portion of our journey(s), she is aware of aspects of myself in her. They do not feel alien or other. She has found a good-enough mother with whom to identify and disidentify. Toward the end of our work together, she left for several weeks to assist her family through a difficult time. This was a multi-tiered graduation for Kate. She was able to contemplate surviving on her own resources within the family system that had threatened to destroy her for so many years. She is doing well, and writes to me of a dream, in which she carries me in a manner that is quintessential Kate:

> Last night I had the greatest dream about us. I was in Florida, but not here, a more rural place. You showed up at my father's house, surprising me. It was a huge sprawling mansion and I was at my wit's end because every time I tried to straighten, clean, or organize, either a sibling or some small child was sabotaging it. I was walking around with you, showing you the beautiful artwork, sculptures, and treasures. We walked out on the veranda, and the dirt road that ran through the town in front of the house was flooded. Up to this point you had said little, and I was just so happy to see you that it took me a while to work up the courage to ask you why you were there. You smiled and said you just needed a longer vacation than you realized. You were wearing this dress of a gorgeous, silky, dark saffron color. We walked down the steps and you hesitated, not wanting to muddy your dress. I picked up the hem of your dress and led you by the arm out into the water. I wasn't sure what you were going to do, or how far you would walk with me into the water. I told you that you could wear one of my dresses while we dried yours, and then you surprised me by diving all the way in. We laughed, and then swam together. I carried you in my arms all the way out to the deepest part, at which point I looked around and thought "this could be gator territory." But then I realized that any gators around here would be small ones, and we were okay. I asked you again why you were here to see me, and you made a suggestive comment, which scared me, but then I just felt this incredibly protective feeling toward you, and I turned around to wade out of the water with you in my arms still and our skirts heavy and dripping.
>
> It was one of those dreams that make you smile when you wake up. Do you think this dream is about more of my hopes/fears about where our work is/is not going?
>
> I was just remembering the terrifying dark water and gator or shark-infested dreams that I had for years, and the contrast now is awesome.

In this dream, Kate once again puzzles over confusions between intimacy and boundary violations. I have become intimately intertwined with her sense of aliveness and vitality, both of which necessitate feeling in and through all parts of her being, even those that have come to seem dangerous. Her father has been tantalizing her during this and previous visits, and both parents have been soliciting her caretaking in various ways. She has been discomforted by her father's sexual innuendos and by his willingness to abandon his wife and young son in order to take her out on the town. She asserts her autonomy with her father, reminding him that he has obligations and that she can take care of herself. "I know that I like spending time with dad," she says, "but not at the expense of his wife. That's pretty murky territory."

Kate has gone "home" to rescue her father/self. She decides that she can "carry" him, without abusing self or other. *She* can keep the boundaries that continue to elude him, she can protect them both. Kate then continues:

> I'm so looking forward to Paul's visit. It will be good to have a real vacation and to reconnect with him. There was a moment last week, when I told Paul that I was somehow comforted by the idea of his staying in my apartment while I was here. "Why do you think that is?" he asked. I thought about it for a while, and said, "Because you hold a piece of me that feels like home." Then I started sobbing into the phone, totally bewildered as to why. I think it must be because I've never allowed that before. It's scary. It's wonderful too. Do you think it's okay that I feel that way? I mean, okay as in appropriate to feel *and* rely on?

There are times when the question becomes its own answer. Kate wonders whether she can get along without me but it is no longer a question, it is merely a regret at having to move along from a portion of her journey that has facilitated a profound transformation for this remarkable young woman. She is no longer the lamentable Kate of the unrealized potential. She has transcended the bonds of childhood that had proscribed her limits and emptied her skin, she has ripped through the clouded covering her stepfather had nailed over her window each winter. Flight no longer necessitates crashing or burning. She has learned to soar on the wings of her very fluid imagination, grounded by her ability to know what she knows through her own common senses, rather than relinquishing the possibility of discovering her own self by seeking self through the other.

As Kate determines to become her own hero in this legend, she challenges those she loves to take their stand as well, to make their own journey, which becomes a pilgrimage to the source, the labyrinthian entrails of our innermost desires and fears, steaming with the breath of our most cherished dragons, lying ever in wait, beyond the next bend, until we catch them at their source, within.

NOTE

1. Portions of this chapter are taken from the article Marilyn Charles, "Through the Unknown, Remebered Gate: Journeys into the Labyrinth," published in *Psychoanalytic Review* vol. 89 (2002): 79–89. The title of this chapter is drawn from the poem "Little Gidding" by T. S. Eliot.

TWELVE

Standing Outside the Gates

Pierre, or The Ambiguities[1]

"[A]ll the great books in the world are but the mutilated shadowings-forth of invisible and eternally unembodied images in the soul; so that they are but the mirrors, distortedly reflecting to us our own things; and never mind what the mirror may be, if we would see the object, we must look at the object itself and not at its reflection"

—Melville, *Pierre*

The hero's quest entails being able to stand outside the gates of conformity to cultural dictates so that one might discover one's own path. Psychoanalysis has had an uneasy relationship with difference, as it has marked territory that falls outside of consensual discourse but also hopes to be authorized as a legitimate "scientific" enterprise. As a discipline, psychoanalysis had its origins at a time when women, in particular, were speaking through their symptoms about problems that could not be put into words. Our history has been highlighted by creative attempts to explore that wordless territory, whether through Klein's (1932) interpolations about the internal workings of the child's mind, Ferenczi's (1949) attempts to bridge the gap between analyst and analysand, or Bion's (1967a) conjectures about the psychotic mind. Each of these efforts was also punctuated by attempts to make sense of self in relation to other—to bridge the unbridgeable gaps—and above all to learn enough to be able to act with integrity.

We are faced with the dual paradoxes that we discover *ourselves* through our interactions with *others*, and that what often seems most true is information taken in through the nonverbal realm, meanings that cannot necessarily be acknowledged, much less put into words. How, then, do we navigate in that slippery terrain in which meaning can be asserted and denied at one and the same time, *and* in which truth is tied, not to logic or even coherence but rather to moments that may be fragile and ineffable? As a woman whose experience has often been that of feeling mad in relation to the larger culture, and also of having insights that seem difficult to put into traditional speech, particularly under opposition, I have been drawn to that which, and those who, stand outside the gates. Like Antigone, I feel torn between the demands of conscience and those of the social structures in which I live. Because of this dilemma, I often find myself, in my clinical work, standing at the edge of what can seem like a terrifyingly strange, lonely, and dangerous abyss. At times, the only mantle I can wrap around myself to give me courage is the call of the othered other, that demand that Adrienne Rich (1978) aptly phrased as the need to *take ourselves more seriously* or die. But, hard as we might try to sustain certainty under fire, the living death of failing to achieve recognition in the eyes of the other can mean a terrible descent into madness.

Increasingly, data affirms how inextricably the self is bound to others. We are born utterly dependent on those around us. Optimally, there is sufficient containment that the child can build her own capacities for affective and cognitive self-regulation. When the parent's availability is inhibited by unresolved mourning, however, it is difficult to build relationships in which meanings can be held reliably. Without that type of containment, tensions can result between individual perception and consensual meanings. At the extreme, these tensions can be literally maddening, increasingly driving the child into a universe remote from others. In such circumstances, finding the words in which meanings can be held by oneself and with another can become a crucial factor in lodging and consolidating the foundations of one's identity. This is a dilemma highlighted by Marquez in *One Hundred Years of Solitude* (1970) when he writes, "Thus they went on living in a reality that was slipping away, momentarily captured by words, but which would escape irremediably when they forgot the values of the written letters" (p. 51). Notably, for Lacan (1977i) the *letter* is a tangible unit of meaning that marks the essence of the thing and distinguishes one word from another. Therefore, this issue of being able to register the *meaning of the letter* becomes of crucial importance in establishing one's identity within the context of the larger narrative of family history.

For those who cannot find recognition of their internal needs and desires with their parents, young adulthood is a particularly precarious time, given the developmental challenge to increasingly stand on one's own and move beyond imposed values to discover one's own values, one's own desires. This process occurs through the ability to both identify and disidentify with parents and to feel recognized and valued by them as a separate being. Much like Winnicott's (1971) observations about the *use of the object*, the adolescent must be able to reject parental authority, to kill off the parent, euphemistically, and find him still standing. For the young man, in particular, there is a need to identify with the father sufficiently to separate from the mother, but also to be accepted as separate from the father in order to find his *own* way. That was a tension we encountered in chapter 10 with Nikolai, whose inability to negotiate the transition from family of origin to relationships with peers left him unable to find a path to separate adulthood.

In this chapter, I will discuss the case of a young man who was able to identify with peers but whose identity was so tied to parental values that he was driven mad by what felt to him to be a forced choice between his identity as his father's son and the new, nascent autonomous identity being developed. As the disparities mounted, identity could be neither fully embraced nor consolidated and he became increasingly unable to function or to know fantasy from reality.

Bion (1977) saw the crucial juncture of development as the constant choice between seeking knowledge and turning a blind eye, highlighting the absence of acknowledgement that is at the core of human vulnerability. Early development includes an evolving transition from reliance on the nonverbal communications of early childhood to increasing reliance on language. Because of this duality of language, what we perceive but cannot validate inevitably entraps us. When there are family secrets, the transition to adulthood is impeded by what cannot be known within the family. There are holes in what may be known that become impediments to development. When the self cannot be known in the family context, one must either lose self or lose home. Either of these choices may severely impede development for the young adult who has not attained sufficient maturity to survive on his own. Unresolved mourning entails a splitting off of whatever has not been worked through, creating a vulnerability in the parent. The child senses this vulnerability, making it difficult to fight off the idealizations and bring the parent down to the human size required for the deidealization that marks the passage into early adulthood (Blos, 1979).

When the parent's narrative has been foreclosed, the untold story cannot be encountered directly but rather becomes known through the ellipses, the gaps that mark the place of what is missing (Charles, 2006a). The inability to narrate one's life story with coherence leaves us estranged and alienated from self and other. Without some means of repairing these ruptures, the fragmentation and alienation are passed along the generations, symbolized through symptoms that await recognition. Working with such individuals can be incredibly difficult, as we encounter the unmetabolized bits and fragments, registering the echoes of cries that are not easily answered, softened, or soothed, and may take very peculiar forms. Working *with* the individual with such problems—rather than *problematizing* him—is an ongoing challenge in an age in which distress and disorder are thought of as aberrant phenomena to be eradicated by any means at hand.

Our stories become the myths and parables through which we mark and pass along our understandings—and also our questions—regarding the complexities of existence. Melville's novel titled *Pierre, or The Ambiguities* (1929) is one such novel in which the author considers ways in which people can be driven mad by family secrets and by social exclusion. The person who eats of the forbidden fruit then stands outside the gates and those inside are haunted by the pain transmitted and its implicit reproach. It is difficult to live in such an alternative reality without feeling as though one is losing one's mind. Psychosis can be seen as precisely that state in which one is lost outside of history in the realm of what Lacan (1977b) calls *the Real*, a realm outside of symbolization. Unarticulated, he says, it is that which "doesn't stop not being written"—and so resides outside space and time, intruding upon us in its own ways (Lacan, 1972–1973, p. 59). When social forces eliminate the subject, narrating the story becomes a way of not only affirming one's being but also one's essential humanity.

At times, these stories enter the consulting room in uncanny ways, as was the case with "Peter," with whom my unconscious spoke most clearly through the intrusion of memories of a film that had been made from Melville's gothic novel. The film was titled *Pola X*, an acronym of the title in French. For some time, *Pola X* had haunted me intermittently, with its dark, apocalyptic warnings about the exigencies of fate and circumstance, depicting all too evocatively what it can mean to stand outside the gates. The allure of mystery and the danger of becoming lost in it was an all too familiar trope. I had hurt my foot recently and, as I hobbled, I felt like Pierre, hobbling outside the social structure that might have provided care but now denied him. Uncannily, then, I found myself faced with the embodiment of Pierre, in the form of a young man who looked as though he had landed from another, far remote time, who was himself ensconced in the literature of that era. Peter had been searching through the literature of the American transcendentalists, including Melville, for a means to escape the piety of his parents. In this way, he hoped to anchor himself in a newly authorized morality that might help him to get out from under the bonds of filial loyalty that were strangling him.

Lacan (1975–1976) uses the term *sinthome* to designate an idiosyncratic solution to the problems of existence that then also becomes the *key* to the meanings displayed and implied by that solution, as we attend to the ways in which the meanings are knotted together for that individual. In this term, I find respect for the meaning being carried. Rather than merely a symptom of pathology, the sinthome is an important puzzle waiting to be explored, a key to the individual's mystery. This move on Lacan's part points to a place where the clinician can stand in relation to an individual who is clearly and firmly embedded in his own reality, one that does not easily coincide with that of the clinician. This stance presumes that there is a logic, a structuring at work, that may be too idiosyncratic to be comprehensible outside the realm of that internal logic.

From this perspective, there is no substitute for our willingness to learn from our patients about where they are stuck. This, according to Lacan (1992), is an inherently ethical stance that insists that one cannot presume authority when questions of individual existence are at stake, a statement of a value system that demands that we recognize the inherent narcissism at the base of our presumptions regarding the "illness of the other" and the proposed solutions that such a model implies. Like Bion, therefore, in Lacan we find a determined slipping away from definite meanings and prescriptions that would pre-define the course of treatment. To the contrary, if we are to face the challenge head on, our task is to *learn the language* of the other sufficiently to be able to recognize the gaps and elisions, the condensations, the ways in which meanings are organized and formulated by that individual. If we can avoid "correcting" or challenging this system of meanings, then perhaps we can recognize the logic sufficiently to be able to invite a conversation that is *in relation to* that system. From such a position, the analytic conversation moves toward obtaining a better sense of the meanings as they exist, the ways in which they function for the person, and then perhaps, but only then, to begin to consider together ways in which that system fails the individual in relation to his own desires. We can see in this stance a return to Freud's model of inquiry, a return to psychoanalysis as a process of discovery rather than as an encyclopedia of terms and techniques.

Through this process of discovery, we may better reflect on the difficult meanings as they surface. Works such as Davoine and Gaudillière's (2004) *History Beyond Trauma* point to an intergenerational story that is spoken through the individual whose vulnerability to psychosis may also speak to his creative potential. For the clinician, being able to listen for the echoes of the family history that may be infusing itself into an individual's life story can be crucial. Our ability to register those echoes and take them seriously helps the person to locate himself in the context in which he is embedded. Otherwise, he remains haunted by phantoms from a past that cannot be formulated sufficiently to be worked through (Abraham and Torok, 1994; Fraiberg, Adelson, and Shapiro, 1975).

Because of my recognition of what is at stake in the negotiation between self and other, I am interested in creativity as such; what opens it up and what shuts it down, particularly in relation to the so-called helping professions, whose ways of understanding can become fundamentally crippling, particularly to one who stands outside the gates. Research shows that individuals with psychotic liabilities, who are also creative, manage moments of insufficient grounding by either constraining and dumbing down, or else by letting go completely, in flows of ideas that have little grounding whatsoever and are difficult for another to follow.

But an interesting stabilization occurs with the support of a responsive other, such that one individual might be able to move beyond the original constrictions, and another might show us the links between the flow of ideas and the referents from which they flow (Charles, Clemence, and Biel, 2011).

When working with individuals who struggle with psychotic symptoms, there is always the question of whether meaning can be made and held between two individuals. As Davoine and Gaudillière (2004) put it:

> The cognitive stakes are considerable, a prelude to the opening or the closing of the field of *logos*. A disingenuous reply or an embarrassed silence, when adamantly repeated, sends the subject into nonexistence on this point. He exiles himself, falls silent, goes crazy. Instead of speaking to him, people speak of him, as an aberration. (p. 70)

It is important for the clinician to be attuned and attentive so that she can track the process in sessions sufficiently to catch those moments when meaning closes down, to recognize them and, if possible, to inquire into them. Even our earnest attempts to discover the problem and recognize what is at stake for the patient can be disorganizing, *writing over* the individual and further obscuring him from view. This dilemma was of concern in my work with this young man I call Peter, after the main character, Pierre, in Melville's novel. Peter wanted a diagnosis that would illuminate the symptoms he had been experiencing but, as he told his story, Pola X intruded so strongly that I bought the novel, trying to make sense of the links.

The story was that of a young man of privilege who becomes disillusioned in the transition to adulthood, when the semblance of the father breaks open and familiar guideposts can no longer be relied upon. Pierre and Peter each struggled to carry forward the paternal injunctions toward a new, less tarnished morality. But breaking with the father's world meant putting himself outside of the culture, and its comforts, into realities that were hard to bear.

In the novel, Pierre is the earnest and idealistic heir to his father's large estate, a person of privilege with the world waiting at his feet. His early efforts at writing have been well received and he plans to marry his childhood sweetheart. This idyllic future is broken into when Pierre meets a mysterious young woman who claims to be the unacknowledged daughter of Pierre's father. Isabel seems to speak of the oneness with nature that Pierre has sought, while also inviting shame and filial loyalty at what she has endured in her life. She says to him, "I feel that there can be no perfect peace in individualness. Therefore, I hope one day to feel myself drank up into the pervading spirit animating all things. I feel I am an exile here" (Melville, 1929, p. 119). Pierre's enchantment with Isabel and his disillusionment with his father and his life are profound, and he gives up everything to take care of her. This break with family and community leaves him at the fringes of society, destitute. He rails against "that doctrine which the world actually and eternally practices, of giving unto him who already hath more than enough, still more of that superfluous article, and taking away from him who hath nothing at all, even that which he hath" (p. 262).

Peter was similarly preoccupied with issues of meaning and morality. He was a refined and sensitive young man of twenty-something who had sought treatment because of a fear that he was losing his mind. He said he had become so adept at imagining himself in the context of the character he was creating in his mind that he sometimes became lost in it. Peter came from a household in which both parents had embraced fundamentalist religion as a way of dealing—or not dealing, according to their children—with the traumas in their own lives. Family life centered on the church, and the house was the center of a youth fellowship group that the father fostered. Peter, however, rather than feeling comforted within this circle, felt impossibly constrained, isolated and alone. He recalled a strong sense of "spirituality permeating the house and family." From early on, he could recall being absorbed by eternal questions such as "the strangeness of death, the mystery of the unknown."

He describes himself as shy and impressionable, a "late-bloomer. It affected my self-confidence, especially about my appearance or in sports. I felt like a small twig. I carried that through high school. I just kept to myself, doing what was needed to keep my parents happy and spending time in my room." By middle school, he was struggling with depression, wishing he could be more like his peers but feeling alienated because of the stringent demands entailed by his role in the family ministry. In high school, he found himself drawn toward music and the arts. "I saw a way that art could redeem—salvation through art."

Increasingly he felt torn by the dichotomy between the life that had been chosen for him and the one he felt drawn to. "I questioned my beliefs in religion," he said, "but that was all buried. . . . There was a comfort in the assurance of going to heaven, holiness." He read the bible avidly and assiduously in an unsuccessful attempt to relieve his increasing distress. His self-hatred grew. In his senior year, he began to focus more on art. "I was more alienated from my family and more worried. The depression physically manifested itself in worry about letting my family and God down. When I stopped the ministry, they said 'It's sad to see you choose death over life.' Because I was brainwashed, I had a hard time overcoming that. I still struggle with it."

Increasingly, Peter turned to dark voices in poetry and music, their melancholy resonating with his own. This was a new type of home, one that seemed to nourish his soul while further undermining his precarious place in his family. So unstable was his equilibrium that the idea of really taking a stand felt like a kind of death: "I started to become more who I am today and saw how hard it was—to be the black sheep of the family—

like coming out as this non-Christian, and I couldn't really do it. I started to feel an inner tug in another direction. I started to follow that at all costs. I was skipping school a lot—it didn't affect my grades. I worked out a system."

Trying to tolerate the tension between these two worlds took a toll. "I started to see different meanings behind certain scriptures. It was a different version but still the God I had grown up with. As though he had pulled me to think more independently. There was a sort of peace. It was fun. I was having fun. I felt that it wasn't wrong." As his new identity grew, however, the tensions increased. "I was still haunted by eighteen years of orthodox Christian beliefs. It was an intoxicating sense of freedom that would wear off, but for that year, I was really enjoying sort of being someone else. I still led Young Life through the first year of college. I was very confused but I felt like I still had commitments. I was living in two different worlds." What little confidence he had faded, and he found himself battling increasingly with depression. "The tide would go in; the tide would go out; it was easiest to play that role."

Much like Pierre, Peter felt a profound affinity with the poor and downtrodden, such that he felt enriched by public service. "I worked at a crossover clinic, doing janitorial work. I cleaned up bloody rags. It was an outreach clinic for the poor. It was a good experience. I had a really good attitude. It was worth having shown part of myself to my parents. You learn a lot that anyone learns being a servant anywhere but it wasn't life-changing to me. I've never had trouble seeing the reward in service like that. Those kinds of acts come kind of naturally to me."

"The one scripture I held onto and struggled with—it's from Paul—'*my preachings were not with words but with demonstrations of the spirit's power*.' That was the only scripture I took with me when I left Christianity. There was always a struggle—a tug of war between the God I felt calling me away from religion, and the God that had been hammered into my being. Psychologically, there wasn't a clear break—and in many ways I still wrestle with many of the questions I had in childhood and adolescence regarding the great sort of 'silence of God.' The spiritual search consumed me in everything I did."

Unable to commit to the life his parents wanted for him or to break free from them, he went to the college they chose, but soon felt suicidal and returned home. He then led the ministry for seven or eight months but the tensions between conflicting identities and moral values became intolerable. "After enlisting into that army, I had a mental breakdown," he says. "I was put in charge of my own high school; I had three people working under me. It wore me down and made me weak. I had been taught to follow God's plan. It was hard to be certain in the face of God's silence. It may be the devil calling."

"I quit. There were four months of night terrors—very real experiences with demons, around sleep. They were terrifying. I didn't know how to interpret it. I was feeling for the first time a real and tangible power from the darker side. I googled it and decided it wasn't a real battle for my soul."

Peter's family values had afforded him a guide to the moral life within particular constraints but left him with no way of defining his own path and also keeping within the proscribed and tremendously constraining system of paternal authority. His depression continued to worsen and he felt that he had no mental space at home to begin to build an internal world that was truly his own. He tried therapy but the therapist who seemed to understand him suddenly died and he did not have the heart or the hope to try again. Although he had friends, he felt as though they wanted something from him that he could not give. There was nowhere, aside from the internal world of his imaginings, where he could be the focus of interest or inquiry. Without a responsive other, however, the isolation was deadly. Increasingly remote, he listened to music that was resonant with his sadness, and at times felt he was going mad. "There had been trials by fire in the church. This felt more like the ashes of that fire, blowing in the wind. I didn't have enough energy to make a pilgrimage to a new place in my soul." After a particularly bad night when he felt dangerously suicidal, he left for New England, the home of the "fathers" he had found in literature.

Although getting away from home was helpful in terms of letting go of the depression, anger, guilt, and shame that had been festering, the underlying distress remained. "Ever since middle school, there's been a noise in my head," said Peter. "It's been gradually getting turned up louder and louder. During those two years, it was so loud, I didn't do much. I started to feel I was losing my mind. I wasn't sleeping much." He tried desperately to make sense of the impasse in which he found himself but only became further lost. "I tried to trace everything back—to see where it went wrong—thinking I could overcome the questions in religion I had. I would think about death, eternity, rebirth—further and further down that rabbit hole—and never really come out."

Like Pierre, Peter was born into an entitlement that wore thin. As he began to look at life through other lenses, he recognized a hypocrisy in his father and his father's faith, and his own faith broke down. His identity was so firmly lodged in the father's world that he was left floundering, though the allegiance to moral principles he had learned in his family held fast. That allegiance helped Peter to find new father figures in the American Renaissance writers, such as Emerson and Thoreau, who represented to him a different religion, a vision of goodness and morality that was unlike that of his own father.

He left home, feeling as though he could not survive in his father's home, finding a series of alternative fathers, both through literature and in the professors who taught it. He audited classes and was apparently compelling enough that the professors took him under their wings and even into their homes. The promise of Pierre seemed also present in the promise of this intense, engaged, and oddly engaging young man who, like Pierre, began to write as a means for self-definition and, in some ways, survival. For each of these young men, the writing they turned to in the hope of resolving the moral questions with which they were faced further embroiled them in the life questions that seemed to have no answer and led them deeper and deeper into a terrible void of dark despair. Peter told me that his writings had become a world he could escape into, a world in which he "has no name." This "having no name" was a way of sloughing off the ill-fitting Name of the Father but also revealed him as unformed and nameless. Like Pierre, he became increasingly unable to survive in the world or even to attend to his basic needs.

When Peter entered treatment, after another spike in suicidality that, once again, frightened him, he was pleased to leave behind his family and close the door on the demands he experienced in their presence. "I cannot be the person they want me to be," he said. He recognized that intensive treatment might help him to work through the terrible state he had come to, but his relief at not having to face his family soon gave way to distress, as he came up against issues of conscience in relation to asking his parents for money for his treatment when he did not want to have anything to do with them. "How do I say 'I hate you. Please pay for this'?" he asked.

Peter's treatment was marked by such extreme changes in mood and demeanor that I was never entirely sure who I would encounter as our hour approached. At one point, he responded to my greeting by saying that he was no longer Peter and could not be called by that name. Peter was dead, he told me. He seemed hyper-alert but not quite present, oddly manic, as he told me that he had decided to leave treatment as a way of completely severing his ties to his family. He said, "I'm fine. I'm so grateful for this opportunity. I was able to do what I needed to do here; I'm a new person; the old Peter is dead." As he spoke of this rebirth he was experiencing, it was as though he had shed his name—and his past—like an old unwanted skin. It seemed as though part of him was already gone, as though he had to kill off the part of himself that was connected to his family in order to survive.

Peter's dilemma was familiar to me. I can remember young adulthood being a time of such upheaval that my internal and external selves at times did not seem to fit together at all. Peter seemed to sense this resonance. On one occasion, he looked at me pointedly and said, "You are like me." In the silence that followed, I puzzled over the possible meanings of that remark. Although I sensed that it was in some ways true, something he had registered in having taken in my habits of speech and, through his gaze, the contents of my bookshelves and the art upon my walls, it also seemed that there were many layers to that remark. Because the remark seemed to be both true and untrue, it seemed worthwhile to try to unpack the layers rather than allowing the confusion to persist through my silence. We were often caught in such moments, in which there was a palimpsest of meanings that were in danger of passing by unexplored if we were not sufficiently alert to the danger of such inattention. At such times, our shared ability to wander inward introspectively could be a hazard if we could not then stumble upon the silence and bring forward something of what we were thinking.

Peter's ambivalence, his desire to speak and not speak, was a force to be reckoned with throughout our time together. This ambivalence drove his distress and also the direction of his various attempts to resolve his intense sense of urgency. Caught between his desires for independence and his utter dependence on his parents, and the financial limits that would require him to leave his treatment that has carried the hope of discovering himself sufficiently to truly stand on his own, Peter's calm turned once again to distress and agitation. He began to talk obliquely about suicide and I recalled his reference to using talk of suicide as a flag to get his father's attention. My sense was that the opportunity that had opened up within our work was closing down and that without that space he was once again finding it difficult to use his mind. Although there was the appearance of cogent speech, it circled around and never quite came to a point. His speech seemed more like a display than a conversation and he seemed to stumble over meanings that could not be articulated or even fully considered.

Having the reliability of our four times weekly psychotherapy meetings helped Peter to recover his capacities for reflection, and he began to talk about his hopes and wishes and to plan for the future. He wondered how to talk to his parents about who he is and what he wants so that he might be able to live with them without such terrible tension. Although there was more of a sense that this might be a possible goal, he was not able to reliably believe in that possibility. It continued to be difficult to imagine how he might straddle the world that called to him and the world of his childhood. He kept trying to build a bridge but the ground remained unsteady. In speaking of trying to communicate to his parents his desire to find another way of serving god, Peter alluded to universal truths and acknowledged that people might think he is crazy for "having a mission." Although he seemed more present, there was an edge of desperation and a sense that he was constructing himself and his speech to fit the demands of the moment. Where, I wondered, is there room for Peter?

Peter worked diligently, trying to stay on the high side of his good intentions, but that very effort left him distanced from his internal self. His resolve to go home and have a better experience strengthened, and he faced his upcoming case conference with a determination that seemed partly bred of desperation. In line with my own framing of his situation, which had been about development gone awry, he said that he didn't think that he was fucked up, rather that it was more like a watermark, that there were particularities about him that characterize him and make him himself.

Peter's openness to what might be offered, along with his desperation, convinced him to try an antipsychotic medication in an attempt to help relieve his agitation. It made him feel intolerably restless and agitated, however, and he quickly discontinued it. He continued to worry about what to say to his parents, talking in such generalities that it was difficult to follow him. When he was able to be more specific, the manic edge was more pronounced, as in his idea of just wanting his own apartment so that he could do intensive therapy and work on the writing he hoped would reveal the truth and perhaps save others. I suggested that he might begin by telling his parents what he wants, to help focus the conversation.

As Peter began to seem more overtly psychotic, I asked about the other world he alluded to, whether it was a constant for him. He said that it was; that he spent a lot of time there but that it was hard to describe. I was trying to get a picture of this world in my mind, and asked about the landscape. He replied that it wasn't so much a landscape but a way of seeing things. He then described this world more in terms of his *relationship* to it rather than the world being different, more a way of being in the world than another reality per se. In that sense, what had seemed psychotic then seemed to be Peter's way of finding a spiritual path that was his own rather than one imposed on him by his father or by the religion of his childhood. He felt propelled by the need to define his own path and spoke of his desire to communicate to his parents his sense that the transcendentalists had not gone far enough, and also of his hope to better communicate those values in his own writing. He hoped that his parents might understand his goals because they, too, were spiritual people.

At that point, Peter was able to recognize that this treatment had provided the vehicle for a major change in him. He spoke of feeling not *re*-born but born for the first time, saying that he wasn't sure how it happened, that it seemed like a gradual process. His depiction was so at odds with my own experience that it gave me pause. When I said that it seemed more explosive to me, that it had been quite turbulent, he smiled and agreed.

Pater was also able to recognize that he really didn't hate his parents and to look forward to talking with them. As he thought back, he could recall sitting in my office on his first day and not being able to look at them, but now could see that his aversion had more to do with the difficulties he was encountering in his relationship to them. I said that he seemed to experience them as oppressive forces when he first came but increasingly felt able to express his own ideas and talk with them as adults. This interpretation seemed relieving to Peter and helped him to go into the family meeting with greater calm. That calm enabled the family to have a conversation in which each person could listen respectfully to the others. Peter was initially relieved and hopeful after talking with his parents but then, as he faced discharge, he felt increasingly frustrated and uncertain. He once again began to pivot between extremes, promising his parents, for example, to "tell them everything." I suggested that it might be important to agree to try to be honest in what he *does* say without promising to say everything, that he would likely need some room for privacy. His identity was still porous enough that the boundaries between self and other could become difficult to distinguish or sustain.

As the case conference approached, he began to worry about what he would say about himself and his desires, vacillating between wanting something and wanting nothing. He spoke of wanting to paint his face in war paint; wanting to be able to be himself; being accustomed to putting on a front but then feeling like two people. In counterpoint, I spoke of the importance of being able to ask for space when he needs it rather than by flagging alarm as he had done in the past, as with talk of suicide.

Peter's concern over "going crazy," over losing his mind as he tried to find it, and over who he might or might not be able to trust in this process was familiar to me. I can recall as a young adult my own wariness of the various health-care professionals who seemed to locate me in ways that demeaned or diminished me, and to stand in the way of my own developmental strivings, inchoate as they might have been. Because of this, central to my clinical work is a profound respect for the authority of the individual with regard to his own desires and motivations, and also to the logic of his perceptions and conclusions. This type of stance can leave the clinician adrift in a world in which certainty can be valued over sensibilities, and yet, it may be a prerequisite for creating a space in which an individual can obtain insight into his own troubles.

Although I am not a Lacanian, I see in that heritage the type of respect for what is at stake that is likely the pivotal underpinning of good clinical work, a stance that our patients at times recognize. Perhaps most important to have in mind has been Lacan's (1977f) idea of the *Subject caught by the desire of the Other.* Lacan sees us lost before we have begun, arriving into a world in which ideas about us precede our entry. We internalize the world as it is given, accommodating to these demands while also rebelling against them. Many of our patients come to us with little sense of internal desire or agency. "What I want" tends to be "what I have learned to want," which makes it important to try to locate each patient in relation to his desires, rather than losing him behind his (or my) ideas of what is or should be wanted. With Peter, this was a salient challenge, how to locate him in relation to an internal chaos that could override him in various directions, whether from his own scripting of his character or from his reversions to the dark side, to once again identify with the persona he believed his parents wanted him to become, within which confinement no life had been possible.

From a Lacanian perspective, we become lost in relation to that desire of the Other that holds the possibility of an unlimited Jouissance. The challenge is to accept the inevitability of lack—of limit—and to recognize and articulate our own particular desire. From this perspective, I try to avoid being caricatured as the One who Knows in some absolute sense, so that I might invite the patient to become the Subject of the inquiry, to literally take his rightful place as the subject of his own experience. I take the position that I have no way of working with a patient unless there is something that he wants to work on. The work, then, can focus around locating a desire that is truly one's own.

When working with someone who struggles with psychosis, it is particularly important to be able to recognize the sinthome—the problem in context—so that we can respect what is being offered while also breaking into what are often concrete and universal presumptions of meaning. In the encounter between one mind and another, there is the possibility of two minds meeting, and recognizing both sameness and difference. This recognition is the ground on which reflective function and resilience are built. If we think of psychosis in terms of an inability to engage with another's mind and keep one's own, the working through of this dilemma is critical to any legitimate developmental process that might take place.

Such are the lessons of psychoanalysis. At best, we are blind companions on a journey, depending on our patients to show us the way. With Peter, being willing to hear his story as he tells it, to allow the reverberations to echo, and to allow the vantage point to change radically without demanding cogency or linearity, remaining as present as I could through it all, helped Peter to know he was not entirely alone, and also helped him to have faith in my faith in him and in what the future might hold.

In psychosis, the symptom is like a dream, concrete in the experience but beautifully layered underneath. If we listen to Peter's story, we hear that the demand imposed by the Name of the Father, for him, was deadly. He needed to find someone who could recognize *his* watermark—the essential pattern of his being—his signature within the knot in which he had become embroiled, a watermark through which he might be recognized sufficiently to call himself into being.

Peter's perspective could shift so radically that he was not able, at times, to know much of anything. Knowing that I could hold the bits without losing any, or foreclosing on some, helped him to accept the diagnosis I eventually offered. Rather than naming his experience as a psychotic process, I chose to call it an identity crisis. In so doing, I took a stand with both Peter and his family, endorsing the importance for Peter of having time and resources to find his way through this crisis, while having a psychoanalytic interpreter to accompany him on that journey. In this way, I hope he will be able to build his sense of his own ideas, his own feelings, and his own mind, in relation to others that may be similar and different in important ways. Peter did return home and, predictably, was once again driven mad within the confines of the family in which he still felt trapped. This time, however, he had my diagnosis and prescription in hand, and called me as a way of establishing once again a conceptual anchor and obtaining a referral to a psychoanalyst in another location who I believed could offer him the type of 'home' he needed in order to re-envision himself.

Within such a home, retreats to safety are no longer quite so devastating because they are not so absolutely private. They can be talked about within the safety of a relationship that may be good enough to negotiate some of the developmental passages that could not be taken up within the confines of his family of origin. Within such a home, hope can be found.

NOTE

1. Portions of this chapter are taken from the article "Working at the Edge: Meaning, Identity, and Idiosyncracy," *Contemporary Psychoanalysis* vol. 50, no. 4 (2014): 548–570.

THIRTEEN

Identity Derailed

The Echo Maker

"In tragic life, God wot,
No villain need be!
Passions spin the plot;
We are betrayed by what is false within."

—George Meredith

In *The Echo Maker,* Richard Powers (2006) explores the farthest reaches of mind and meaning, deconstructing aspects of identity through the character of Mark Schluter. Mark sustains a traumatic brain injury in a near-fatal automobile accident and his sister reluctantly returns to their hometown to be by his side. When he emerges from a protracted coma, Mark recognizes his sister's face but not her person, and comes to believe that she must be an imposter. Distressed by her brother's failure to recognize her, Karin finds an expert who is famous for his studies of rare brain disorders. Dr. Weber identifies the problem as Capgras Syndrome, a rare disease in which the visual and emotional recognition of the face are separated.

Powers offers us two separate stories, each with their own layers of complexity, that threaten to entwine. We encounter Mark's story in juxtaposition to the story of the spring migration of the sandhill cranes.

> In fact, "echo maker" is the Ojibwa-Anishinabe name for the sandhill crane. My obsession with the primitive processes that underpin cognition began when I discovered these birds. . . . I looked out into a barren field along the side of Interstate 80 and saw this carpet of birds, three feet tall, spreading in all directions. I thought I was hallucinating from highway hypnosis, and I almost drove off the road.

> The sight was absolutely thrilling, partly because I didn't know what I was looking at and partly because the gathering was just so primordial. They really did look like some prehistoric remnant, something absolutely indifferent to human time. (Powers, 2007)

Because the two stories are not explicitly linked, they loom upon the reader, threatening to collide. In this novel, the protagonist's own reality has been literally shattered, creating a duality from what is usually experienced as one. The split in the story line is echoed in the split within the mind of the main character. In this way, Powers invites us to consider two disparate strands of signification that speak both singly and collectively toward a larger meaning that can be intuited though it is never entirely revealed. This enigma would seem to be a model of the life journey, as we struggle to put the pieces together into a story through which both sense and meaning can be achieved. Mark's injury leaves him with a visual memory for faces but no emotional connection with the person behind that visage. Sensing the gap, he assumes that the lack is in the other, that this woman who looks like his sister must be an imposter. His sister, who had only reluctantly come to be by his side, finds herself unsettled by her brother's failure to recognize her. As the novel progresses, we begin to discern the sense beyond the non-sense in Mark's accusation.

On the one hand, this novel can be read as an interesting depiction of a rare syndrome or, on another, as a mystery novel. For my purposes here, I will focus on the duality pointed to between what is presented and what may be revealed, between the mask we present to the world and the truths that may be hidden even from ourselves. That type of duality became a terrible gap that "Will" finally fell through in young adulthood. Will had been a bright child in a high-achieving family, who had been unable to meet many of the developmental challenges with which he was faced. His mother had tried to understand and accommodate to his needs but none of her efforts had ever really been effective in either making the difficulties more apparent or helping to relieve them. Her efforts had become increasingly protective, leaving Will, in turn, increasingly unable to meet life's challenges himself. Instead, he had learned to hide his frustration, distress, and shame behind an affable exterior that his family at times found maddening, as he failed to meet very basic expectations regarding managing his living environment or financial affairs. Fast forward to his early thirties, Will was still dependent on his family for survival and on his mother for assistance in accommodating to the minimal expectations still in place for this young man who had finished college but whose addiction to amphetamines had left him unable to sustain employment.

When I first met Will, he had come to an impasse that occurred between himself and his family. He had asked them for assistance when his life began to fall off the cliff but then there had been a terrible collision between his own ideas of what "help" might mean versus those of his parents, which also revealed that they did not see him as he had imagined they might. His conclusion, at the time, was that he had been terribly lied to, a type of twilight truth that, similar to Mark's position with his sister, spoke quite lucidly at the level of metaphor about the difficulties at the core of the familial relationships. His parents literally did not recognize him as a legitimate agent in his own right, and ignored his stated requests rather than addressing them. They then proceeded to manage his problems in their own ways, in direct opposition to their son's stated desires.

Will's subsequent collapse, although terrible and painful, also opened up the opportunity for him to move beyond the impasse in which he had been caught by his inability to advocate for his own perceived needs. Intensive psychoanalytic psychotherapy afforded him a process through which he was able to discover for himself how to read what was offered by others. First, however, he had to learn to recognize and make sense of his own internal affective signals, signals that somehow had not been sufficiently registered and regulated in the early parent child relationship. Oddly similar to Mark in *The Echo Maker,* for Will, a face was something that could be looked *at* but could not be looked into, the type of terrible dilemma pointed to by Winnicott (1971) and Hesse and Main (1990) in their depictions of child development gone awry.

Will's affable style was initially engaging to those around him but soon wore thin because of the lack of depth or follow-through. What seemed like a pleasant exterior actually masked his utter fear of encountering demands he was not able to meet. Initially, the mask held sway but as we continued to work together, Will could let me see that he was aware of the mask and was troubled by it. He had little idea of what might lie underneath that mask, aside from a terrible chasm of darkness that he feared falling into. His feelings were largely undifferentiated, which left him confused and frightened by the strong feelings he encountered within. It took some time for Will to recognize his anger, in particular, because of his fear that if he got too close to this anger it would overpower and engulf him. It was as though if he were angry, that would be all he could be, an angry, hateful, 'bad' person with no further possibility. It took some time for him to be able to entertain the idea that he might be able to be angry and have other feelings as well.

When we first started working together, Will had no real language for his feelings, which were not easily or clearly distinguishable from one another. Feeling, itself, seemed dangerous. Early on, when I would ask Will what he thought or felt about something, he would turn the question back on me. "What do *you* think?" he would inquire. It was hard for him to know how he felt or to imagine himself as a legitimate source of inquiry. Soon, he realized that I was most interested in his experience and did not want mine to erase or overpower his own. At that point, he would turn to me to inquire as to what I thought. "I'm just asking you your *opinion*," he would say, reserving some space for the possibility that he might have his own ideas and feelings.

Over the course of several years of four times weekly sessions, I began to realize that what had been occurring over time was the development of reflective function. I had been studying metacognitive function for a research project, and so the relevant parameters were salient in my mind. Such was the pace of development that it was only in retrospect that I could appreciate that Will had begun to recognize, first his own thoughts and feelings, and then those of others. Increasingly, then, he was able to distinguish between the two, and to recognize that there was not necessarily a right way to think or feel but rather differences in character, preference, and values. His ability to sustain relationships in spite of conflict was enhanced and he was increasingly able to speak up regarding his own opinion rather than fearing that he would be ridiculed, humiliated, or proven wrong.

In their studies of metacognition, Lysaker and his colleagues (Dimaggio et al., 2007; Lysaker et al., 2014) have found that, much as Mark was unable to have a sense of the emotional sensibilities of his sister, deficits in emotional recognition are linked to psychotic spectrum disorders and also to personality disorders. The inability to "read" others is a serious handicap, making it difficult for the individual to find his or her way into the social world (notably, Capgras Syndrome is also linked with psychotic disorders). From this perspective, I could begin to make better sense of something that had eluded me in my early work with Will, during which time it had been difficult to understand where, precisely, the trouble lay.

Being able to discern emotional meanings is crucial in being able to develop sound and resilient relations with others. Children with deficits in these areas often encounter interpersonal difficulties, which can lead to bullying and marginalization in childhood (Charles, 2013). Good peer relationships are so crucial to the development of self-esteem and identity formation that marginalization of this sort has also been linked with the development of severe and chronic emotional and social difficulties in later life. Although Will had been well-liked, his development had been tinged by the recurrent shame he experienced in relation to repeated failures. Without the type of mastery experiences that lead to persistence under duress, Will learned to give up and avoid challenges that arose. His mask had come to hide the underlying deficits all too well, and he had been unable even to consider that he might move beyond them until he entered into intensive psychoanalytic treatment and began to face the difficulties underneath.

Lysaker and his colleagues (2014) have found that difficulties in emotional recognition can be linked to metacognitive difficulties in terms of the capacity to form complex, coherent representations of self and others.

These difficulties then impede social, emotional and self-development. When I encountered Will in adulthood, he had largely failed to accomplish these primary developmental tasks. Much like Mark in *The Echo Maker*, others' faces did not reveal much about their internal worlds or experience. The false self he had developed left him similarly impenetrable to others. Although he was able to sustain engagement one on one, he tended to find social groups either entertaining or boring, and he became largely mute in treatment groups that required active personal engagement. His silence began to make others uncomfortable, inviting misreadings of his feelings and intentions that became increasingly hostile. As we discussed ways in which his silence was becoming untenable, Will struggled to make his voice heard and to tolerate discrepancies between his perceptions and ideas, and those of others. No longer was there one right way or idea but rather there could be collisions of subjectivities and desire that could be understood in terms of the particularities one could discern in the people involved.

Perhaps most important, Will began to be able to consider a question that could not even be thought about when we first met regarding his own desires. The idea of a future had seemed so remote that he had not even dared to imagine it. We could talk about how his history of repeated failures had left him unable to imagine mastery, making hope a terrible trap to be avoided at all costs. As time went by, however, he could begin to think about the future and imagine what he would and would not like in that future, what he would need in order to feel fulfilled, what types of environments might or might not be sustaining, what resources might be needed. Crucial to those considerations was Will's growing ability to attend to his own needs and well-being. Increasingly, he learned to catch himself in familiar patterns and think things through for himself, and to avoid overriding his own needs by deferring to the other.

Will's growing ability to track his needs and feelings and the ways in which they were or were not being met in a given relationship helped to safeguard important relationships and to let go of relationships that were not sufficiently satisfying. Over time, Will was able to build strong attachments to people that he was able to sustain even through conflict, something that had been impossible when we first met, when he would withdraw and feel nothing at the first sign of disappointment. At that point, relationships were no longer solely driven by the other's needs and demands. Will could say yes and he could say no, and could make decisions about how much and when. He was even been able to make his peace with his parents. Even though he was still angry and recognized their failings, he could also recognize their limits and their good intentions. As he became increasingly able to attend to these subtleties in their engagement, he could also locate himself caught in similar relationships in which there might be more that is promised than could be delivered. He could recognize ways in which disappointments in current relationships could be a function of the other person's current constraints, much as his mother often had been constrained by her own emotional burdens precisely at the times when he had needed her most. Through his ability to recognize these types of discrepancies between a person's desire and their ability to follow through, and between love and the ability to know another person's heart, mind, or desire, Will could better navigate the at-times difficult terrain of personal relationships.

Through my work with Will, I was able to recognize ways in which developmental failures can become self-perpetuating tropes that drive further failure and despair. I also learned a great deal about resilience, a resilience that is built through the development of the reflective functions that enable us to make sense of self and world, thereby helping us to adapt to changing circumstances and the challenges that life brings. This, I think, is what psychoanalysis builds, the very basic capacities on which resilience and reflective function depend.

Turning back to the novel, Mark's traumatic accident cuts the tie between his cognitive registration of a familiar visage and his emotional connection to the person the face represents. That disconnection can be seen to parallel the disconnection that occurs for children when their parents are too caught up in unresolved mourning to be able to be reliably present for the child. As Winnicott (1971) notes, it is a terrible thing when the child cannot find him or herself in the parent's face. When a face can only be looked at but cannot be looked into, we cannot find ourselves reflected there. There is no experience of the human connection, no way of making sense of feelings in relation to another living being.

The attachment literature has pointed to the particular difficulties of the child whose parents are largely available but who become preoccupied by their own unresolved grief, such that they are unreliably available (Main and Hesse, 1990). That type of unpredictable reinforcement is particularly frustrating. For Will, his mother's love and devotion, which he could sense, was countered by her inability to truly assist him in meeting many of the developmental challenges with which he was faced. Rather, her well-intentioned efforts merely further obscured and overrode his own independent efforts. Similarly, his father had not been able to help the son to move beyond the developmental impasse he encountered, making him unavailable as a source for a positive identification. Much like Mark in the novel, there was no way to 'become a man' directly through his own actions or in his father's eyes. Thus, the parents' care was countered by their inability to sufficiently recognize his needs, as he experienced them. Unable to help him find ways to meet them and to work effectively with life challenges, their efforts served to further frustrate and debilitate him, confirming for Will his utter insufficiency. In many ways, he encountered with each parent a face that could not be looked into because the relationship had become a pseudo relationship in which each accommodated to the limits of the other without being able to acknowledge and work with those limits. In spite of the failures, comfort could be found during times of strain, which had offered emotional sustenance but at a high price in terms of self-development.

That comfort was broken into at the point where he desperately needed his parents' assistance. Their ideas about what was needed were in direct opposition to his own, such that the assistance they provided was offered in relation to the son in their minds rather than in relation to Will's needs as he experienced and expressed them. The parents' failure to confront that gap left him in a terrible chasm, cut off from his primary support, which had been revealed as utterly lacking. The father offered only judgment, whereas the mother's own distress at that particular point in time had made her angry at the increased demands made by her adult son, enabling her to ignore him while ostensibly helping him. That empty care, experientially, seems to have been functionally similar to Mark's experience of his sister's emptiness, an emptiness that could be traced to a brain injury but, at a deeper level, likely pointed to an emptiness in the relationship itself.

Similarly, it had been easy for Will's parents to discount his desires because they did not take him seriously as an active agent, an individual subject with his own needs and desires separate from their own. His failure to become the child they had hoped he might be left him seemingly empty to them in spite of their ostensible care. It is easy for subtleties of meaning to hide behind appearances. The sense of love and intention of care can obscure an inattentiveness that can make that care deadly for the dependent person because of the lack that is hidden. This type of disrespect also happens in the consulting room, when the clinician's limits are projected onto the patient. Most clinicians have encountered, in their consulting rooms, refugees from that type of impossible therapy relationship that can prove so deadly. There is no substitute for the clinician's integrity, particularly when it comes to being able to recognize and work with our own failings in relation to the person who comes to us for something we may not be able to offer in spite of our best intentions. There is no substitute for recognizing the other as other and trying to listen across that gap and develop a sense of that person's own unique needs, desires, and limits.

In my work with Will, the line between what he desired or needed versus what he thought should have value was never quite clear. That confusion made me very intent on trying to track his feelings as they manifested themselves in speech, behavior, dreams or symptoms. I tried to be very transparent regarding my own thinking and how I was making meaning from his past and current experience, trying to invite him to pay closer attention to his own internal world and take himself more seriously. His lack of faith in himself made him very susceptible to the authority of others, even when he bristled against that type of control. In this regard, it became important to distinguish between good intentions and impact, and also to be able to consider to what extent authority was real or misplaced. He began to be better able to reflect on ways in which intention may or may not be sufficient to sustain a relationship or, to the contrary, may become a trap that held him captive in relationships that were utterly unsatisfying and at times even destructive. We learned to recognize that it was precisely the hook he felt to the empty relationship that could tell him something profound about his early experiences in his family, as he desperately tried to manage the anger that was called forth in him by the allure of the empty promise. Increasingly, we could recognize that his symptoms and his dreams pointed to something important, illuminating crucial meanings that he was trying to reveal to himself.

In *The Echo Maker*, the sub plot tells the story of the migration of sandhill cranes, whose magnificent journey is being obstructed by a civilization that threatens to break into the miracle of that migration, a migration embedded in a history that is carried across the generations with no words, only an underlying language encoded in the body. In Powers' (2006) tale, this utter knowing that comes from being present in one's being is contrasted with the characters who cannot be known because they are not sufficiently centered within themselves to be locatable beyond whatever façade they present. Thus, Karin, who has fought to be recognized by her brother, eventually concedes defeat in what she comes to accept as a false enterprise, as she comes to an appreciation of

> why her brother stopped recognizing her. Nothing to recognize. She has twisted herself past recognition. One small deceit laid on another, until even she can't say where she stands or what she's working for. . . . She is nothing. No one. Worse than no one. Blank at the core. (p. 407)

In this novel, there is a crisis during which pretense collapses and there is the possibility of encountering a truth beyond what had been known previously. There is something in Mark's utter lack of guile in the wake of his injury that touches those he encounters, but it is ultimately in the characters' encounters with the cranes that their illusions falter and become empty and meaningless, obstructing life rather than supporting it. Mark's intuition that there is something in the cranes of which he is in dire need can be seen as an acknowledgement that, when we move too far from our roots in nature, we threaten both the planet and the quality of our life on it. Ironically, we move away from precisely what has most value, something that is more visible in the dance of the cranes than in the engagements between human beings.

In crisis there is opportunity but, as occurs too often in life, there is a narrow margin for this type of deep and profound meeting, and Karin discovers her own truth too late to save the relationship that had been offered. She had hidden all too well behind her own mask, leaving her lover to collide terribly with the truths that she had finally faced too late to afford the possibility of repair. Even with her brother, she finds herself too late to meet him in the place where he had been. He has "recovered" sufficiently to be out of reach, once again. Even if they can find one another, she recognizes that soon enough "her brother will be gone again, or his sister will, some place the other won't be able to follow. But for a little while, now, they know each other, because of their time away" (p. 447).

Much like Karin and Mark, Will and his brother took time away from one another, something Will insisted on as he came to realize how invisible he had become within his family, and how easily he lost himself further in their presence. He waited until he felt that he knew himself sufficiently to be able to survive the encounter with a family member before beginning to take them on slowly, one at a time. In our initial family meeting, when he first entered treatment, we had seen the care and concern but also the profound difficulty family members encountered in trying to see past their ideas about one another. It was as though the caricatures had become so firmly ensconced that there was no room to encounter growth or difference. Given the ways in which Will's desires and preferences had been misread by his family as indicating only a hostile lack of interest in other people's needs and feelings, it was difficult for Will to face his own aggression without feeling as though his family was utterly correct, that that was all he was. From that perspective, his own desire disappeared under the perceived reactivity to the other's desire. There was no Will to be discovered, which helped to make sense of his tendency to retreat to a neutral corner where only his affability might be revealed.

Collaborating with Will in a retelling of his life story, such that we could recognize his increasing frustration at the repeated failures he encountered, helped Will to recognize his own retreat. Being able to find himself in a story in which, in spite of his intellectual potential and his parents' earnest efforts, mastery had eluded him, helped him to think of himself not as a failure but rather as someone whose ideas about himself had been painfully marked by those failures. In *this* story, we could consider his strengths and also his weaknesses, and think about what types of supports he might need in order to meet some of the life challenges he had been avoiding. One factor that came through quite pointedly was his reactivity to being treated like an object, as had occurred all too often in his family. Because of that history, encouragement was easily experienced as pushing and overriding his nascent autonomy and desire, and could close down those capacities. Together, we worked to help those who believed he needed pushing to recognize that he actually fared much better when left to his own devices. From that position, he could invite assistance when he needed it and could also obtain recognition for the accomplishments he had managed in his own way, in his own time.

Will's family missed him and were grateful when he began, slowly, to let them back into his life. They learned to listen to him rather than overriding him by turning to the 'authorities' for information and, as they listened, they began to get to know him and to respect the person he was becoming. That respect had been something Will had not truly imagined he could obtain but, as his family began to recognize his strengths, he was able increasingly to build on those strengths and to demand respect in his other relationships as well, and to speak up about his own particular needs, desires, values and interests.

In a family in which intellect had been prized over and above and even to the exclusion of emotion, the anger that had been a sign of Will's early frustrations became a marker, not of his distress but rather of an ostensible evil that lurked inside him. In adulthood, he was unable to recognize or tolerate any strong emotion, softening it with substances. At the point where his anger at his mother became undeniable, he retreated into what was largely a self-induced coma and did not emerge until he came upon the possibility of a treatment through which he might make sense of the mysteries that had eluded him. He emerged ready to begin work. At that point in time, however, deep feeling signified anger, which signified badness, an utter and unrelievable black chasm that threatened to overtake him utterly.

Much as the darkness held the keys to the story through which we were able to make sense of Will and his experience, in *The Echo Maker*, the story of the sandhill cranes confront us with something archaic in living beings that holds our prehistory. The cranes stand for the undeniability of the meanings held in our bodies, for the importance of recognizing and cherishing those underlying meanings that hold some of the most primary significations regarding what it means to be human, and what it means to be a living being among other living beings, dependent on a fragile and precious ecology. Mark intuitively senses that there is a meaning inside him that he does not have access to. In his least rational moments, he has access to truths he cannot encounter through his rational mind. Although he leaves himself a message, he cannot decode it from the other side. His sister discovers the note, which had appeared as if by magic. "No one could tell her when it had appeared. Some messenger had slipped into the room unseen, even while Karin was shut out. The writing was spidery, ethereal; immigrant scrawl from a century ago" (p. 10).

In the story, we move back and forth between the humans who ostensibly can parse the story of their lives and the cranes who ostensibly cannot. We encounter the young bird whose father is shattered by bullets, then

> locates his mother. He hears her calling, half a mile off, circling traumatized. They wait two more days, searching, sounding some ghost of the

> unison call. Nothing can tell them; no way they can know. There is only circling and calling, waiting, a kind of religion, for the dead one to show. When he doesn't, there is only yesterday, last year, the sixty million years before that, the route itself, the blind, self-organizing return. (p. 278)

Although the cranes no longer stop in that place, there is still the memory of absence:

> Her mate is not in this place, either. She grows jittery again, remembering that ancient accident, the trauma of last spring. . . . Her edginess rubs off on this year's colt. Contagious distress lifts him into a leap. He kicks out at the surrounding emptiness. . . . for the first of a thousand times in his life, he dances. In the falling dark, other species might mistake it for ecstasy. (p. 278)

Similar to the young crane, Will suffered from the absence of his father and had no way of making sense of it. He and his mother joined together for comfort but, in contrast to the cranes, they did not truly recognize the terrible absence created by the father's disinterest in his son and remoteness from his wife. Much as Mark experiences with Karin, there is the appearance of the father but the essentials behind the face, whatever more primary, visceral, affective meanings might bind them together, are not perceptible. In this absence, Will could not find himself, first as a son and then as a man. His mother's comfort, rather than easing his burden, suffocated his potency and agency and left him hidden behind his own mask. It was only years later, when the defense fails and his life was in ruins, that he could begin to consider what it might take to invest in his life sufficiently to perhaps make meaning from his experience.

The Echo Maker is a story of crisis and opportunity, an edge that is always present in human experience, an edge that challenges us to make the most of what has been offered. In contrast to Will's lament over what had been lost, I told him that I thought that the collapse of his world had been inevitable, that he needed his previous resolution to come apart in order to make way for something new. We do the best we can with what we have but then, in order to develop, we need to be able to break through our habits in order to learn and to grow.

Much like Will, Mark was described as having "long ago taken every wrong turn you could take in life, and from the wrong lane" (p. 5). The parent who gives life but also obstructs it by obstructing development poses an impossible dilemma for the child. Much as Will struggled to find himself as a man in relation to a father who was unavailable, Mark was searching for a father who eluded him, who tried to teach him to be prepared for what life might offer by almost drowning him and then introduced him to the wonder of the cranes but also killed them. Much as Will depended on his mother for protection from his father, so, too, Mark had depended on his sister. "Saved my life once," he said. "My father came this close to snapping my neck like a pencil" (p. 63).

We begin life as sensory beings. Like the cranes, we learn to make meaning from the echoes we encounter in those around us. Optimally, when all goes well, our parents are attentive enough to our signals that they can respond to our needs sufficiently that meaning can be made and held between us. That is the ground on which the self is built. When these types of primary meanings cannot be reliably exchanged and held, the dependent child moves toward attending to the other over and above the self. Thus decentered, the self is essentially destabilized, and meaning becomes something to be interpreted through an external translation system rather than an internal one. Trauma that is not worked through disrupts these meaning systems and creates a call that reverberates outward precisely because there is no containing other on whom the echo might resound. Will's story, much like Mark's, shows us that even when insufficient meaning can be made in the early years, being able to echo in the mind and heart of another human being can help to ease the brittleness of our defenses such that the reflective functions so crucial to human resilience can be built, and the development that has been waylaid can proceed.

VI

Relatedness, Aging, and Generativity

FOURTEEN

Identity, Community, and Object Choice, Part I

Mrs. Dalloway and *All Passion Spent*[1]

"Turning mortal for thy love . . ."

—William Shakespeare

Through her encounters at middle age with two lost loves, we can recognize the limits of a woman's ability to know herself sufficiently to truly love another. . . . A middle-aged woman with grown children falls in love with a new friend who seems to "get" her in a way no one ever has. Although she loves her husband, she begins to discover herself in a new way that is compelling. She struggles to be true to herself without hurting her family.

We live in a world in which change may be the only constant. The family structures on which our ancestors relied have been increasingly deconstructed, opening up new questions about the lives that we will choose, and yet, many of the struggles we encounter today were also present in previous generations. We can see in her writings, for example, ways in which Virginia Woolf struggled with her own questions regarding gender and sexual identity. Although the conventions and contextual pressures have shifted and changed, opening up the possibility of such choices inevitably invites encounters with tensions between individual needs and the "rules" associated with love in a monogamous and largely heterosexual society. We tend not to question love and the rules we make about it and yet these rules, along with their protective functions, may also serve to circumscribe and deny vital parts of self. After considering the search for identity in the preceding chapters, in this chapter we will explore how culture constrains views of love and gender in ways that can impede efforts to build satisfying relationships.

Western values of heterosexuality and monogamy have resulted in clashes between individual needs and the need to conform to the strictures of culture, particularly as these cultural mores are increasingly challenged. There are also tensions between our ideas of love as intra- versus interpersonally driven, and sexuality as both a social construction and, according to Foucault (1978), a scientific construction that reifies the labels imposed. As these constructions come under question, conservative forces react against the instability thus invoked, creating increasing constriction in some quarters.

Monogamy, as an ideal, has served as a stabilizing force in Western civilization but also represents an illusion of symbiotic oneness that is fed by a regressive desire. Although we may want exclusive love, it is unrealistic to expect to love only one person or to be loved exclusively by another over the course of an adult lifetime. That type of exclusivity seems to be driven more by regressive longings and Hollywood fantasies rather than real-life experience, in which families tend to be more stable when extended kin or friendship relationships augment parental care.

The high divorce rates in American culture suggest that individuals are searching for relationships that will satisfy multiple needs, many of which are defined and promulgated by the culture—most obviously through media representations but in myriad more subtle forms, as well. The fallacy of the ideal of monogamy lies in

> the assumption that the monogamous relationship should fulfill all the partners' sexual and romantic needs and the greater part of their emotional needs. . . . If either partner does feel a need for outside liaisons, this is taken as a sign that the relationship is not working properly. In other words, sexual and romantic monogamy—institutionalized in the legally recognized marriage—becomes the hallmark of the successful romantic partnership. (Rust, 1996, p. 131)

However, the expectation that one person should fulfill our multiple needs for sex, intimacy, idealization, and meaning often leads us to devalue the self and the relationship for falling short of this ideal (Person, 1991).

Monogamy has been linked to prescribed notions of gender that delimit both intrapsychic and relational potential, through the type of dichotomized relationships between self versus other that tend to result in splitting and false-self relations to self (Dimen, 1991; Goldner, 1991), and in sado-masochistic relations with others (Benjamin, 1988). Proscribed ideas about gender and object choice have come under scrutiny in a world in which increased freedom reveals the inherent uncertainty underlying many of our presumptions (Gherovici, 2010). Even more recent works that have opened up these questions have tended to dichotomize possibilities rather than considering gender and sexuality in terms of a continuum that includes the notion of bisexuality posited so long ago within psychoanalytic theory (Callis, 2009).

In spite of this scrutiny, we find a regressive trend in Western culture, in which literature, films, and popular music have supported the notion that one person might, somehow, meet all of our affiliative needs. That tempting illusion invites us to stretch and twist our perceptions of beloved (and of self) in vain attempts to find that mythical union. The industrial complex that supports our capitalistic economy promotes our efforts to create an illusory self, as though the right car, the right clothing, the right physique, or the right perfume might be the crucial factor in bringing us our heart's desire.

In relation to these myths, it is easy for two illusory selves to become lost in the reciprocal fantasy of mutual adoration and reflective self-adoration that becomes the affirmation of being loved. The illusion that one perfect other should, could, or might fill all our needs is reflected in the staggering divorce rate in this country, now estimated at about 50 percent. This illusion also makes it difficult for people to talk with one another about their disappointment and disillusionment, much less the grief, shame, guilt, and anger that accompanies their failure to live up to the ideal. At just the moment when our dreams come crashing and we need the support of family and friends, we are most likely to hide our troubles and put on the type of protective armor that inhibits our ability to work through the distress. The sense of betrayal when the illusion falters can be so regressive that it is difficult to even consider the other person's needs or feelings. When couples come into my office, each individual tends to feel a sense of betrayal at being largely unseen and unheard by the other, with little awareness that their dilemmas are intertwined, that the self who loves is fed by the self who is loved.

We are inevitably defined within the context of relationships that, in turn, are prescribed and proscribed by societal norms and values. In profound ways, there *is* no self outside of relationship. We learn who we are in relation to those others who care for and about us. According to Butler (2000), this dependency is inevitably "ambivalent. The price of self-knowledge will be self-loss, and the Other poses the possibility of both securing and undermining self-knowledge" (p. 286). Our gaze always cuts at an angle, looking for what we hope to find while dreading finding those aspects of self that we have not yet come to terms with (Charles, September 20, 2014; Lacan, 1977g). Because we know that those dreaded qualities are also part of us, relationships that do not acknowledge that duality are inevitably unstable.

Literature provides a means for exploring these entanglements between self and other, thereby providing a forum through which to better understand not only questions of identity but also relationships and ways in which illusion can inhibit engagement. In a novel, we can see the character being written, not only by the author's intention but also by the evolving identity of the character, herself, and also the ways in which other characters play upon her. In this way, the novel, through its very structure, mirrors an essential aspect of human life, that we have some freedom within which to write the narrative of our lives but that freedom is fundamentally constrained by inheritance and experience. In many ways, we are written *by* our lives, much as Kafka (1946) describes it: "Does he know his sentence? . . . No . . . There would be no point in telling him. He'll learn it on his body" (p. 145).

Characters are also a means for considering aspects of personality, their interplay with context, and ways in which these factors play out in relationship. In *One Hundred Years of Solitude*, for example, Marquez (1970) uses the same name over successive generations to designate something consistent that plays out over time in myriad ways. There are primarily two male characters, one wild and striving for conquest, the other more quiet and solitary. The women, alternatively, provide a container for sexual desire or for home. There is little space for anyone to fulfill her own desire, which then seems to empty out and close in upon itself. "After searching for it uselessly in the taste of the earth, in the perfumed letters from Pietro Crespi, in the tempestuous bed of her husband, she had found peace in that house where memories materialized through the strength of implacable evocation and walked like human beings through the cloistered rooms" (p. 161). The inability to bring together these dualities or to work through the relationships between one another, mirrored by the wars and tensions raging in the outer society, ultimately brings an end to the dynasty. As the characters are written and rewritten, a pattern emerges in which we can see that it is the very solitude—the failure to bring new life into the household—that ultimately brings collapse. In the end, even the attempt at new life empties out and turns to dust. There is nothing to sustain it. "Time was not passing. . . it was turning in a circle" (p. 335).

Woolf, too, uses her characters as ways of playing out her ideas within the text. In some of her novels, as in *The Waves* (1931, see chapter 2), the characters are not entirely characters at all, but rather aspects of self-experience playing out over time. This effort to make sense of self-in-relation seems to be part of a larger struggle with the demands of self-fulfillment versus societal demands, to make sense of herself as an artist but also as a woman in relation to those she loved. The tension between those various roles permeates Woolf's writing, in her considerations of the individual versus the social, what it means to love a man versus a woman, or what it means to be a man versus a woman. Her identity seemed to be fluid and porous, something that may have tripped her up personally but also gave her characterizations a profound and enduring vitality through her efforts to envision herself into them.

For Woolf, bringing a moment or a character to life was a profound and vital undertaking. Although she sought to capture the profound and the ephemeral, she did not distance that truth from the mundane and momentary, as in her description of a woman she sees in passing, playfully dubbed "Mrs. Brown": "Your part is to insist that writers shall come down off their plinths and pedestals, and describe beautifully if possible, truthfully at any rate, our Mrs. Brown. You should insist that she is an old lady of unlimited capacity and infinite variety . . . for she is, of course, the spirit we live by, life itself" (1984, p. 212).

The tension Woolf experienced as a forced choice between relational needs and becoming more fully herself remained an unresolved dichotomy for her, whereas in current times the possibilities are more openly various. In spite of the tendency to dichotomize and simplify life into discrete categories, there is increasing recognition that gender, sexuality, and love relationships exist along a continuum, with many variables. Viewing gender and sexuality as containing possibilities rather than being entirely fixed, Butler (1997) suggests that "masculine and feminine are not dispositions, as Freud sometimes argues, but indeed accomplishments" (p. 135) that are inevitably formed in relation to cultural ideals and values.

Although men also suffer from bifurcated beliefs about the possibilities entailed in gender and object choice, the dilemma of self versus other has been particularly problematic for the woman, whose role has traditionally been one of protected protector. Much as Woolf (1915) depicts in *The Voyage Out*, for many women marriage can seem equivalent to death; the price of love, servitude. However, this price is exacted in relation to fears that can keep the individual imprisoned behind walls that are, ultimately, self-imposed. Recalling Butler's observations regarding the search for recognition, we can see how our mirrored reflections become ways of both perceiving and misperceiving self and other. As Grotstein (2009) notes, what we term perception is often more aptly named apperception. Our lenses are inevitably colored by our experience, which in turn is shaped by culture.

Woolf's (1925) preoccupation with these issues comes forward in the novel *Mrs. Dalloway,* in her depictions of ways in which the characters both rely on and lose themselves within their projections regarding how they are reflected by others who, in turn, are seen in relation to their own hopes and fears. When there is too little faith in self, the reflected view easily becomes an annihilating force. That type of condensation or *symmetrization* (Matte-Blanco, 1975) between recognition and misrecognition is a crucial issue. We have ideas about recognition and reflection that are based on an idea of a mirror as veridical reflector rather than an idiosyncratic refractor of images (Charles, 2003b). However, recognition is a process that is based upon the relative agreement between parties as to the veracity of whatever it is that is being seen. As Butler (2000) notes, these agreements are inherently conditional and therefore unstable, depending as they do on a search for recognition that is always in some sense a search for misrecognition in the hope that we might be seen as more, better, or other than we believe are.

Even when there is agreement that something important is recognized by another, we also have beliefs about the price of that recognition, patterned on our past experiences. Insufficient self-regard leaves us vulnerable to our own lack of faith in self, grounded in the suspicion that the recognition is an illusion rather than a real reflection. This dilemma is at the core of what Klein (1946) has described in terms of our persecution either by the bad, split-off aspects of self, or by our fear that the good aspects of self are not really ours at all. When our internal foundation is shaky, recognition can seem like a possession of the other rather than a reflection of the self, leading into battles for psychic survival built on fictions so densely warded off that we cannot even encounter them. These reflections then seem, rather, to loom or to intrude on us in ways that evoke anger, fear, panic, or other ways of desperate not-seeing.

The tension between the allure of relationship and the fear of the price of actual engagement can make it difficult for either person to truly make a home for him or herself within the relationship. This is the dilemma described by Woolf (1925) in *Mrs. Dalloway,* in which there is a deadly tension between the self that the title character was yearning to create and the self being evoked by those most near and dear. Woolf notes Clarissa's difficulty in doing things for herself but rather trying "to make people think this or that" (p. 201). We see the clash between issues of servitude and self-realization but there is also the tension between the monogamous ideal and Clarissa's love for Peter and, even more, her love for Sally. This love for Sally was in some ways the most intense of her experiences, perhaps because the most forbidden. In looking back on her life, Clarissa recalls a particular moment with Sally that illustrates for her something lacking in her own passions. Though highly ephemeral, something profound had been stirred by Sally in a moment that had left its mark

> like a faint scent . . . she did undoubtedly then feel what men felt. Only for a moment; but it was enough. It was a sudden revelation, a tinge like a blush . . . Then, for that moment, she had seen an illumination; a match burning in a crocus; an inner meaning almost expressed. But the close withdrew; the hard softened. It was over—the moment. (p. 47)

Clarissa thinks back on this love, which had a particular purity and integrity, "not like one's feelings for a man" but rather more protective and chivalrous that "sprang from a sense of being in league together, a presentiment of something that was bound to part them (they spoke of marriage always as a catastrophe)" (p. 50). She recalls her entrancement, her giddiness at the thought of being with Sally. "But nothing is so strange when one is in love (and what was this except being in love?)" (p. 51). Clarissa recalls "the most exquisite moment of her whole life" when "Sally stopped; picked a flower; kissed her on the lips. The whole world might have turned upside down! The others disappeared; there she was alone with Sally" (p. 52). In contrast, Peter makes Clarissa feel strange and criticized, and she becomes uncomfortably self-aware, whereas Peter thinks of Clarissa as the love of *his* life. Having chosen social status above her heart, Clarissa is left with a terrible emptiness. When we encounter her in middle age, love seems remote to her. It is only in her hatred of Kilman, her perceived rival for her daughter's affection, that she feels real. "She hated her; she loved her. It was enemies one wanted, not friends" (p. 148).

Clarissa seems caught by her failure to move beyond a place of desired self-recognition toward a more mature form of love. That failure is marked perhaps most notably by her inability to parent her daughter sufficiently to accept the daughter's needs when they oppose her own. This failure is highlighted in the hateful jealousy aroused by the daughter's infatuation. Clarissa's reminiscences focus on the state of *being in love,* which is quite different from the *loving* that requires sufficient differentiation between self and other that each can be known and valued (Chasseguet-Smirgel, 1985). Loving requires the capacity for relatedness between two separate beings, as described by Winnicott (1971), whereas Clarissa's desire seems to be in line with what Lacan (1982) describes as the desire for the desire of the other, a symbiotic, largely narcissistic, self-reflective immersion. When the illusion of symbiotic oneness cannot be renounced, the loss cannot be mourned and love, constrained by idealization, can neither grow nor evolve (Altman, 1977; Bak, 1973). In Clarissa, we find the type of renunciation without real mourning that is the cornerstone of idealized, *romantic* love, in which the very impossibility of fulfillment fuels the love (Ireland, 1986), versus Sally's apparently more mature capacity to find fulfillment in her relationships.

In contrast to the romantic vision of love, which may preclude and even be spoiled by contact with the beloved, Kernberg (1974) describes mature love in terms of an identification with the values for which the person stands. Inherent in that conceptualization, however, is the hazard that cultural imperatives will impede each individual's ability to acknowledge idiosyncratic needs and work conjointly toward mutual fulfillment. As problematic as the ideal of symbiotic monogamy may be, we still attempt to accommodate to it, often coming up hard against the cultural constraints that can complicate our efforts to build mutually satisfying relationships.

The monogamous ideal can encourage men and women to use their partners as crutches through which they might meet life's challenges vicariously rather than confront them personally. We see in *Mrs. Dalloway* the enactment of the traditional woman's role of giving up her own needs in favor of the other (see Horney, 1967). In that era, devotion to duty seemed to prevail over fulfillment of personal needs as we see in another novel from that time, Vita Sackville-West's (1931) *All Passion Spent*. In that novel, we encounter Lady Slane after her husband has died, at just the point when she is free to live the life she chooses, rather than one proscribed by obligation. In retrospect, we can see ways in which Lady Slane denied many of her own desires so profoundly that they no longer left a conscious trace, though she did still feel a desire for freedom and for solitude.

Making choices between the needs of self and other remains a struggle for many women, who are faced with competing demands for their time and attention. In today's world, gender and sexuality become increasingly porous dimensions of human experience, further complicating questions regarding object choice (Gherovici, 2010). As societal constraints loosen, we are increasingly confronted by tensions between our various desires and the possibilities regarding how these might be filled. For example, I worked with a woman who had married and raised four children into adulthood. She had a good relationship with her husband, who in many ways was her best friend. Although "Cassie" had struggled to foster the type of intimate communication in her marriage that she desperately needed, her husband remained unable to talk with her about feelings or relational issues in any depth. Once her children were grown and she moved further into the external world in search of satisfaction, she discovered a woman who seemed to understand her in a way she had never imagined possible. This recognition was so exciting and stimulating that she found herself in the wonderful and terrible territory she could understand only in terms of being in love.

Although Cassie had been able to find the type of mutual interactive engagement she craved in many relationships outside the marriage, over time this lack in her marriage became untenable, particularly in contrast to the vitality she was discovering in her new relationship. A gifted artist and academician, Cassie was reluctant to give up on her twenty-year marriage, which had been an important source of safety and succor for her. She described her husband as her best friend, and had secured her most positive sense of identity through the dual roles of wife and mother. The thought of giving him up, along with these roles as they had existed, was horrendous but seemed imminent and ultimately necessary. Her husband's inability to move beyond his own affective constrictions or, alternatively, to acknowledge them and welcome his wife's ability to meet her needs in other ways (he was jealous of time she spent with friends), became an insurmountable barrier in their relationship. Her children were horrified and felt betrayed by what they saw as their mother's infidelity, not only to her husband but also to her role as mother. Increasingly frustrated, Cassie wondered whether the limits she experienced were a function of her own unresolved issues or merely inherent in the relationships she had built with her husband and her children.

It became increasingly clear that Cassie and her husband had provided for one another's regressive needs for love and security at the price of growth. They seemed to be relatively unable to integrate their own development as individuals into the relational structure they had built together. Cassie eventually decided that she needed more freedom in order to better delineate her own needs in intimate relationships, and the couple decided to separate. The intensity of the affect in her intimate relationships had felt like a forced choice between all or nothing, which most often left her with nothing. This was the way that relationships had been patterned in her family of origin. Greater awareness of these patterns helped reduce her dependence on what had been a mutual blind acceptance of regressive and destructive aspects in her intimate relationships. She was better able to move away from the disjunctive subject versus object, dichotomized relationship in which important aspects of self had been sacrificed as a condition of being in relationship, toward one of greater mutuality between two subjects. Her ability to stand stronger as a subject in her own right also helped her to work through the difficulties she was encountering with her children.

As we have seen, Cassie's attempts to define her needs as both subject and object in her relationships called into question familial and cultural imperatives and prohibitions. She had been struggling with competing fulfillments that she experienced as a disjunction between relationships with men versus women. Although her relationships with women were more problematic, she also felt that they were more authentic. Women seemed better able to confront obstacles they encountered in the search for intimacy and emotional bonding at deep and fundamental levels. I have encountered this type of split in my work with many women, for whom highly disparate but equally important needs are met in their relationships with men versus women. The multiplicity of needs is often experienced as a forced choice in a culture in which heterogeneity is suspect and people tend to be dichotomized into disjunctive categories of self versus other (see Goldner, 1991). To complicate matters, the choice of a life with another woman would necessitate a disjunctive break with family and tradition for many women, leaving them cut loose from important sources of sustenance and identity.

Cassie's new love relationship flourished until she tried to put into words the feelings she was experiencing. These words seemed to be untenable to her friend, who was also married, and the friend began to distance herself. The emotional instability that ensued brought Cassie into my consulting room. Through our work together, she was able to move beyond the position of the rejected lover who needed the beloved in order to obtain value, so that she could consider the gaps in herself that left her in such need. Unlike Mrs. Dalloway, Cassie was able to recognize that her current dilemma was predicated on an internalization of societal values based on self-abnegation. She was also able to actively consider the tensions she experienced between the possibility of love and fulfillment opened by her homosexual desires versus the conflicting demands and desires of the husband and children whom she loved and valued.

That tension, between one's own evolving desires in later age versus the expectations of one's family, is beautifully captured in Sackville-West's (1931) novel, *All Passion Spent*, in which the heroine is threatened with further entombment at the hands of her children after the death of her husband. Her liberation after his death is impossible for her children to imagine, precisely because they have never truly thought of her as a being in her own right but rather as an appendage to the needs of others. "She had been a lonely woman, always at variance with the creeds to which she had conformed. Every now and then she had known some delicious encounter with a spirit attuned to her own. Such encounters had been rare" (p. 87).

Although Lady Slane gives up on her own children, she does sense in one great granddaughter such a kindred spirit.

> She caught herself wondering whether she could afterwards recapture the incantation of this hour sufficiently to render it into terms of music. Her desire to render an experience in terms of music transcended even her interest in her great-grandmother as a human being; a form of egoism which she knew her great-grandmother would neither resent nor misunderstand. . . . On some remote piano the chords were struck, and they were chords which had no meaning, no existence, in the world inhabited by her grandfather and her great-aunt Carrie; but in her great-grandmother's world they had their value and their significance. (p. 177)

Like Lady Slane, Cassie, having tasted an attuned encounter, was determined to find a way to live her own life in relation to her needs and preferences as she experienced them, to move toward the music she intuited inside, and to hope that this determination could ultimately provide a guidepost to her own children.

As definitions shift, possibilities open. Increasingly, there is a multiplicity of patterns that inform our experiences of gender and sexuality, shaping the meanings of desire along with the sense of self (Harris, 1991). Through our early encounters of self with other, we derive notions of what it means to love or be loved, as well as the relative safety and price of that safety. These notions inform our object choices. In households in which one can identify with both parents, there may be more freedom of choice. Even when parents are the same sex, they often take different roles, affording greater diversity of possible identifications. In households in which the same sex parent is devalued, otherness may be valued over whatever is perceived as *same* or *self*. In such cases, the child of the devalued gender is faced with an impossible choice, in that disidentification with the deprecated parent repudiates important aspects of self. This was the case for Kate (described more fully in chapter 11), who as a young child was faced with a forced choice between mother or father. Her parents tantalized her in their acting out with one another and also with Kate, thereby objectifying the self and substituting desire for relatedness.

In her denial of the parents' desire and hatred, Kate remained unable to integrate her own love, hatred, and desire for either parent. Her femininity was tainted such that she could be the subject only to the extent that she played the dehumanized and dehumanizing role of father as seductor. Disowning her rage kept her ostensibly safer but also denied the power of the mother self, which had become demonized. Working through these identifications and counteridentifications took many years, as she struggled to move beyond her desperate need for a recognition that was really a misrecognition, a denial of her femininity, to a place in which she could stand sufficiently strongly to be recognizable as herself. At that point, she was able to engage in more open and honest relationships in which each person's needs and feelings could be considered. Without sufficient self-recognition, dependence on the other validates the fear that recognition is a gift bestowed by the other, rather than a reflection of one's own internal resources. There is always a price for failing to come recognize and come to terms with one's own desire.

NOTE

1. Portions of this chapter are amended versions of passages from "Monogamy and Its Discontents: On Winning the Oedipal War," *American Journal of Psychoanalysis*, 62 (2002): 117–41. Reprinted with permission of the editor. Excerpts from *Mrs. Dalloway* by Virginia Woolf. Copyright 1925 by Houghton Mifflin Harcourt Publishing Company. Copyright © renewed 1953 by Leonard Woolf. Reprinted by permission of Houghton Mifflin Harcourt Publishing Company. All rights reserved.

FIFTEEN

Identity, Community, and Object Choice, Part II

Possession[1]

"The poet, therefore, is truly the thief of fire."

—Arthur Rimbaud

Two poets meet; they enjoy the interactive stimulation of mind meeting mind. The man becomes possessed by his urgency to reencounter this woman and urgently needs to believe that he can possess her without betraying his love for his wife. . . . A young man spends a semester abroad and meets and falls in love with another student. Within this idyllic setting, they create a seductive fantasy of their time together, as though they could be all things to and for one another; as though they could freeze time and space.

The Western ideal of individualized and idealized love relationships can be seen as an ascetic turn that appeals to the desire to be lifted from the mundane into idealized substrates, thereby bringing love into the realm traditionally associated with mystical experience (Brehm, 1988) and also with platonic ideals. In Plato's time, romantic, spiritual, and sexual love between men were valued over heterosexual love, and sublimated, spiritual, transcendent love, or *agape,* was love at its highest level: "an affair of the soul" (Ireland, 1986, p. 17). Christianity maintained the valuation of a transcendent love but added a devaluation of sex and a firm devotion to heterosexual relations (1986). The price of this idealized notion is that it glorifies union without contact, thereby inviting an idealized self at the price of self-development, particularly for women (Kristeva, 1941).

This type of ascetic asexuality provides one solution to the problem of monogamy. For some individuals, exorcising sexuality from the equation seems to be a viable means for accommodating their love of more than one person. The problem then becomes discovering which partner will tolerate that exclusion; who will be willing to be sacrificed in order to fit the form. This is a theme with which A. S. Byatt (1990) plays in her novel *Possession,* in which she struggles with tensions between love and abstinence within a monogamous culture. For each person, there is a price for both action and inaction. As Byatt considers the notion of the *muse,* and what it means to find and to lose her, she also explores the disparate price for the man versus the woman, in terms of the relative ease with which a man can play with the idea of love without necessarily having to bear (literally and figuratively) the reality of it. Also depicted are Byatt's own musings as to the price of acting out the love rather than utilizing it in the service of one's art, a study in the virtues and hazards of sublimation.

Kristeva (1941) also explores this issue of sublimation, suggesting that Christianity solves the oedipal dilemma by eliminating both mother and father from the primal scene and thereby from the arena of envy. This type of conceptualization highlights an intense ambivalence and discomfort over knowing ourselves as sexual beings. Even analysts, who have ostensibly sought to integrate sexuality into the individual's self-experience, have tended to be uncomfortable with the actuality of experienced sexual feelings, in spite of their ubiquity (Davies, 1998; Tower, 1956). There are some indications that sexual feelings may be more difficult for women to acknowledge, whereas loving feelings may be more problematic for men (Gabbard, 1992). As we search for some more neutral form of love, our definitions become a means for denying the diversity, richness, and intensity of our feelings (Charles, 1999).

Although resolutions of the oedipal dilemma have been linked conceptually to growth and development, they are also linked to a capitulation to the authority of the other and to a renunciation of one's desire to be desired (Lacan, 1977g). This move too often represents an internalization of the feared external controls rather than the development of the capacity to make one's own judgments. As Benjamin (1988) puts it: "The sanitized view of oedipal authority denies the fear and submission that paternal power has historically inspired" (p. 141). What is at stake is the capacity to become the subject of one's own desiring rather than merely capitulating to the greater will of the other and thereby trading the fear of external authority for an internalized version. "Paternal authority . . . is not merely rooted in the rational law that forbids incest and fratricide, but also in the erotics of ideal love, the guilty identification with power that undermines the son's desire for freedom" (Benjamin, p. 143). The woman, too, is impacted by her relationship to paternal privilege that obstructs her sense of sovereignty over her body and her desire, thereby delimiting her ability to freely choose. In this way, a further aspect of the oedipal dilemma entails developing the capacity to move beyond idealizations and enforced compliance toward a view of love that is not blinded by guilt or fear. We see this relationship to paternal authority in the possibility of freedom that the Magus points to by making visible the constraints to which one is closing one's eyes (Fowles, 1977).

In her novel *Possession,* A. S. Byatt (1990) explores the intertwining themes of passion and productivity through the personae of two poets who chance to meet. The man (Ash) is enchanted and pursues the woman (LaMotte), who has chosen to live a celibate life with another woman in pursuit of their respective arts. Ash, in parallel, is living a life of enforced celibacy with a woman whom he loves. Tensions within their individual relationships leave each poet vulnerable to a growing passion that finds its way into their letters and poetry, and pushes increasingly toward realization in the flesh. As Ash becomes more active in his pursuit, LaMotte worries over what this might mean for her art. "My Solitude is my Treasure, the best thing I have. I hesitate to go out. If you opened the little gate, I would not hop away—but oh how I sing in my gold cage" (Byatt, p. 137). She finds her talents being diverted from her poetry into her letters and is loath to lose what is most precious to her. "I cannot let you burn me up, nor can I resist you. No mere human can stand in a fire and not be consumed" (Byatt, p. 239).

This dilemma as exemplified through the character of LaMotte points to an ongoing question for the artist: To what extent is the richness of our legacy from Dante in direct proportion to the inaccessibility of Beatrice? Both Byatt (1990) and Sarton (1965) bring these issues into focus most specifically in regard to the female, who has historically been forced to choose between the often highly disjunctive paths of woman, wife, and mother versus creator (Zerbe, 1992). "Love opens the doors into everything, as far as I can see, including and perhaps most of all, the door into one's own secret, and often terrible and frightening, real self," writes Sarton. "Sometimes the world you create on the page seems more friendly and alive than the world you actually live in" (p. 25).

In a society in which women are treated as devotees rather than as individuals in their own right, the woman faces particular difficulties in her quest to find her own voice and often colludes with her own exclusion, as love becomes confused with devotion (Le Doeuff, 1987). We see this tension in *Possession,* as LaMotte watches her own voice as a poet become overshadowed and diminished by the siphoning of her passion into her letters and lover. That dilemma is further complicated as her life literally is taken over as another life begins to grow inside her. "We must come to grief and regret anyway—and I for one would rather regret the reality than its phantasm, knowledge than hope, the deed than the hesitation, true life and not merely sickly potentialities" (p. 196).

Historically, the woman's role in Western society has made it much more difficult for her than for her male counterpart to find active support for her creative development (Zerbe, 1992). The devaluation of the woman's voice often results in what is experienced as a forced choice between identifying with the devalued mother or the overvalued father (Benjamin, 1988). Kavaler-Adler (1995) suggests that the alienated instinct becomes the bad object, as whatever cannot be loved becomes a split-off aspect of the self. Further, creative women are haunted by these split-off ghosts of themselves, "shaped by the particular personality of the women writers' actual father, which is condensed with the imprint of the dysfunctional mother as it remains in the psyche" (p. 75). Although Kavaler-Adler (1995) focuses on women's "longings for transcendence . . . (via) merger with a male god muse" (p. 75), in my own work with creative women, I have found that the split-off feminine aspect can be more problematic than that of the male (Charles, 2001). In the deferred mourning of the absent or assaultive mother, the female aspect becomes the needed and feared muse.

In *Possession,* LaMotte's decision to renounce the world of men and family in order to devote herself to the world of women and to her art represents, in part, an affirmation of self. However, it also presumes that there can be no successful resolution of the split between the needs of the man and those of the woman, thereby affirming the type of bondage relationship described by Benjamin (1988) in *Bonds of Love.* As LaMotte is pulled increasingly toward Ash, the tension between self and other—between self-dominion and domination—increases. Dimen (1991) notes that pleasure is derived from a cycling of this type of tension within an optimal range. LaMotte and Ash each experience the productivity associated with this cycling, as well as its lack when the tension either becomes too severe or is resolved. To some extent, this coupling with the idealized other, in the guise of the muse, is depicted in the novel in terms of the realization of the incestuous phantasy in which some proscribed distance might be necessary in order to ensure survival. Through that type of resolution, the affirmation of monogamy as a cultural ideal helps to keep us safe from our own yearnings, as we relinquish hopes for more direct satisfaction of desire, and comfort ourselves with the richness that Kernberg (1974) links to our frustrations. "Renunciation and longing may also add a dimension of depth to the life of the individual and the couple, and the redirection of longings and fantasies and sexual tensions within the couple's relationship may constitute an additional, obscure, and complex dimension to it" (p. 767). But it can also, as we saw in the case of Cassie, be a source of suffering, self-abnegation, and despair.

As noted in part IV, cultural values become lenses constraining and modifying the perceived needs and feelings of the individual. Meanings are derived within the larger social context, which defines what it means to adapt to or resist the prevailing myths of the time (Walker, 1993). These myths structure reality and assign values along with penalties for failure to conform, thereby encouraging the compromise of individuality for the sake of safety. As we saw with Cassie, the price of this safety is often the annihilation of important aspects of self, as the individual surrenders "the private kernel of his being, his *absolute* particularity, in order to enter a social reality in which he [is] comparable to others" (Copjec, 1999, p. 251). As conformity becomes confused with consensus, the othered voice is easier to devalue, causing further rigidity and a lack of viable alternatives.

In this way, mass culture tends to have a regressive impact on the individual, which can result in the type of conventionality characteristic of the latency age (Kernberg, 1989). True maturity requires our ability to locate ourselves in relation to these conventions, rather than losing ourselves within them. When these efforts fail and a more actively integrative path is foreclosed, consensual prohibitions and prescriptions of the chosen group tend to be accepted as self. It is then easy to appeal to some external authority to bolster our precarious sense of self-worth, as we see in many of the novels we have considered. In that process, however, we abdicate some measure of control for reality testing, as well as decision making. Freud (1921) pointedly describes some of the pitfalls of cohesion in groups, in which there are "a *number of individuals who have put one and the same object in the place of their ego ideal and have consequently identified themselves with one another in their ego*" (p. 116; italics in original).

Ideology can encourage identification with an idealized other or, alternatively, a surrender of self in the service of vicarious self-aggrandizement (Hernandez, 1988). Identification with the idealized other becomes the illusion of potency attained, paradoxically, via the assertion of impotence implicit in the surrender of self to other. There is a tragedy at the heart of this type of enactment of the myth of symbiotic oneness, in which lack is denied rather than confronted. From a Lacanian perspective, lack is at the heart of the human dilemma and must be encountered and faced in order to be able to discover our own particular desires. Failing that confrontation, we too easily become enslaved to the man or woman we believe will complete us (Abelin-Sas, 1994). When the price of relationship is the self, no one emerges the victor.

Through the character of Mrs. Dalloway, we have considered ways in which a woman can become enslaved in relation to her capitulations to convention. In contrast, in Western cultures, men's achievement needs are overvalued to the relative neglect of their affiliative and emotional needs. Many men depend on their partners to translate for them relational needs within the family, though these translations are inevitably idiosyncratic and may serve self better than other. At times, as we saw in the case of Tom in chapter 7 and will continue to explore through the case of Guy in chapter 16, relying on the partner to make meaning of affective experience creates further tension in the relationship. In such partnerships, the woman who is relied on in turn relies on her partner's greater relational constriction and inhibitions in order to enhance her own esteem needs. In such cases, the very insufficiency of the other can affirm idealized self-fantasies, which are perpetuated to the extent that neither partner is free to test these realities in other relationships. The monogamous ideal is such that many individuals refrain from seeking out further possibilities, impeding both self-awareness and growth.

Constraining oneself in relation to convention not only can preclude self-knowledge but also inhibits creativity. As we saw in *Possession,* creative individuals often struggle intensively with rules proscribing the limits of relationships. At times, individual needs are sacrificed for the sake of peace within the relationship, but always at a price. When the passionate feelings of being in love give way to less fervent emotions, disillusionment in the love relationship often ensues. Bak (1973) suggests that this difficulty may be linked to the type of "early loss or deprivation . . . [that can] promote fusion with the object and thus create a difficulty in the transition from 'in love' to loving" (p. 6). He notes that for some individuals, it is the intensity of the feeling that is most important, rather than the particular affective quality.

Although Bak views this characteristic in pathological terms, it may also be seen as one facet of what might be called an *artistic temperament.* I have seen artists struggle with the need to maintain or re-attain sufficient affective intensity through which to forge their creations. Such inspiration often comes in the form of a muse or idealized other, much as has been depicted by Sarton (1965) in her novel *Mrs. Stevens Hears the Mermaids Singing:* "you only feel safe and able to function when you can attach yourself with fierce concentration to one person and not necessarily—this is the point—to someone with whom you could ever share your life on any deep level. . . . Someone who captures the imagination" (p. 121). "I write for one person, but the person changes" (p. 125). The title of the novel is taken from a line from T. S. Eliot's (2009) "Love Song of J. Alfred Prufrock," in which the poet alludes to the elusive nature of the muse, such that one might drown in those very human voices that awaken our love and longing.

In Sarton's novel, much as we found in *All Passion Spent,* the creative woman pays a price for remaining in relationship. "She was caged, caged by being in love with, and married to, a man whose life pattern seemed to her both trivial and confining" (Sarton, 1965, p. 42). We meet Hilary Stevens also in later age but in a different era than Lady Slane, an era in which there has been greater freedom to try out the various possibilities she has entertained. Hilary Stevens has been able to live and love relatively freely and to make use of her creative capacities, though she recognizes ways in which she also has been used by them. That is the paradoxical moment in which we encounter her, when she is confronted by someone who would like to know *about* her with little capacity to *know* her.

Duty versus passion is a theme that plays through many of these novels. When conventional values are rigidly adhered to, excessive guilt can inhibit passion or, alternatively, encourage enactments of triangular relationships (Kernberg, 1988). Although triangular relationships can be problematic, they can also provide important fodder for the creative mind. Tensions between fidelity and passion can pose particular challenges for the creative individual who depends on the muse for inspiration without necessarily understanding which aspects of that relationship might be vital to his ongoing creativity. One young writer, for example, struggled before his marriage to work through the losses inherent in giving up a previous lover. Giving up the woman, herself, was a far easier task than what "Nick" experienced as a demand that he disavow all that she had come to represent to him, for him, and about him. The novel that had grown out of their time together was repeatedly set aside as those aspects of himself were concomitantly repudiated. This disavowal resulted in increasing anxiety and extreme writer's block.

The underlying hostility surfaced in vividly intense, aggressive and assaultive nocturnal and daydreams that began to plague Nick and disrupt his waking life, as well. The dreams served both discharge and obfuscating functions, enabling him to ignore the underlying yearnings that were being killed off. Particularly problematic were the regressive longings for intimacy with his mother, the residue of an early relationship that had been both idealized and sexualized. Memories of snuggling in her bed watching television during her sojourns at home between hospital visits brought mixed feelings of gratification and guilt. The type of highly charged fantasies evoked by these memories seemed to be an important source of his writing but became strangled as he struggled to bear the yoke of being the "successful husband" for his mother, as she made increasing demands on him, using him as a confidante regarding the problems she was experiencing with his father. This ostensible oedipal victory entailed complicity in vilifying the father for his lack of success, thereby impeding his ability to identify with the devalued, displaced father.

Nick's attempts to write this novel (which required working through his ambivalence over renouncing the "other woman" in his life) were complicated by his fantasies of having his wife read the novel. As he began work on the sexual part of the novel, the other woman and his feelings about her too vividly came to life. Previously, he had managed to derealize her, to make of her a symbol, a cipher, an empty space rather than a person. Her unreality had made her acceptable, which had enabled him to marry his wife. But now the other woman had become real, as he continued to write of her, dream of her, and fantasize about her. He would then feel nothing for his wife and tremendous guilt would fill the space that might formerly have contained other feelings. He could build no excitement, for there was no spontaneity. There can be no excitement without the playfulness that had been given up for the perceived "reality" of marriage, which he experienced in terms of entrenched, deeply internalized memories of the dull, empty, lifeless, mechanized existence of his parents.

During this time, there was no room for play in our work, either. My words became endorsements or prohibitions of one path or another. Talking was treacherous. What I had taken to be choices with consequences were heard by him as, alternatively, prescriptions or admonitions. There was no room for free choice, no space he could step into where he could take ownership of his own urges, needs, feelings and desires—to act on them and accept the consequences or, alternatively, to imagine them and make decisions based on his own imaginings. His reflective capacities were at times so impaired that he would find himself in a room with no recollection of why he had entered. Similarly, milk would appear in the cupboard, already warm and spoiled. It was hard to know where he was, easier to track where he had been. Nick's incapacity for thought in our sessions mirrored the incredible paucity of play in his current life. When I reflected to him this lack in contrast to the previous importance that play had held in his life, he could not hear me but merely affirmed the equation of marriage and responsibility. There was no room now for such childishness.

That session highlighted for me once again this dilemma with which we were faced. I became the other woman, the secret woman with whom he shares his inner life with such austere intimacy. I became the person for whom he leaves his wife and with whom he talks about things that his wife would prefer he not say. The very vitality of that session stretched his limits and he missed the next. He was feeling ill, he said. In his absence, I wondered what it was like for him to be presented with this offer of space and to what extent he experienced it as a seduction, overly stimulating and disorganizing, like his relationship with his mother. During this period of our work together, the muse, for Nick, was a sinister seductress, both desired and feared. This tension kept her out of reach, resulting in a period of acute and paralyzing artistic block.

As Nick became better able to integrate these disowned aspects of self, his muse assumed a more benign maternal image in his dreams, uniting past with future sources of creativity. This new maternal image replaced the intense erotic imagery that replayed his early experiences of tantalization at the hands of an absent yet seductive mother. His wife's jealousy and his own guilt and fear had sorely impeded this facet of his own self-discovery, as well as his ability to work creatively. As he became less frightened that re-discovering these aspects of self would result in the loss of his marriage (and self), the novel resurfaced, and he was better able to reconnect with the fundamental issues he was exploring there.

This dichotomization between good and bad, self and other, father and mother, continues to both fuel and impede Nick's progress as a writer. Much like the mother who cannot tolerate the reality of the child's separate autonomous existence, Nick was able to finish his novel but found it difficult to bring it forth into the world. For Nick, being separate meant becoming lost. His mother's frequent illnesses and absences throughout his childhood gave rise to fears that she might die and be gone forever. His father's financial difficulties were experienced as an elimination of the powerful, loving, and present father, with whom he had identified. That father was suddenly eradicated, gone.

Much like Aron in *The Book of Intimate Grammar* (Grossman, 1991), Nick has played with the idea of *being gone* by isolating himself in various forms throughout his childhood and adult life. His intensely aggressive dreams are cathartic, in that they kill the need for the other, but also terrifying in that they affirm for him his ultimately evil and uncontained self that was responsible for having been, in many ways, motherless and fatherless. The dreams also serve as attempts to kill the ties to his mother, which were too sexualized to be of enduring comfort, and those to his father, who became too deprecated to provide sustenance. Nick's ability to vivify and kill his phantasies in dreams and novels seems to provide him with some equilibrium. However, this equilibrium carries a high price, achieved through a split between the all-good relationships with his wife and son and the need to kill the seductive mother/lover and his desire for her, keeping him depleted and fearful of being invaded from the outside by what has been deemed unacceptable within. In turn, this intense focus on his entanglement with the women in his life keeps him from exploring the treacherous territory of his intense love for his father, which is largely hidden behind the aggressive entanglements in his dreams. Aggressive contact seems to become a way of being close without transgressing boundaries that seem terrifying to breach.

In our struggles to make sense of our own desire—its meanings, forms of expression, and ramifications—cultural values often obscure our efforts. Conceptualizations of gender, in particular, can impede attempts to forge meaningful ties with others. In a culture that is largely heterosexual and homophobic, the intensity of ties with same-sexed friends may be intimidating because of difficulties in discriminating intimacy needs from sexual desire. The intensity of attachments to other-sexed individuals may also become problematic as we grapple with fears as to what that attachment might mean for or about a primary relationship. Often, the values assigned by culture to relational needs make them difficult to recognize and define without trying to squeeze them into socially acceptable containers. Insofar as the other comes to carry the face of culture and to stand for its injunctions and imperatives, fears of losing the other can be most pressing, even when our needs and feelings are devalued. Ironically, finding what we seek becomes its own dilemma. We search for love, and yet, too often, when it comes it is neither neat, orderly, nor comfortable. In consequence, we develop rules to help bring order to this inherently disorderly realm of experience.

Psychoanalysis, in the exposition of preferred or ostensibly healthier or more mature forms of love, has been complicit in creating a palimpsest in which the multiple realities of loving relationships are obscured by the overlay of value. Although Kernberg (1980), for example, explicitly attempts to refrain from taking a moralistic stand, his rendition of love is forged within the constrained visions of a monogamous culture. Further, his focus on sexual needs over other intimacy needs suggests a male vantage point, in which infidelity or triangulation of the couple's relationship is depicted largely in sexual rather than emotional terms. Whereas men tend to equate sexual and emotional intimacy, women are more likely to use emotional intimacy as the standard or hallmark of the quality of the relationship (Harris and Christenfeld, 1996). In contrast to Kernberg (1980), Lacan (1982) attempts to depict a more feminine view, reminiscent of platonic themes, in which the sexual is merely one aspect of love and certainly not the focal point:

> The soul's existence can, therefore, be placed in question *[mise en cause]*—cause being the appropriate term with which to ask if the soul be not love's effect. In effect, as long as soul souls for soul [*l'ame ame l'ame*], there is no sex in the affair. Sex does not count. (p. 155)

Lacan (1982) brings to the forefront an issue that confronts many of our patients: the passionate, and yet in many ways *asexual,* genderless experience of love. He depicts courtly love as ungendered: "rooted in the discourse of fealty, of fidelity to the person" (p. 141). Lacan suggests that it is through courage and patience that we persist in the search for 'the Good' in which we hopelessly confuse the good in ourselves with our notions of god. This search for the good becomes the search for the good/god in the other, which becomes the possibility of love. "It is by their courage in bearing this intolerable relation to the supreme being that friends, φίλοι, come to recognize and choose each other. The outsidesex [*hors-sexe*] of this ethic is so evident. . . . such is mankind on whom the soul did speculate" (Lacan, 1982, p. 155).

In these passages, we find the intrinsic dilemma in which the search for self becomes the quest for the reciprocal love that should have been found in the face of the early other. When the search for love becomes confused with sex, it becomes a devaluation of self and soul, severely diminishing the capacity for relatedness to self or other (Charles, 2001). However, efforts to omit the sexual and sensual from the equation diminish our experience, as well.

Whether or not a relationship includes a sexual component, it is often difficult to share the affection of those we love. The oedipal dilemma, ultimately, is about knowledge: our willingness to know whatever might be uncomfortable to know (Bion, 1963). It is also about our confrontations with the *Law of the Father*, and the price of such hubris. For Lacan (1977b), the Law of the Father is what saves the individual from being caught as a function of the mother's desire. The struggle, then, is to keep from becoming caught within reciprocal idealizations of desire and to be able to stand separate as the subject of one's own desiring and the object of another's. At one level, this is the war we cannot afford to win (in terms of taboo violations); at another level, this is the war we must win (in terms of becoming the subject of our own desiring). The reciprocity inherent in adult relationships requires that we give up the illusions inherent in idealization in favor of what might be known if we are willing to be less blind.

Thinking critically about our assumptions regarding mature or desirable forms of loving relationships may enable us to help our patients better meet the needs of both self *and* other within the multiplicity of their loving relationships. There is a crucial difference between being *aware* of cultural values and being ruled by them. We should be cautious about presuming that our limitations should be prescriptive to others. Whereas the novelist may take on the task of instructive warnings via morality plays, the clinician's task is constrained by the needs and capacities of the individual who invites us into his or her world. Even within the analytic space, prescribed and proscribed notions of health and maturity can make us blind and deaf to the actuality of the other's experience. In this way, our own idealized and dichotomized views of self and relationship impede our ability to know self and other in the moment. This hazard cautions us to be particularly wary of *any* givens, whether through cultural or analytic prescriptions, and to remember that it is exactly whatever feels fixed, certain, and most immutable that should invite our inquiry.

NOTE

1. Portions of this chapter are amended versions of passages from "Monogamy and Its Discontents: On Winning the Oedipal War," *American Journal of Psychoanalysis*, 62 (2002): 117–41. Reprinted with permission of the editor.

SIXTEEN

Aging and Death

The Map and the Territory, All Passion Spent, *and* The Sense of an Ending

"As we grow old, the beauty steals inward."

—Emerson

Like psychoanalysis, the novel affords the possibility of casting backward to consider ways in which meanings change with increasing age, much as we find in *Mrs. Dalloway*, as Clarissa looks back on her life and loves. Challenges and priorities change with advancing age, as we encounter loss increasingly in its many forms, and face the limits of our own capacities and even life itself. Faced with the inevitability of an ending, we are invited to consider both the quality of our life as we live it and also our potential legacy, what we would hope to leave behind. For example, in Houellebecq's (2010) novel *The Map and the Territory*, we pick up some of the same themes offered by Fowles (1977) in *The Magus*, in terms of what it means to look to some larger authority than oneself for answers to questions of meaning and identity. Whereas Fowles points to freedom and to love as the keys to resolution of that mystery, Houellebecq seems less certain. Notably, Fowles focuses on the young man seen from the vantage point of greater age. In contrast, as we follow Jed Martin, the central character in Houellebecq's novel, over time, we watch his development as it manifests across the span of his life and work. For Jed, love remains ungrounded, the potential containment lost in the wake of his mother's suicide when he was a young child. Jed seems to be searching indirectly for a father who might be able to offer what he is missing. He cannot find it in his own father, who remains an empty vessel, eventually committing suicide, as well, without allowing his son to even say goodbye. The only outstretched arm he is able to offer to his son comes in the form of a story of the dreams of his own youth, which were left behind when he turned instead toward commercial success.

In the last part of the novel, we see that Jed goes back to his father's work in the last period of his own life. He uses that work as a jumping-off point to search in his own way for the keys to meaning in a universe in which meanings are elusive and so complex that one can try to catch them only through the instruments at hand. Although these tools are inevitably imperfect, they do capture something of the essence of that mystery. In the first phase of Jed's work, he is preoccupied with capturing images of the material objects created by people. In his second phase, he is preoccupied with the maps that give the lay of the land. In his third phase, he captures the people, like his father, who are absorbed in their work. In his final phase, he attempts to capture some essence of what goes on within the territory that cannot be seen in the still overlay captured in the map but rather requires our ability to factor in the passage of time.

In Jed's quest for engagement with an environment to which he seems utterly unattached, we can wonder to what extent his abandonment by mother and by father has left him struggling to survive in a world of material objects, literally without a map, to make his way through the complex landscape of human relationships. Our identities are formed within the context of our early experience. When that early experience includes a terrible emptiness, the effects are profound. I encountered the emptiness left in the wake of a mother's suicide early in my career, in my work with "Simon" (see Charles, 2002a). Simon's last moment with his mother was of being handed off to his grandmother before the suicide. The rest was absence. Although he was then raised by a series of "mothers," each became lost to him in their own way and the loss of the other became equivalent to the loss of self. As was the case with Jed Martin, Simon's father was preoccupied with moving on with his life in ways that cut him off emotionally from his son. The parent's failure to mourn creates a terrible absence that the child internalizes as his own, as a fundamental and fathomless flaw.

Our work together seemed to require a self-discovery process that could be linked with the very early relationship between mother and child, as Simon anxiously sought my gaze at the beginning of each session. Having had no acknowledgement of his loss and no opportunity to grieve, he struggled between an utter dependency and a desire to need nothing. Over time, he began to recognize that his fascination with mattering to me was a way of discovering the possibility of mattering to himself. Like Aron in *The Book of Intimate Grammar* (Grossman, 1991), he seemed to be trying to disappear in order to be found. I suggested to him that his attempt to disappear was both a way of avoiding being left and also a way of trying to find the lost mother. It was a way of trying to keep her with him. "She wasn't there to be refound," I said, "and becoming her has been a way of not feeling the pain of that." These words seemed to help Simon to locate some ground under his feet. Like Jed Martin, he had been trying to organize an understanding of a world in which there were no reference points. Whereas Jed sought out those reference points in the external world by first fixing the objects, and then the locations and the people in their positions, Simon sought to discover himself, to organize an understanding of the world in which he might have a tangible place.

When I first met him, it had been impossible for Simon to imagine being valued for himself. Over the course of our work together, however, he began to discover himself, first in relation to the disappearing mother and then in relation to the father who had not been able to help him find his way into adulthood. For Simon, psychoanalysis afforded the possibility of discovering himself sufficiently to be able to take up the tasks of adulthood and to create a life for himself in relation to his needs, feelings, and desires. In contrast, Jed had been largely lived by his life. Much as he had waited to be taken over by his artistic pursuits, he also had waited to be taken over by the world of feelings and human desire. That latter world had largely eluded him.

> Life sometimes gives you a chance, he thought, but when you are too cowardly or too indecisive to seize it life takes the cards away; there is a moment for doing things and entering a possible happiness, and this moment lasts a few days or even a few months, but it only happens once and one time only, and if you want to return to it later it's quite simply impossible. There's no more place for enthusiasm, belief and faith, and there remains just gentle resignation, a sad and reciprocal pity, the useless but correct sensation that something could have happened, that you just simply showed yourself unworthy of the gift you had been offered. (Houellebecq, 2010, p. 164)

Simon was able to recognize ways in which he had lost the faith of his childhood and thereby was able to work to discover faith in himself and, through that, the ability to have faith in others and in relationship itself. In contrast, Jed lived out his life entirely alone, shut off into the territory he had created for himself that closed in on him increasingly as time went by.

Jed and Simon, each in their own ways, were caught within the patterns inscribed in them by their lives, and tried to discover the pattern sufficiently to be able to live. Many authors have used the novel as a way of marking ways in which our reading of those patterns can change over time in relation to the perspective afforded by experience. Much as Jed's final project entailed trying to obtain an image of life in motion that also recognized its decomposition, the novel can afford the reader such a glimpse. In his final project, Jed juxtaposes images so as to depict the idiosyncrasy of the view, using the technique of double-exposure to enable him to "superimpose up to ninety-six videotapes, by setting for each of them the brightness, saturation and contrast; by making them, also, progressively pass to the foreground, or disappear in the depth of the image" (p. 289).

> This technique allowed him to juxtapose living matter with created objects, so that the industrial objects seem to drown, progressively submerged by the proliferation of layers of vegetation. Occasionally they give the impression of struggling, of trying to return to the surface; then they are swept away by a wave of grass and leaves and plunge back into a plant magma, at the same time as their surfaces fall apart, revealing microprocessors, batteries, and memory cards. (p. 289)

As Jed was dying, he played with death and decay by taking photographs of the people who had figured prominently in his life and placing them outside to decay and decompose. In the end, despite our preoccupation with our creations and the tyranny of their debris, "the triumph of vegetation is total" (p. 291).

In contrast to the sealed-off universe in which Houellebecq's character finds himself, in Julian Barnes' (2011) *The Sense of an Ending,* the main character looks back on a life characterized by relationships that largely elude his understanding. We see the story evolve and alter from the narrow scope of adolescence, through the greater wisdom of age, and then finally coalesce through the recognition of alternative viewpoints that highlight ways in which memory can seal over the past, much as Jed Martin's vegetation sealed over the paths that had been left by civilization. In Barnes' novel, time is at the forefront. "We live in time—it holds us and moulds us—but I never felt I understood it very well" (p. 3). It is not abstract theories of time that Barnes is trying to understand but rather the ways in which experience and emotion color and alter our sense of it.

The narrator of the novel, Tony, looks back on his adolescence and contrasts his own youthful myopathy with the vantage point of Adrian, his friend and nemesis.

> Time first grounds us and then confounds us. We thought we were being mature when we were only being safe. We imagined we were being responsible but we were only being cowardly. What we called realism turned out to be a way of avoiding things rather than facing them. Time . . . give us enough time and our best-supported decisions will seem wobbly, our certainties whimsical. (Barnes, 2011, p. 93)

Early in the novel, the young men are in class considering the nature of history. In contrast to the general trend toward glib misunderstanding, Adrian objects to the notion of ascribing responsibility. "That's one of the central problems of history, isn't it, sir? The question of subjective versus objective interpretation, the fact that we need to know history in order to understand the version that is being put in front of us" (p. 12). This novel is very much about history, the lies we tell ourselves and the ways in which we rewrite history to soften and shape the past. The character of Adrian Finn seems to fulfill the function of the Greek chorus, commenting from the side and shaping our understanding of what is to come. "History," he says, "is that certainty produced at the point where the imperfections of memory meet the inadequacies of documentation" (p. 17).

In Adrian's pronouncement, he foretells the denouement of the novel. In much the same position Mr. Conchis takes in relation to Nicholas in *The Magus*, Adrian challenges Tony to move beyond his own limited understanding and attain further perspective. The characters in *The Sense of an Ending*, as in *The Magus*, tend to be unidimensional. They are, literally, characters positioned to stage a drama such that some larger truth can be revealed. In *The Sense of an Ending*, the characters reflect back to Tony his imperviousness to alternative meanings that are framed from some context beyond his ability to understand them. As he ages, Tony becomes more consciously aware and accepting of his limits. He can recognize that Adrian had an intelligence that left Tony behind. He also recognizes his own mediocrity and ways in which he had traded comfort for understanding. "In Adrian's terms, I gave up on life, gave up on examining it, took it as it came" (p. 99). He can recognize ways in which he had lost his friends, love, and ambitions. "I had wanted life not to bother me too much, and had succeeded—and how pitiful that was" (p. 100).

Barnes wonders, through Tony,

> Does character develop over time? In novels, of course it does; otherwise there wouldn't be much of a story. But in life? I sometimes wonder. Our attitudes and opinions change, we develop new habits and eccentricities; but that's something different, more like decoration. Perhaps character resembles intelligence, except that character peaks a little later: between twenty and thirty, say. After that, we're just stuck with what we've got. We're on our own. If so, that would explain a lot of lives, wouldn't it? And also—if this isn't too grand a word—our tragedy. (p. 103)

At the end of the novel, Tony is left with his shame at the enormity of what he had been unable to see, what he had been unable to face. The reader, however, is left with the larger picture of what remains invisible, largely because of Tony's inability to move beyond the frame of his own imaginings. He looks to others to tell him what he is missing. But he does not seem to really be searching for answers but rather redemption, a redemption that is not in the other's hands to offer. "You are on your own, now," says his ex-wife, recognizing that he is looking for something she cannot give him. She can offer him only the benefit of her perspective but Tony is seeking redemption in an impossible place: precisely from the woman who had found him wanting in the first place. He had "wanted to prove to her, even at this late stage, that she had got me wrong" (p. 130).

However, from the reader's vantage point, the problem seems to be that she had got him *right* and that he had never really gotten *her* at all. By the end of the novel, the characters largely remain characterizations because Tony still, even though he had "got" the story, did not really "get" the people who had been involved. He had never really known them, much as he had not known himself. At the end of the novel, he is still mystified by the bits and fragments, the secret gestures, and the "cresting wave of water, lit by the moon, rushing past and vanishing upstream" (p. 149). The rest, he says, is a "great unrest" (p. 150).

In contrast to Tony, who comes to later age with little ability to know self or other, Vita Sackville-West's (1931) *All Passion Spent* tells the story of an elderly woman who seems exceptionally self-aware. It is her family who fails to recognize her as a person in her own right and so are surprised when Lady Slane quite competently and intentionally makes a life for herself after her husband's death, refusing their efforts to take her on as an obligation. Told in three parts, Lady Slane's musings on her life come into sharper relief in part three when she meets Mr. FitzGeorge, who reminds her more pointedly of who she had been in her younger days, and what she gave up in order to live the life she chose. Whereas Nick (chapter 15) was able to continue to struggle to make room for his creative self along with his relational needs, Lady Slane had foreclosed the former. Thus, the challenges of later adulthood depend in part on the sacrifices that have been made that have subverted the individual's development in particular ways. Reclaiming what has been lost or left to the side can become a rewarding challenge in later age.

Sackville-West's (1931) *All Passion Spent* tells a story that is ostensibly beyond passion, perhaps more specifically beyond the passion that drives the young adult toward the type of intense engagement that underlies the commitment needed to invest in creating a family. In later age, as we face the limits imposed by aging, we are invited to reflect on the values our lives affirm and to think about how we might choose differently, to consider what might matter if we were to reflect more deliberately on what our lives might eventually *mean*. Much as we described in relation to "Cassie" in chapter 14, there is a different challenge that faces us in mid and later life, as we begin to grapple with issues of aging, generativity, and thoughts of what we hope to leave behind. It is not only women who find themselves caught in relationships that feel increasingly constraining as time goes by. One of the primary challenges of older age, as highlighted by Erikson and Erikson (1982), is to think forward to the impact one might have on successive generations. That type of thinking forward helps us to tolerate imagining a world that goes on without our presence.

"Guy," an aging artist, struggles to locate himself in a story in which his humor and creative capacities have effectively masked the shame hidden at his core that seems to have been passed along from father to son. Aging puts us in the odd position of reconsidering ourselves in relation to changing ideas about our parents. Particularly for those who become parents, themselves, the demands of parenthood increasingly call into question convenient truths culled from our childhoods. It is often precisely at this juncture—when we consider ourselves in relation to both parent and child—that we can obtain a better glimpse of relational patterns and character styles that had previously eluded us. This was certainly the case for Guy, who entered treatment in his seventies because of anger issues in relation to what he experienced as impossible demands from his wife, "Lee." Like Tom (chapter 5), Guy relied on his wife's understanding of him but then felt betrayed by her misunderstanding. In this way, we see Guy positioned in the place of Lacan's hysteric, who searches for the answer *in the other* that can be found only in the self. The wife's interpretations, culled from her own years in psychoanalysis, were wearing thin and he sought assistance.

Over time, Guy could recognize ways in which these interpretations impeded rather than facilitated self-knowledge. He could see the ways in which his deeply buried and avoided sense of shame had left him unable to insist on being accepted as he is. He could recognize that he had been asking his wife a question that could never be answered to his satisfaction because she had no way of overriding his own lack of self-acceptance. Our work together helped to provide Guy with a third perspective through which to observe ways in which he became further lost in relation to this question his wife could never answer. By virtue of the reflective space afforded by that distance, Guy was able to look inside rather than outside and so to connect more directly with needs and feelings that had been suppressed, often written over by his delightful and very quick sense of humor. Relegated to the background had been threads of pain that emerged in our sessions, particularly in relation to his struggles with his adult son.

As is often the case, Guy's dreams captured this primary dilemma, in which he was caught in a lineage of gifted and talented men who were not able to sufficiently make their mark to feel truly at home in the world, in spite of their great achievements. Early on, his dilemma in relation to women is apparent in his dreams:

> I'm in a dream of being in an extended argument with Lee, after which we are just not speaking. I was the new guy in a Teutonic military school. My group has filed in and another guy's ornament has caught on my shirt. I felt isolated. We needed to see a movie. Four faces were talking down to us. There was visual distortion because of the low angle. The faces were wrinkled and female. I have to climb up to get to traverse across to leave.

In this dream, we can see the visual acuity, the attention to detail through which Guy views the world. We also can recognize how he locates himself in relation to women.

Whereas in the preceding dream there is a sense of distance from, and a lesser place in relation to, the world of women, in other dreams, his confrontations with Lee emerge as a source of real acrimony and loss of control. In one such dream, he was being cornered and that word opened up for him greater insight into ways in which

> I lose it because I can't get away. Just that word "cornered," having no exit, no way out, that's when I get—that's what escalates the animus. It brought back those times early on in the city when, in order to get away, I would run to my studio and lean against the door to prevent Lee from shouldering her way into my room. I remember panting and trying to figure out how I got into that. In cooler moments, I could see that I had generated her panic, her fear of being abandoned.

Increasingly, Guy is able to recognize details about his wife, including how she both invites and wards off engagement. His dreams reflect his growing awareness of ways in which he suffers in relation to her need to be in control and her lack of recognition of his own competencies. He has a dream in which his wife is driving but not well, and he is trying to assist her but she ignores him. It is dark and

> the car starts rolling faster and faster, and I'm bracing for the impact or drop-off, and I wake up and realize it's a dream. The adrenaline is pumping and my heart is racing. I relax, and then I'm back into the dream. We come to a stop at a precipice. There's a lake below. I wait for Lee to back away but instead she turns the wheel and goes over the cliff.

As they are falling, Guy's focus is on his wife, telling her how to survive the incident. He checks her door to make sure it opens before he opens his own and swims to the surface. "I get to the surface, I'm waiting for Lee. No Lee. I don't know what to do. I'm shocked that I'm without her and then I wake up again and realize that it's a dream." In Guy's associations to the dream, what comes up are ways in which Guy feels constrained by views of himself as deficient (or lazy) and therefore requiring intervention. He is supposed to be grateful for these offerings, even when he has said he does not want them. Where, then, is there room for his own autonomy, his own desire, to be recognized as valuable in his own right?

Confronting this situation with his wife leaves Guy hard against the major dilemma, for him, of what it means to be a man, his own man, and to value himself as he is. We see this theme play out in his dreams, in relation to the father he identifies with and loves and admires, but he also recognizes ways in which his father felt demeaned and diminished in his own life. These same themes emerge in Guy's conversations about his adult son, who has trouble taking in the ways in which he is valued by others for his own achievements.

Early on in our work together, Guy dreams about his father:

> There's a manila envelope hanging on a door knob. I slip out a *Time* magazine. My father is on the cover. I'm stunned. I think "it's a trick." I'm flipping through the pages. Then I think "wow, it's real." Someone has found out. I need to show it to him. Where is he? I'm excited. It's a good picture. This is too much! He's standing, half-sitting, at the edge of a table, not looking at us, natty, in a tweed jacket, with pipe in hand. The picture is sort of weathered, in sepia tones. The picture is bordered. It has an antique quality. It *is* antique. What of it?

I ask for his associations. "It's him as he wanted to be. It's him at his best. It made me feel good and I was really eager to bring the good news. It was a nice thing."

In a later dream, the "natty" dresser theme is picked up in a "snappy" car:

> I dreamed I went to a kind of woodshop by bicycle and tried to leave surreptitiously without disturbing the class. It was nighttime. It was tough going. Then, all of a sudden, I had this snappy convertible with the windows laid flat on the hood. It was parked in an expanse by the seashore, on a bluff overlooking the seashore.
>
> I was looking for a restaurant. It was boarded up and closed. I go back to the car and my father's in the car. I'm going to give him a lift home. The car barely starts. I tell him to steer and I'll push. I barely get it going into traffic and I steer slowly. That's it. There's a feeling of dissatisfaction and acceptance of the status quo in a resigned kind of way. I hadn't anticipated how dark it would be. I remember having to kind of feel my way. There were some other people outside the restaurant and I gestured to them like "who knew?" The whole mood is bleak, spare, shut. The convertible was kind of snappy but it didn't go.

Still later:

> My car is falling apart in increments. I'm letting it happen. I'm letting it happen. I think I'll be left alone. There will be no outside input. I'll be able to hear myself think. There will be no obligations, no judgment (you have no space). It seems like it. There is nothing to contend with. It feels like survival mechanism (like you're contending with something?) Like if I fight less, less energy will be expended, less energy to expend. There is no space but I'm sort of reducing so I'm not hampered by no space, reducing myself at the same rate I'm being hemmed in.

In his dreams, Guy seems to come up against the ways in which he has allowed himself to be devalued in his own mind, to have his learning difficulties misread as a "laziness" that left him with no means for overcoming the actual difficulties he encountered. Decades later, through our work, he has been able to encounter this accusation as a misappelation rather than a shameful secret. In this way, the natty, snappy car that doesn't work can be recharacterized in ways that allow Guy to be in the driver's seat to the extent that he can take the wheel and drive in his own way, rather than allowing his wife to do all the steering. Finally, he is able to confront her unwillingness to accept his preferences and desires and to refuse to be rewritten or overwritten by her preferences and desires. Instead, he demands to be accepted as he is and engaged with rather than ignored. In this process, he begins to recognize that he is the person standing in his way rather than his wife.

Through the dream in which Lee is steering, for example, he realizes that she knows how to take care of herself. It is Guy who does not. Somehow, he has to learn to do it in spite of her resistance, which feels like death to him at times but opens up when he refuses to capitulate to it. Recognizing how his fear of loneliness and isolation keeps him imprisoned, Guy fights for his autonomy, insisting on his right to be listened to respectfully rather than overridden and ignored, demeaned and diminished, as though he were a child who is either recalcitrant or impaired. In refusing to accept this position, he repositions himself and fights for the space he needs in order to be able to regain and make use of his creative capacities. Through these efforts, he discovers that his wife not only accepts this repositioning but also seems in many ways relieved by his resilience that enables her to speak to him without destroying him.

Most recently, Guy reports what he calls a "weird dream":

> I was trying to make love to a good looking guy with female genitals. I decided it was a weird idea. I was lying on his chest. I got up and went out into the street. It was a commercial loft building area. I went into a large truck garage. There was a door in the back that was off limits. I wanted to get in. There were a couple of people who were protective of the place. I talked my way in. I went up the back stairs—it had a dangerous feel about it. I went through a doorway into a large upstairs apartment. I could see down the hallway. Something was going on but I only had a partial view. A guy came and asked me what I was doing there. I felt threatened. I said "I'll be back another time." I left, relieved. I went into the street, into a neighborhood that was unfamiliar. I woke up in a kind of fright, afraid I'd be late coming here.
>
> Somehow, I think it has to do with my father, but why I should have the dream at this moment puzzled me. I was thinking that I miss him. I would like to show him how terrific things are and whatever groundwork he laid, whatever tough stuff he had to go through, paid off.

Guy then began to talk about a conversation with his wife, in which she had remarked on what seemed to her to be cycles of depression he went through. He spoke about having been called lazy as a child, which made her cry. Lee's emotion resonated in Guy, as well. "It made me tear up. Being characterized like that and buying into it and it wasn't really the case." We talked about this accusation of character that obscured the learning difficulties he was having and made surmounting them seem even more impossible. I noted that that accusation of character had been passed along to his son, who was implicated in this male lineage, as well. Seeing how his son stumbles over his own fears about himself makes Guy want to confront his own internal impasse more effectively so that he might, perhaps, ease the way for his son. Unlike Jed in *The Map and the Territory*, Guy had been afforded sufficient nurturance in his family of origin to have wanted to pass along this love to the next generation. This generativity leaves him struggling to find a balance between caring for those he loves and living his life well. It also, however, strengthens his resolve to become more fully himself and, in that way, to support his son's ability to more truly accept himself and become more fully engaged in living his life.

As we age, time becomes shorter and there is, as Barnes puts it, *the sense of an ending*. That limit invites us to consider the quality of our life as lived and also to reflect on what we are leaving behind and what we might yet build that will not so easily be taken over and usurped by the fecundity and ruthlessness of the natural world. In Houellebecq's novel, the map is a guide to a territory that cannot be fixed by whatever means we find to capture it. The territory—*the Real*, as Lacan terms it—can be approached, theorized, and struggled with but remains elusive, a mystery, a labyrinth to be encountered successively by each generation to come.

Epilogue

"And you? When will you begin that long journey into yourself?"
—Rumi

Psychoanalysis provides a space in which the unconscious can be valued. Previously, as Joseph Campbell notes, it was always "the prime function of mythology and rite to supply the symbols that carry the human spirit forward, in counteraction to those other constant human fantasies that tend to tie it back (1949, p. 11). Given the diversity of religious symbols and structures in current times, psychoanalysis affords a means for making sense of the signs and symbols, both idiosyncratic and consensual, through which meanings are—or might—be made. Psychoanalysis takes a stand for the possibility of making meaning from even the most ephemeral of signs and signals, the primacy of the unconscious that "sends all sorts of vapors, odd beings, terrors and deluding images up into the mind-whether in dream, broad daylight, or insanity. . . . Psychoanalysis, the modern science of reading dreams, has taught us to take heed of these insubstantial images" (Campbell, 1949, p. 8).

At the end of the difficult work that is psychoanalysis, there is left the pleasure in self-knowledge that enlarges more than it distresses. As we gain familiarity with the cues whose signals are increasingly recognizable, we have more room to choose whether to follow the habit of our defenses or to turn the wheel and make a new choice. The possibility of choice affirms our agency, authority, and autonomy in spite of our limits and lacks. Psychoanalysis is an intensive process that becomes compelling, almost a way of life, and yet, as in Barnes' title, there comes at some point *the sense of an ending*. And so, Guy finds himself at a point, three years in, where he realizes he has little to say, he is in such a different place than when he first came in. The problems that had been driving him relentlessly have softened and eased, and he finds himself, for the first time, comfortable in his life and in his own skin. "I can do nothing now," he says. "I always thought I was being inauthentic. I felt guilty about doing nothing. There isn't that edge of being afraid of getting caught anymore."

"I think back to when I first came in. Everything was so dire. It was driving me crazy. I'm feeling more like myself now and the stakes aren't as high as I thought. I can see clearer what's changed in my attitudes, my sense of possibilities and even probabilities." Guy talks about his various accomplishments, perhaps most notably being able to hold his own with his wife and to accept her difficulty as her difficulty rather than becoming lost in it. He also reflects on his growing acceptance of himself. His ability to maintain self-knowledge helps to stem Lee's anxiety, creating a stabilizing force in the relationship. That greater stability leaves him freer to make choices about how to spend his time, rather than feeling utterly constrained by his wife's choices, as though he could only conform or rebel. From that vantage point, he can recognize the value of pleasing her but also of pleasing himself and leave room for each value as he makes decisions. "I went out to lunch the other day with some people I just met," he says. "They hadn't heard my jokes before and they really enjoyed them. It was fun."

I said that I could imagine that it was important to be able to encounter *himself* in that way, the pleasure of being able to encounter oneself anew as if for the first time. "Yes," he said. "It's nice to feel free to live one's life, make adjustments, speak up with conviction and a sense of substance." Guy was enjoying being able to meet new people and see them enjoy being with him, being able to make people laugh spontaneously, from something that emerges within the context of the moment, within the relationship, and to have it received.

With a broad smile, Guy reminds me of the final line of Bellows' (1969) novel *Portnoy's Complaint*: "So," he says, his eyes sparkling. "Now vee may perhaps to begin. Yes?" He says it wryly, caught up by the sense of the ending but not knowing exactly how that ending should occur. That, I think, will be our final project, to come to the ending that suits his needs, that bears his stamp. At this point in the journey, we can agree to trust in the process through which that ending will be revealed.

References

Abelin-Sas, C. (1994). "The Headless Woman: Scheherezade's Sorrows." In A. K. Richards and A. D. Richards (Eds.), *The Spectrum of Psychoanalysis: Essays in Honor of Martin S. Bergmann* (pp. 161–82). Madison, CT: International Universities Press.

Abraham, N., and Torok, M. (1994). *The Shell and the Kernel*. N. T. Rand (Trans.). Chicago: University of Chicago Press.

Akhtar, S. (1995). "A Third Individuation: Immigration, Identity, and the Psychoanalytic Process." *Journal of the American Psychoanalytic Association*, 43: 1051–84.

Altman, L. A. (1977). "Some Vicissitudes of Love." *Journal of the American Psychoanalytic Association*, 25: 35–52.

Amador, X. F., Strauss, D. H., Yale, S. A., Flaum, M. H., and Gorman, J. M. (1993). "Assessment of Insight in Psychosis." *American Journal of Psychiatry*, 150: 873–79.

Apprey, M. (1993). "The African-American Experience: Forced Migration and the Transgenerational Trauma." *Mind and Human Interaction*, 4: 70–75.

Atkinson, J. (2002). *Trauma Trails, Recreating Song Lines: The Transgenerational Effects of Trauma in Indigenous Australia*. North Melbourne: Spinifex Press.

Atwood, M. (2000). *The Blind Assassin*. New York: Random House.

Bak, R. C. (1973). "Being in Love and Object Loss." *International Journal of Psychoanalysis*, 54: 1–8.

Barnes, J. (2011). *The Sense of an Ending*, New York: Random House.

Bell, Q. (1972a). *Virginia Woolf: A Biography*. Vol. 1: Virginia Stephen 1882–1912. London: Hogarth Press.

———. (1972b). *Virginia Woolf: A Biography*. Vol. 2: Mrs. Woolf 1912–1941. London: Hogarth Press.

Bellows, S. (1969). *Portnoy's Complaint*. New York: Random House.

Benjamin, J. (1988). *The Bonds of Love*. New York: Pantheon.

Bezoari, M., and Ferro, A. (1999). "The Dream Within a Field Theory: Functional Aggregates and Narrations." *Melanie Klein and Object Relations*, 27: 333–48.

Bion, W. R. (1957). "Differentiation of the Psychotic from the Non-Psychotic Personalities." *International Journal of Psycho-Analysis*, 38: 266–75.

———. (1963). *Elements of Psycho-Analysis*. London: Heinemann.

———. (1965). *Transformations*. London: Heinemann.

———. (1967a). *Second Thoughts*. London: Heinemann.

———. (1967b). "Notes on Memory and Desire." *Psychoanalytic Forum*, 2: 271–80.

———. (1963). *Elements of Psycho-Analysis*. London: Heinemann.

———. (1965). *Transformations*. London: Heinemann

———. (1970). *Attention and Interpretation*. London: Heinemann

———. (1977). *Seven Servants*. New York: Jason Aronson.

———. (1989). *Two Papers: The Grid and Caesura*. London: Karnac.

———. (1990). *Brazilian Lectures*. London and New York: Karnac.

———. (1992). *Cogitations*. London: Karnac.

Bloos, I. D. and O'Connor, T. St. J. (2002). "Ancient and Medieval Labyrinths and Contemporary Narrative Therapy: How Do They Fit?" *Pastoral Psychology*, 50: 219–30.

Blos, P. (1979). *The Adolescent Passage: Developmental Issues*. Madison, CT: International Universities Press.

Bollas, C. (1987). *The Shadow of the Object: Psychoanalysis of the Unthought Known*. New York: Columbia University Press.

Borges, J. L. (1962). *Labyrinths: Selected Stories and Other Writings*. New York: New Directions.

Brehm, S. S. (1988). "Passionate Love." In R. J. Sternberg and M. L. Barnes (Eds.), *The Psychology of Love*, 232–63. New Haven: Yale University Press.

Burke, K. (1957). *The Philosophy of Literary Form: Studies in Symbolic Action*. Oakland, CA: University of California Press.

Butler, J. (1997). *The Psychic Life of Power: Theories in Subjection*. Stanford, CA: Stanford University Press.

———. (2000). "Longing for Recognition: Commentary on the Work of Jessica Benjamin." *Studies in Gender and Sexuality*, 1: 271–90.

Byatt, A. S. (1990). *Possession*. New York: Random House.

Callis, A. S. (2009). "Playing with Butler and Foucault: Bisexuality and Queer Theory." *Journal of Bisexuality*, 9: 213–33.

Campbell, J. (1949). *The Hero with a Thousand Faces*. New York: Princeton University Press.

———. (1988). *The Power of Myth* (with B. Moyers). New York: Doubleday.

Caruth, C. (1991). "Unclaimed Experience: Trauma and the Possibility of History." *Yale French Studies*, 79: 181–92.

Cassirer, E. (1957). *The Philosophy of Symbolic Forms: Volume Three: The Phenomenology of Knowledge*, London: Oxford University Press.

Celan, P. (1978). "The Meridian." Ed. J. Glenn, *Chicago Review*, 29:29–40.

Charles, M. (1999). "The Promise of Love: A View Among Women." *Psychoanalytic Psychology*, 16: 254–73.

———. (2000a). "The Intergenerational Transmission of Unresolved Mourning: Personal, Familial and Cultural Factors." *Samiksa: Journal of the Indian Psychoanalytical Society*, 54: 65–80.

———. (2000b). "Convex and Concave, Part I: Images of Emptiness in Women." *American Journal of Psychoanalysis*, 60: 5–28.

———. (2001). "Reflections on Creativity: The 'Intruder' as Mystic or Reconciliation with the Mother/Self." *Free Associations*, volume 9, part 1 (no. 49): 119–51.

———. (2002a). *Patterns: Building Blocks of Experience*. Northvale, NJ: Analytic Press.

———. (2002b). "Bion's Grid: A Tool for Transformation." *Journal of the American Academy of Psychoanalysis*, 30: 429–45.

———. (2003a). "A Beautiful Mind." *Journal of the American Psychoanalytic Association*, 63: 19–35.

———. (2003b). "Mirroring from the Perspective of the Theories of Matte-Blanco." *Psychoanalytic Review*, 90: 791–809.

———. (2004a). *Constructing Realities: Transformations Through Myth and Metaphor*. Amsterdam/New York: Rodopi.

———. (2004b). "'The Hours': Between Safety and Servitude." *American Journal of Psychoanalysis*, 64: 307–21.

———. (2004c). *Learning from Experience: Guidebook for Clinicians*. Northvale, NJ: Analytic Press.

———. (2006a). "Terror and Truth." *Psychoanalytic Review*, 93: 191–200.

———. (2006b). "Silent Scream: The Cost of Crucifixion—Working with a Patient with an Eating Disorder." *Journal of the American Academy of Psychoanalytic and Dynamic Psychiatry*, 34: 261–85.

———. (June 27–28, 2007). *Fear*. Invited Speaker, Interdisciplinary Conference: "*Fear*." Hosted by the Michigan State University Department of Philosophy, East Lansing, MI.

———. (2008a). "The Masquerade, the Veil, and the Phallic Mask: Commentary." *Psychoanalysis, Culture, and Society*, 13: 24–34.

———. (2008b). "A View from Riggs: Treatment Resistance and Patient Authority: VIII. System Pressures, Ethics, and Autonomy." *Journal of the American Academy of Psychoanalysis and Dynamic Psychiatry*. 36: 547–60.

———. (2010). "When Cultures Collide: Myth, Meaning, and Configural Space." *Modern Psychoanalysis*, 34: 26–47.
———. (2011). "Remembering, Repeating, and Working Through: Collage: Piecing Together the Fragments of Traumatic Memory." In L. DellaPietra (Ed.), *Perspectives on Creativity, Volume II*, 145–75. Newcastle upon Tyne: Cambridge Scholars Publishing.
———. (2012). *Working with Trauma: Lessons from Bion and Lacan*. New York: Jason Aronson.
———. (2013). "Bullying and Social Exclusion: Links to Severe Psychopathology." In M. O'Loughlin (Ed.), *Working with Children's Emotional Lives: Psychodynamic Perspectives on Children and Schools*, 207–26. New York: Jason Aronson.
———. (2014). "Trauma, Fragmentation, Memory and Identity." In M. O'Loughlin and M. Charles (Eds.), *Fragments of Trauma and the Social Production of Suffering*, 25–44. New York: Rowman and Littlefield.
———. (2014b). "The Intergenerational Transmission of Trauma: Effects on Identity Development." In N. Tracey (Ed.). *Transgenerational Trauma and the Aboriginal Preschool Child: Healing through Intervention*, 133–52. New York: Rowman and Littlefield.
———. (September 20, 2014). "The Oblique Angle: Psychoanalysis and the View from the Side. 2014 Bernard N. Kalinkowitz Memorial Lecture, NYU Postdoctoral Program. New York.
Charles, M., Clemence, J., and Biel, S. (2011). "Psychosis and Creativity: Managing Cognitive Complexity on Unstructured Tasks." In L. DellaPietra (eE.), *Perspectives on Creativity, Volume II*, 107–22. Newcastle upon Tyne: Cambridge Scholars Publishing.
Charles, M. and O'Loughlin, M. (In progress). *Listening to the Disease of Psychosis: An Interdisciplinary Research Study*.
Charles, M. and Telis, K. (2009). "Pattern as Inspiration and Mode of Communication in the Works of Van Gogh." *American Journal of Psychoanalysis*, 69: 238–62.
Chasseguet-Smirgel, J. (1985). *The Ego Ideal: A Psychoanalytic Essay on the Malady of the Ideal*. New York: Norton.
Cohen, T. (1999). "Identifying with Metaphor: Metaphors of Personal Identification." *Journal of Aesthetics and Art Criticism*, 57: 399–409.
Copjec, J. (1999). "More! From Melodrama to Magnitude." In J. Bergstrom (Ed.), *Endless Night: Cinema and Psychoanalysis, Parallel Histories*, 249–72. Berkeley: University of California Press.
Cox, K. (2006). "What Has Made Me? Locating Mother in the Textual Labyrinth of Mark Z. Danielewski's *House of Leaves*." *Critical Survey*, 18: 4–15.
Danielewski, M. Z. (2000). *House of Leaves*. London: Anchor.
David, A. S. (1990). "Insight and Psychosis." *British Journal of Psychiatry*, 156:798–808.
Davies, J. M. (1998). "Between the Disclosure and Foreclosure of Erotic Transference-Countertransference: Can Psychoanalysis Find a Place for Adult Sexuality?" *Psychoanalytic Dialogues*, 8:747–766.
Davoine, F., and Gaudillière, J.-M. (2004). *History Beyond Trauma: Whereof One Cannot Speak, Thereof One Cannot Stay Silent*, S. Fairfield (Trans.). New York: Other Press.
DeLillo, D. (2007). *Falling Man*. New York: Scribner's.
Derrida, J. (1995a). *The Gift of Death*, D. Wills (Trans.). Chicago: University of Chicago Press.
———. (1995b). *Archive Fever: A Freudian Impression*, E. Prenowitz (Trans.). Chicago and London: University of Chicago Press.
Dimaggio, G., Procacci, M., Nicolò, G., Popolo, R., Semerari, A., Carcione, A., and Lysaker, P. H. (2007). "Poor Metacognition in Narcissistic and Avoidant Personality Disorders: Four Psychotherapy Patients Analysed Using the Metacognition Assessment Scale." *Clinical Psychology and Psychotherapy*, 14: 386–401.
Dimen, M. (1991). "Deconstructing Difference: Gender, Splitting, and Transitional Space." *Psychoanalytic Dialogues*, 1: 335–52.

Eliot, G. (1856/1963). *Essays of George Eliot*, T. Pinney (Ed.). New York: Columbia University Press.
Eliot, T. S. (1943). *On Poetry and Poets*. New York: Farrar, Straus and Giroux.
———. (2009). *Collected Poems 1909–1962*. New York: Harcourt, Brace and World.
Ehrenzweig, A. (1967), *The Hidden Order of Art: A Study in the Psychology of Artistic Imagination*. London: Weidenfeld and Nicolson.
Erikson, E., and Erikson, J. M. (1982). *The Life Cycle Completed (Extended Version)*. New York: W. W. Norton.
Fabiani, M., Stadler, M. A., and Wessels, P. M. (2000). "True but Not False Memories Produce a Sensory Signature in Human Lateralized Brain Potentials." *Journal of Cognitive Neuroscience*, 12: 941–49.
Farrell, E (1995). *Lost for Words: The Psychoanalysis of Anorexia and Bulimia*. London: Process Press.
Felman, S. (1995). "Education and Crisis, or the Vicissitudes of Teaching." In C. Caruth (Ed.), *Trauma: Explorations in Memory*, 13–60. Baltimore, MD: Johns Hopkins University Press.
Ferenczi, S. (1949). "Confusion of the Tongues between the Adults and the Child." *International Journal of Psycho-Analysis*, 30: 225–30.
Ferrer, D. (1990). *Virginia Woolf and the Madness of Language*, G. Bennington and R. Bowlby (Trans.). London: Routledge.
Fivush, R. (2007). "Maternal Reminiscing Style and Children's Developing Understanding of Self and Emotion." *Clinical Social Work Journal*, 35: 37–46.
Fivush, R., Habermas, T., Waters, T. E. A., and Zaman, W. (2011). "The Making of Autobiographical Memory: Intersections of Culture, Narratives, and Identity." *International Journal of Psychology*, 46: 321–45.
Fogel, A. (1992). "Movement and Communication in Human Infancy: The Social Dynamics of Development." *Human Movement Science*, 11: 387–423.
Foucault, M. (1978). *The History of Sexuality: Volume One*. New York: Vintage.
Fowles, J. (1977). *The Magus: A Revised Version*. New York: Little, Brown and Company.
Fraiberg, S., Adelson, E., and Shapiro, V. (1975). "Ghosts in the Nursery: A Psychoanalytic Approach to the Problems of Impaired Infant-Mother Relationships." *Journal of the American Academy of Child Psychiatry*, 14: 387–421.
Freud, S. (1900). "The Interpretation of Dreams." In J. Strachey (Ed. and trans.), *The Standard Edition of the Complete Psychological Works of Sigmund Freud*, 24 volumes, 4.5. London: Hogarth Press, 1971.
———. (1900–1901). *The Forgetting of Dreams*. In J. Strachey (Ed. and Trans.), *The Standard Edition of the Complete Psychological Works of Sigmund Freud*. 24 vols, 5: 512–32. London: Hogarth Press, 1971.
———. (1921). "Croup Psychology and the Analysis of the Ego." *The Standard Edition of the Complete Psychological Works of Sigmund Freud*, 24 volumes, 18: 69–143. London: Hogarth Press, 1971.
———. (1916). "Letter dated '25.5.16.'" In *Letters*, E. Pfeiffer (Ed.), W. Robson-Scott and E. Robson-Scott (Trans.), 45. London: Hogarth Press, 1966.
———. (1924). "Neurosis and Psychosis." *The Standard Edition of the Complete Psychological Works of Sigmund Freud*, 24 volumes, 12: 148–53, 1971.
Gabbard, C. O. (1992). "On Love and Lust in Erotic Transference." *Journal of the American Psychoanalytic Association*, 42: 385–403.
Gadamer, H.-G. (1988). "The Ontology of the Work of Art and Its Hermeneutical Significance. 1. Play as the Clue to Ontological Explanation." In *Truth and Method*, 91–119. New York: Crossroads.
Gallese, V. (2009). "Mirror Neurons, Embodied Simulation, and the Neural Basis of Social Identification." *Psychoanalytic Dialogues*, 19: 519–36.
Gault, B. (2003). "Reasons, Emotions, and Fictions." In M. Kieran and D. M. Lopes (Eds.), *Imagination, Philosophy, and the Arts*, 15–33. London: Routledge.
Gerrig, R. J., and Rapp, D. N. (2004). "Psychological Processes Underlying Literary Impact." *Poetics Today*, 25: 265–81.

Gherovici, P. (2010). *Please Select Your Gender: From the Invention of Hysteria to the Democratization of Transgenderism.* New York: Routledge.

Goldner, V. (1991). "Toward a Critical Relational Theory of Gender." *Psychoanalytic Dialogues,* 1: 249–72.

Gräss, G. (1961). *The Tin Drum.* New York: Random House

Grinberg, L., and Grinberg, R. (1989). *Psychoanalytic Perspectives on Migration and Exile.* New Haven and London: Yale University Press.

Grossman, D. (1991). *The Book of Intimate Grammar,* B. Rosenberg (Trans.). New York: Riverhead Books.

Grotstein, J. S. (1981). "Wilfred R. Bion: The Man, the Psychoanalyst, the Mystic, a Perspective on His Life and Work." In J. S. Grotstein (Ed.), *Do I Dare Disturb the Universe,* 1–35. Beverly Hills: Caesura Press.

———. (1995a). "Orphans of the 'Real': I. Some Modern and Post-Modern Perspectives in the Neurobiological and Psychosocial Dimensions of Psychosis and Primitive Mental Disorders." *Bulletin of the Menninger Clinic,* 59: 287–311.

———. (1995b). "Orphans of the 'Real': II. The Future of Object Relations Theory in the Treatment of Psychoses and Other Primitive Mental Disorders." *Bulletin of the Menninger Clinic,* 59: 312–32.

———. (1996). "Bion's 'Transformations in "O,"' the 'Thing-in-Itself,' and the 'Real': Toward the Concept of the 'transcendent position.'" *Journal of Melanie Klein and Object Relations,* 24: 109–41.

———. (1997a). "Klein's Archaic Oedipus Complex and its Possible Relationship to the Myth of the Labyrinth: Notes on the Origin of Courage." Journal of *Analytic Psychology,* 42: 585–611.

———. (1997b). "Integrating One-Person and Two-Person Psychologies: Autochthony and Alterity in Counterpoint." *Psychoanalytic Quarterly,* 66: 403–30.

———. (1988). "The Numinous and Immanent Nature of the Psychoanalytic Subject." *Analytical Psychology,* 43:41–68.

———. (2009). *"But at the Same Time and on Another Level . . .": Psychoanalytic Theory and Technique in the Kleinian/Bionian Mode. Volume I.* London: Karnac.

Hanfling, O. (1996). "Fact, Fiction, and Feeling." *British Journal of Aesthetics,* 36: 361–63.

Harari, R. (2001). *Lacan's Seminar on "Anxiety."* New York: Other Press.

Harris, A. (1991). "Gender as Contradiction: A Discussion of Freud's 'The Psychogenesis of a Case of Homosexuality in a Woman.'" *Psychoanalytic Dialogues,* 1: 197–224.

Harris, C. R., and Christenfeld, N. (1996). "Jealousy and Rational Responses to Infidelity across Gender and Culture." *Psychological Science,* 7: 378–79.

Hernandez, M. (1988). "Group Formation and Ideology: Text and Context." *International Journal of Psychoanalysis,* 69: 163–70.

Hesse, H. (1969). *The Glass Bead Game,* R. Winston and C. Winston (Trans.). New York: Holt, Rinehart and Winston.

Hirstein, W., and Ramachandran, V. S. (1997). "Capgras Syndrome: A Novel Probe for Understanding the Neural Representation of the Identity and Familiarity of Persons." *Proceedings: Biological Sciences,* 264 (1380): 437–44.

Horney, K. (1967). *Feminine Psychology.* New York: W. W. Norton.

Houellebecq, M. (2010). *The Map and the Territory.* New York: Random House.

Hutterer, J., and Liss, M. (2006). "Cognitive Development, Memory, Trauma, Treatment: An Integration of Psychoanalytic and Behavioral Concepts in Light of Current Neuroscience Research." *Journal of the American Academy of Psychoanalysis and Dynamic Psychiatry,* 34: 287–302.

Ireland, W. (1986). "Eros, Agape, Amor, Libido: Concepts in the History of Love." In J. F. Lasky and H. W. Silverman (Eds.), *Love: Psychoanalytic Perspectives,* 14–30. New York and London: New York University Press.

Jamison, K. R. (1995). *An Unquiet Mind.* New York: Knopf.

Jung, C. G. (1919). "Instinct and the Unconscious." In *Collected Works,* 8. Princeton, NJ: Princeton University Press.

Kafka, F. (1946). "In the Penal Colony." In *Kafka: The Complete Stories*, W. Muir and E. Muir, T. Stern and J. Stern (Trans.), 140–67. New York: Schocken Books, 1971.
Kakar, S. (1989). "The Maternal-Feminine in Indian Psychoanalysis." *International Review of Psycho-Analysis*, 16: 355–62.
Kavaler-Adler, S. (1995). "Women, the Instinctual Self, and the Demon Lover." *American Journal of Psychoanalysis*, 55: 74–81.
Keats, J. (1935). *Complete Poems and Selected Letters of John Keats*, C. D. Thorpe (Ed.). Westerville, OH: Odyssey Press.
Kernberg, O. F. (1974). "Mature Love: Prerequisites and Characteristics." *Journal of the American Psychoanalytic Association*, 22: 743–68.
———. (1980). "Love, the Couple, and the Group: A Psychoanalytic Frame." *Psychoanalytic Quarterly*, 49: 78–108.
———. (1988). "Between Conventionality and Aggression: The Boundaries of Passion." In W. Caylin and E. Person (Eds.), *Passionate Attachments: Thinking about Love*, 63–84. New York: Free Press.
———. (1989). "The Temptations of Conventionality." *International Review of Psychoanalysis*, 16: 191–205.
Klein, M. (1932). *The Psycho-Analysis of Children*. London: Hogarth Press and the Institute of Psycho-Analysis, 1952.
———. (1935). "A Contribution to the Psychogenesis of Manic-Depressive States." In *Love, Guilt Reparation and Other Works, 1921–1945*, 262–89. London: Hogarth Press, 1975.
———. (1946). "Notes on Some Schizoid Mechanisms." In *Envy and Gratitude and Other Works, 1946–1963*, 1–24. London: Hogarth Press, 1975.
———. (1957). "Envy and Gratitude." In *Envy and Gratitude and Other Works, 1946–1963*, pp. 176–234. London: Hogarth Press, 1975.
Kris, E. (1952). *Psychoanalytic Explorations in Art*. New York: International Universities Press.
Kristeva, J. (1941). *In the Beginning was Love: Psychoanalysis and Faith*, A. Goldhammer (Trans.). New York: Columbia University Press, 1987.
Krystal, H. (1988). *Integration and Self-Healing: Affect, Trauma, Alexithymia*. Hillsdale, NJ: Analytic Press.
Kuiken, D., Miall, D. S., and Sikora, S. (2004). "Forms of Self-Implication in Literary Reading." *Poetics Today*, 25: 173–203.
Lacan, J. (1972–1973). *The Seminar of Jacques Lacan, Book XX*, J.-A. Miller (Ed.), B. Fink (Trans.). New York: W. W. Norton, 1998.
———. (1974–1975). *Seminar XII: RSI*. C. Gallagher (Trans.). http://www.lacaninireland.com/web/published-works/seminars.
———. (1975–1976). *Seminar XII: Joyce and the Sinthome*. C. Gallagher (Trans.). http://www.lacaninireland.com/web/published-works/seminars.
———. (1977a). "Anamorphosis." In *The Four Fundamental Concepts of Psycho-Analysis*, 79–90. A. Sheridan (Trans.). New York: W. W. Norton.
———. (1977b). *Écrits: A Selection*, A. Sheridan (Trans.). New York: W. W. Norton.
———. (1977c). "The Subject and the Other: Alienation." In A. Sheridan (Trans.), *The Four Fundamental Concepts of Psycho-Analysis*, 203–15. New York: W. W. Norton.
———. (1977d). "Aphanisis." In A. Sheridan (Trans.), *The Four Fundamental Concepts of Psycho-Analysis*, 216–29. New York: W. W. Norton.
———. (1977e). "The Function and Field of Speech and Language in Psychoanalysis." In A. Sheridan (Trans.), *Écrits*, 30–113. New York: W. W. Norton, 1977.
———. (1977f). "The Freudian Unconscious and Ours." In A. Sheridan (Trans.), *The Four Fundamental Concepts of Psycho-Analysis*, 17–28. New York: W. W. Norton.
———. (1977g). "The Line and Light." In A. Sheridan (Trans.), *The Four Fundamental Concepts of Psycho-Analysis*, 91–104. New York: W. W. Norton.
———. (1977h). "Of the Subject who is Supposed to Know, of the first Dyad and of the Good." In A. Sheridan (Trans.), *The Four Fundamental Concepts of Psycho-Analysis*, 230–43. New York: W. W. Norton.

———. (1977i). "The Agency of the Letter in the Unconscious or Reason since Freud." In A. Sheridan (Trans.), *Écrits*, 146–78. New York: W. W. Norton.
———. (1977j) "The Subversion of the Subject and the Dialectic of Desire in the Freudian Unconscious." In A. Sheridan (Trans.), *Écrits*, 292–325. New York: W. W. Norton.
———. (1982). *Feminine Sexuality*. J. Mitchell and J. Rose (Eds.), J. Rose (Trans.). New York: Norton.
———. (1988). *The Seminar. Book I. Freud's Papers on Technique, 1953–54*. John Forrester (Trans.). New York: W. W. Norton.
———. (1992). *The Ethics of Psychoanalysis. 1959–1960*. D. Porter (Trans.). New York: W. W. Norton.
———. (2004). *Le Séminaire de Jacques Lacan. Livre X. L'Angoisse*. Paris: Éditions du Seuil.
LaCapra, D. (1999). "Trauma, Absence, Loss." *Critical Inquiry*, 25: 696–727.
Langer, S. K. (1947). *Philosophy in a New Key*. Cambridge, MA: Harvard University Press.
———. (1953). *Feeling and Form*. New York: Scribner's.
Laub, D. (1995). "Truth and Testimony: The Process and the Struggle." In C. Caruth (Ed.), *Trauma: Explorations in Memory*, 61–75. Baltimore, MD: Johns Hopkins University Press.
Lawrence, W. G. (2004). "The Language of Social Dreaming and Childhood." In J. Szekacs-Weisz and I. Ward (Eds.), *Lost Childhood and the Language of Exile*, 270–78. London: IMAGO MLPC and Freud Museum Publications.
Le Doeuff, M. (1987). "Women and Philosophy." In T. Moi (Ed.), *French Feminist Thought: A Reader*, 181–209. Oxford: Basil Blackwell.
LeDoux, J. (1996). *The Emotional Brain The Mysterious Underpinnings of Emotional Life*. New York: Touchstone.
Lessing, D. (1972). *Briefing for a Descent into Hell*. New York: Knopf.
———. (1974). *Memoirs of a Survivor*. New York: Knopf.
Levin, G. (1986). "The Musical Style of *The Waves*." In H. Bloom (Ed.), *Modern Critical Views: Virginia Woolf*, 215–22. New York: Chelsea House.
Lévinas, E. (1978). "Being and the Other: On Paul Celan." *Chicago Review*, 29: 16–22.
Lévi-Strauss, C. (1984). *Anthropology and Myth*. Oxford, UK: Basil Blackwell.
Liotti, G. (2004). "Trauma, Dissociation, and Disorganized Attachment: Three Strands of a Single Braid." *Psychotherapy: Theory, Research, Practice, Training*, 41: 472–486.
Lippmann, P. (2000), *Nocturnes: On Listening to Dreams*. Hillsdale, NJ: Analytic Press.
Lysaker, P. H., Buck, K. D., Carcione, A., Procacci, M., Salvatore, G., Nicolò, G., and Dimaggio, G. (2011). "Addressing Metacognitive Capacity for Self Reflection in the Psychotherapy for Schizophrenia: A Conceptual Model of the Key Tasks and Processes." *Psychology and Psychotherapy: Theory, Research, and Practice*, 84: 58–69.
Lysaker, P. H., Leonhardt, B. L., Brüne, M., Buck, K. D., James, A., Vohs, J., Francis, M., Hamm, J. A., Salvatore, G., Ringer, J. M., and Dimaggio, G. (2014). "Capacities for Theory of Mind, Metacognition, and Neurocognitive Function are Independently Related to Emotional Recognition in Schizophrenia." *Psychiatry Research*, 219: 79–85.
Lysaker, P.H., and Lysaker, J. T. (2011). "Narrative Structure in Psychosis: Schizophrenia and Disruption in the Dialogical Self." *Theory and Psychology*, 12: 207–20.
Lysaker, P. H., Roe, D., and Yanos, P. T. (2007). "Toward Understanding the Insight Paradox: Internalized Stigma Moderates the Association between Insight and Social Functioning, Hope, and Self-Esteem among People with Schizophrenia Spectrum Disorders." *Schizophrenia Bulletin*, 33: 192–99.
Main, M., and Hesse, E. (1990). "Parent's Unresolved Traumatic Experiences are Related to Infant Disorganized/Disoriented Attachment Status: Is Frightened and/or Frightening Parental Behavior the Linking Mechanism?" In M. Greenberg, D. Cicchetti, and E. M. Cummings (Eds.), *Attachment in the Preschool Years: Theory, Research, and Intervention*, 161–82. Chicago: University of Chicago Press.

Mar, R. A., and Oakley, K. (2008). "The Function of Fiction is the Abstraction and Simulation of Social Experience." *Perspectives on Psychological Science,* 3: 173–92.

Marceau, M. (November 19, 1965), *Wall Street Journal.*

Marquez, G. G. (1970). *One Hundred Years of Solitude,* G. Rabassa (Trans.). New York: Harper and Row.

———. (1988). *Love in the Time of Cholera,* E. Grossman (Trans.). New York: Knopf.

Matte-Blanco, I. (1975). *The Unconscious as Infinite Sets: An Essay in Bi-Logic,* London: Duckworth.

———. (1988). *Thinking, Feeling, and Being: Clinical Reflections on the Fundamental Antinomy of Human Beings and World,* London: Routledge.

Maurois, A. (1962). "Preface." In J. L. Borges, *Labyrinths: Selected Stories and Other Writings,* xiii. New York: New Directions.

McConnell, F. D. (1986). "'Death among the apple trees': *The Waves* and the World of Things." In H. Bloom (Ed.), *Modern Critical Views: Virginia Woolf,* 53–65. New York: Chelsea House.

McDougall, J. (1989), *Theaters of the Body.* New York: W. W. Norton.

McWilliams, N. (2005). "Preserving our Humanity as Therapists." *Psychotherapy: Theory, Research, Practice, Training,* 42: 139–51.

Melville, H. (1929), *Pierre: or, The Ambiguities.* New York: Grove Press, 1957.

Miall, D. S., and Kuiken, D. (1994). "Beyond Text Theory: Understanding Literary Response." *Discourse Processes,* 17: 337–52.

Milner, M. (1957). "The Ordering of Chaos." In *The Suppressed Madness of Sane Men.* London and New York: Tavistock Publications, 1987.

———. (1969). *The Hands of the Living God: An Account of a Psycho-Analytic Treatment.* New York: International Universities Press.

———. (1987). *The Suppressed Madness of Sane Men.* London: Tavistock Publications.

Molino, A. (2004). *Culture, Subject, Psyche: Dialogues in Psychoanalysis and Anthropology,* Middletown, CT: Wesleyan University Press.

Muller, J. P. (2007). "A View from Riggs: Treatment Resistance and Patient Authority-IV: Why the Pair Needs the Third." *Journal of the American Academy of Psychoanalysis and Dynamic Psychiatry,* 35: 221–41.

Murakami, H. (1997). *The Wind-Up Bird Chronicle,* J. Rubin (Trans.). New York: Alfred A. Knopf.

———. (2005). *Kafka on the Shore,* P. Gabriel (Trans.). New York: Alfred A. Knopf.

Murillo, L. A. (1959). "The Labyrinths of Jorge Luis Borges: An Introductory to the Stories of *The Aleph.*" *Modern Language Quarterly,* 20: 259–26.

Newmark, K. (1995). "Traumatic Poetry: Charles Baudelaire and the Shock of Laughter." In C. Caruth (Ed.), *Trauma: Explorations in Memory,* 236–55. Baltimore, MD: Johns Hopkins University Press.

Nieh, H. (1981). *Mulberry and Peach: Two Women of China,* J. P. Yang and L. Lappin (Trans.). Boston: Beacon Press.

Oatley, K. (1999). "Why Fiction May be Twice as True as Fact: Fiction as Cognitive and Emotional Simulation." *Review of General Psychology,* 3: 101–17.

Obeyesekere, G. (1990). *The Work of Culture: Symbolic Transformation in Psychoanalysis and Anthropology,* Chicago: University of Chicago Press.

Olds, D. D. (2008). "Identification: Psychoanalytic and Biological Perspectives." *Journal of the American Psychoanalytic Association,* 54: 17–46.

Olivier, B. (2008). "Trauma and Literature: Derrida, 9/11 and Hart's *The Reconstructionist.*" *Journal of Literary Studies,* 24: 32–57.

Person, E. S. (1991). "Romantic Love: At the Intersection of the Psyche and the Cultural Unconscious." *Journal of the American Psychoanalytic Association,* 39: 383–411.

Peterson, D. R. (2004). "Science, Scientism, and Professional Responsibility." *Clinical Psychology: Science and Practice,* 11: 196–210.

Piercy, M. (1976). *Woman on the Edge of Time.* New York: Alfred A. Knopf.

Pontalis, J-B. (1993). "Dream as an Object." In S. Flanders (Ed.), *The Dream Discourse Today,* 108–121. London: Routledge.

Powers, R. (2006). *The Echo Maker*. New York: Farrar, Straus and Giroux.

———. (2007). Interview. www.believermag.com/issues/200702/?read=interview.

Rayner, E. (1981). "Infinite Experiences, Affects and the Characteristics of the Unconscious." *International Journal of Psychoanalysis*, 62:403–412.

Resnik, S. (1987). *The Theatre of the Dream*. London: Tavistock Publications.

Read, J., van Oss, J., Morrison, A. P., and Ross, Ca. A. (2005). "Childhood Trauma, Psychosis and Schizophrenia: A Literature Review with Theoretical and Clinical Implications." *Acta Psychiatric Scandinavica*, 112:330–350.

Rhode, E. (1998). "The Enigmatic Object: The Relation of Understanding to Being and Becoming." *Journal of Melanie Klein and Object Relations*, 16: 257–72.

Rich, A. (1978). *The Dream of a Common Language: Poems 1974–1977*. New York: Norton.

———. (1981). *A Wild Patience Has Taken Me This Far: Poems 1978–1981*. New York and London: Norton.

———. (1984). *The Fact of a Doorframe: Poems Selected Old and New*. New York: Norton.

Richter, H. (1985). "Hunting the Moth: Virginia Woolf and the Creative Imagination." In M. Beja (Ed.), *Critical Essays on Virginia Woolf*, 199–211. Boston: Hall.

Ricoeur, P. (1970). *Freud and Philosophy: An Essay on Interpretation*. Chicago: University of Chicago Press.

———. (1984). *Time and Narrative: Volume I*, Chicago: University of Chicago Press.

Ritsher, J. B., and Phelan, J. C. (2004). "Internalized Stigma Predicts Erosion of Morale among Psychiatric Patients." *Psychiatry Research*, 129: 257–65.

Rizzolatti, G., and Craighero, L. (2004). "The Mirror-Neuron System." *Annual Review of Neuroscience*, 27: 169–92.

Rose, G. J. (1980). *The Power of Form*. New York: International Universities Press.

———. (1996). *Necessary Illusion: Art as Witness*. Madison, CT: International Universities Press.

Rubenstein, R. (1976). "Briefing on Inner Space: Doris Lessing and R. D. Laing." *Psychoanalytic Review*, 63: 83–93.

Rust, P. C. (1996). "Monogamy and Polyamory: Relationship Issues for Bisexuals." In B. A. Firestein (Ed.), *Bisexuality: The Psychology and Politics of an Invisible Minority*, 127–48. Thousand Oaks, CA: Sage.

Sackville-West, V. (1931). *All Passion Spent*. London: Hogarth Press.

Sarton, M. (1965). *Mrs. Stevens Hears the Mermaids Singing*. New York: Norton.

Savitz, C. (1991). "Immersions in Ambiguity: The Labyrinth and the Analytic Process." *Journal of Analytical Psychology*, 36: 461–81.

Schachtel, E. G. (1966). *Experiential Foundations of Rorschach's Test*. Hillsdale: NJ: Analytic Press, 2001.

Scott. M. (2008). "Lacan's 'Of the Gaze as Objet Petit a' as Anamorphic Discourse." *Paragraph*, 31: 327–43.

Segal, H. (1957). "Notes on Symbol Formation." *International Journal of Psycho-Analysis*, 38: 391–97.

———. (1991). *Dream, Phantasy, and Art*. London and New York: Routledge.

Shafer, R. (1997). *The Contemporary Kleinians of London*. New York: International Universities Press.

Shapiro, E. R. (1982). "On Curiosity: Intrapsychic and Interpersonal Boundary Formation in Family Life." *International Journal of Family Psychiatry*, 3: 69–89.

Shklovsky, V. (1917). "Art as Technique." In L. T. Lemon and M. J. Reis (Eds. and Trans.), *Russian Formalist Criticism: Four Essays*. Lincoln: University of Nebraska Press.

Sikora, S., Kuiken, D., and Miall, D. S. (2011). "Expressive Reading: A Phenomenological Study of Readers' Experience of Coleridge's *The Rime of the Ancient Mariner*." *Psychology of Aesthetics, Creativity, and the Arts*, 5: 258–68.

Steiner, J. (1985). "Turning a Blind Eye: The Cover-Up for Oedipus." *International Review of Psycho-Analysis*, 12: 161–72.

Stern, D. A. (1985). *The Interpersonal World of the Infant: A View from Psychoanalysis and Developmental Psychology*. New York: Basic Books.

Stolorow, R. D., and Atwood, G. E. (1993). "Psychoanalytic Phenomenology of the Dream." In S. Flanders (Ed.), *The Dream Discourse Today*, 213–28. London and New York: Routledge.

Tedeschi, R. G., and Calhoun, L. G. (2004). "Posttraumatic Growth: Conceptual Foundations and Empirical Evidence." *Psychological Inquiry*, 15: 1–18.

Thomas, D. M. (1981). *The White Hotel*. New York: Viking Press.

———. (1993). *Pictures at an Exhibition*. New York: Charles Scribner's Sons.

Tomkins, S. S. (1962). *Affect, Imagery, Consciousness: Volume 1: The Positive Affects*. New York: Springer.

———. (1987). "Script Theory." In J. Aronoff, A. I. Rabin and R. A. Zucker (Eds.), *The Emergence of Personality*, 147–216. New York: Springer.

Tower, L. E. (1956). "Countertransference." *Journal of the American Psychoananlytic Association*, 4: 224–55.

Transulis, C., Corin, E., and Kirmayer, L. J. (2008). "Insight and Psychosis: Comparing the Perspectives of Patient, Entourage and Clinician." *International Journal of Social Psychiatry*, 54(3): 225–241.

Trevarthen, C. (1989). "Development of Early Social Interactions and their Effective Regulation of Human Growth." In C. von Euler, H. Forssberg and H. Lagerkrantz (Eds.), *Neurobiology of Early Infant Behaviour*, 191–216. New York: Macmillan.

———. (1995). "Mother and Baby: Seeing Artfully Eye to Eye." In R. Gregory, J. Harris, P. Heard and D. Rose (Eds.), *The Artful Eye*, 157–200. Oxford: Oxford University Press.

Turvey, M. (2006). "Imagination, Simulation, and Fiction." *Film Studies*, 8: 116–25.

van Ijzendoorn, M. H., Schuengel, C., and Bakermans-Kranenburg, M. J. (1999). "Disorganized Attachment in Early Childhood: Meta-Analysis of Precursors, Concomitants, and Sequelae." *Development and Psychopathology*, 11: 225–49.

Volkan, V. D. (2001). "Transgenerational Transmissions and Chosen Traumas: An Aspect of Large-Group Identity." *Group Analysis*, 34: 79–97.

Walker, A. (1998). *By the Light of My Father's Smile*. New York: Random House.

Walker, J. (1993). *Couching Resistance: Women, Film and Psychoanalytic Psychiatry*. Minneapolis: University of Minnesota Press.

Winnicott, D. W. (1971). *Playing and Reality*. London: Hogarth Press.

———. (1974). "Fear of Breakdown." *International Review of Psychoanalysis*, 1: 103–107.

Wolf, E. S., and Wolf, I. (1979). "We Perished, Each Alone: A Psychoanalytic Commentary on Virginia Woolf's *To the Lighthouse*." *International Review of Psychoanalysis*, 6: 37–47.

Woolf, V. (1915). *The Voyage Out*. London: Hogarth Press. Reprinted by permission of The Society of Authors as the Literary Representative of the Estate of Virginia Woolf.

———. (1925). *Mrs. Dalloway*. London: Hogarth Press. Reprinted by permission of The Society of Authors as the Literary Representative of the Estate of Virginia Woolf.

———. (1927). *To the Lighthouse*. London: Hogarth Press. Reprinted by permission of The Society of Authors as the Literary Representative of the Estate of Virginia Woolf.

———. (1931). *The Waves*. London: Hogarth Press. Reprinted by permission of The Society of Authors as the Literary Representative of the Estate of Virginia Woolf.

———. (1937). *The Years*. London: Hogarth Press. Reprinted by permission of The Society of Authors as the Literary Representative of the Estate of Virginia Woolf.

———. (1953). *A Writer's Diary*. L. Woolf (Ed.). London: Hogarth Press. Reprinted by permission of The Society of Authors as the Literary Representative of the Estate of Virginia Woolf.

———. (1976a). "The Waves: The Two Holograph Drafts." Transcribed and edited by J. W. Graham. Toronto: University of Toronto Press. Reprinted by permission of The Society of Authors as the Literary Representative of the Estate of Virginia Woolf.

———. (1976b). *Moments of Being*. J. Schulkind, ed. Sussex: Sussex University Press. Reprinted by permission of The Society of Authors as the Literary Representative of the Estate of Virginia Woolf.

———. (1984). "Mr. Bennett and Mrs. Brown." In M. A. Leaska (Ed.),*The Virginia Woolf Reader*, 192–212. San Diego: Harcourt Brace Javanovich (original work published in 1924). Reprinted by permission of The Society of Authors as the Literary Representative of the Estate of Virginia Woolf.

Yeats, W. B. (1983). *Collected Poems*. New York: Simon & Schuster.

Zerbe, K. J. (1992). "The Phoenix arises from Eros, not Ashes: Creative Collaboration in the Lives of Five Impressionist and Post-Impressionist Women Artists." *Journal of the American Academy of Psychoanalysis*, 20: 295–315.

Žižek, S. (2008). *Violence: Six Sideways Reflections*. New York: Picador.

Index

About the Author

Marilyn Charles is a staff psychologist at the Austen Riggs Center and a psychoanalyst in private practice in Stockbridge, MA. She is a training analyst with the Chicago Center for Psychoanalysis (CCP) and serves as contributing editor of *Psychoanalysis, Culture, and Society* and as a member of the editorial boards of numerous psychoanalytic journals. As co-chair of the Association for the Psychoanalysis of Culture and Society (APCS) and president of Division 39 (Psychoanalysis) of the American Psychological Association, Marilyn is actively engaged in mentoring and promoting community involvement for those in the helping professions including her consultation work with Gunawirra in Sydney, Australia. A poet and artist herself, Marilyn has a special interest in the creative process. Other research interests include psychosis, resilience, and the intergenerational transmission of trauma. Marilyn has presented her work nationally and internationally, publishing over ninety articles and book chapters, and five other books, including: *Patterns: Building Blocks of Experience, Constructing Realities: Transformations through Myth and Metaphor, Learning from Experience: A Guidebook for Clinicians*, and *Working with Trauma: Lessons from Bion and Lacan*, and an edited volume with co-author Michael O'Loughlin, *Fragments of Trauma and the Social Production of Suffering*.

www.ingramcontent.com/pod-product-compliance
Ingram Content Group UK Ltd.
Pitfield, Milton Keynes, MK11 3LW, UK
UKHW012036150926
475560UK00001B/41

9 781442 231832